Family Welfare Association (Great Britain)

On the Best Means of Wealing with Exceptional Distress

Family Welfare Association (Great Britain)

On the Best Means of Wealing with Exceptional Distress

ISBN/EAN: 9783337025748

Printed in Europe, USA, Canada, Australia, Japan

Cover: Foto ©Lupo / pixelio.de

More available books at **www.hansebooks.com**

ON

THE BEST MEANS OF DEALING

WITH

EXCEPTIONAL DISTRESS

THE REPORT OF A SPECIAL COMMITTEE

OF THE

Charity Organisation Society

(15 BUCKINGHAM STREET, STRAND, LONDON, W.C.)

NOVEMBER 1886

CASSELL & COMPANY, LIMITED
LONDON, PARIS, NEW YORK, & MELBOURNE
1886

ALL RIGHTS RESERVED

SPECIAL COMMITTEE

OF THE

Charity Organisation Society,

ON THE

BEST MEANS OF DEALING WITH EXCEPTIONAL DISTRESS.

I.—THE COMMITTEE.

Mr. ALBERT PELL, *Chairman.*

Rev. BROOKE LAMBERT.	Dr. G. B. LONGSTAFF.
Hon. and Rev. Canon LEGGE.	Sir JOHN TILLEY, K.C.B.
Mr. J. H. ALLEN.	Rev. DONALD FRASER, D.D.
Mr. J. R. HOLLOND.	Rev. M. S. A. WALROND.
Hon. C. W. FREMANTLE.	Mr. A. G. CROWDER.
Mr. E. PETERS.	Hon. and Rev. A. C. STANLEY.
Mr. F. J. S. EDGCOMBE.	Mr. GEORGE SHIPTON.
Rev. W. CURTIS HAYWARD.	Mr. C. S. LOCH, *Secretary.*

Mr. R. HEDLEY, in attendance on behalf of the Local Government Board.

II.—CONTENTS.

	PAGE		PAGE
THE REPORT	i	WITNESSES—*continued*:	
WITNESSES:		Mr. F. J. DOVE	89
Mr. A. P. FLETCHER	1	Mr. R. ROBERTS	89
Mr. R. A. VALPY	12	Miss F. R. WILKINSON	98
Mr. J. R. J. BRAMLY	19	Mr. G. COLLIE	101
Mr. W. M. ACWORTH	27	Mr. G. T. WESTBROOK	106
Rev. W. CURTIS HAYWARD	33	Mr. G. DEW	113
Mr. W. VALLANCE	40	Mr. M. STEPHANY	118
Mr. T. GAGE GARDINER	49	Mr. J. D. POWELL	123
Mr. W. H. O. JACK	56	Mr. A. S. ANDREWS	128
Hon. and Rev. Canon LEGGE	62	Mr. N. MOSS	131
Mr. T. MACKAY	68	INDEX.	
Mr. T. W. MARCHANT	72	FORMS:	
Mr. W. HEALE	75	APPLICATION FORM, A.	
Miss M. M. GEE	80	RELIEF IN KIND FORM, B.	
Mrs. AVIS	82	INQUIRY OF EMPLOYERS FORM, C.	

EXCEPTIONAL DISTRESS.

REPORT.

THE reference to your Committee was 'to report upon the best means of dealing with exceptional distress, should it occur in a future year.' In the past winter much new experience should have been gained on this subject, and it was thought well to try and gather it together, to put it in a permanent form, and to draw conclusions on many questions of principle and detail, on which there had been differences of opinion and varieties in practice. The Committee have had before them documents showing what was done at other periods of exceptional distress; they have received letters, notes, and reports from many quarters; and they have examined 22 witnesses, whose evidence is appended to this Report. Information has been collected from persons in all classes of society, and, it is believed, upon most of the points of importance in regard to exceptional distress so far as it concerns the metropolis. Some of the readers of this Report, and students of charitable and social questions, will, the Committee hope, refer to the evidence itself, of which a careful index has been made. They will find that the situation is extremely grave; that there are permanent causes of distress which it is impossible for philanthropy to cope with, or even in any sufficient degree to palliate by schemes of direct relief; and that those causes suggest other remedies, beyond the scope of this Report, in regard to which the public and individuals must make their decision, if much of what is now termed 'exceptional distress' is not to assume a chronic form.

The Reference.

By 'exceptional distress' the Committee do not mean such distress as was experienced at the time of the Cotton and Irish Famines, but such as there was last winter in London, and *e.g.* in the years 1860–61 and 1878–79.

'Exceptional Distress.'

The Committee propose to consider

Plan of the Report.

I. Exceptional Distress in 1860–61, and the difficulties then encountered.

II. Several points of general importance in connection with Distress in the Metropolis, viz.:

(1) Charitable feeling and non-fulfilment of local responsibilities;
(2) The necessity of training in the work of almsgiving;
(3) The differences of different parts of London;
(4) Arrangements for obtaining information as to the existence or nature of distress;
(5) The 'chronic' or 'permanent' poor, and their participation in public alms;
(6) The independent artisan and labourer; the improvement in his social position, contrasted with a reduction in the amount distributed in wages and a demand for cheaper goods; his safeguards against distress, and the alternative courses which his position suggests.

III. The Agencies for Relief.

(1) The Poor Law, and its function generally: (*a*) its provisions for dealing with Exceptional Destitution; (*b*) the Workhouse; (*c*) the Labour Yard.

ii

(2) Relief by Employment : (*a*) last winter's experiences at Whitechapel, at Wandsworth, and in connection with the Public Gardens Association ; (*b*) suggestions as to rates of wages, &c.

(3) Charitable Relief : (*a*) existing agencies ; (*b*) a Central Committee for dealing with Distress ; (*c*) [Appendix] Local Committees and their rules.

I. EXCEPTIONAL DISTRESS IN 1860-61.

Evidence of Mr. T. Paynter, 1861.

In 1861 it was estimated that about £40,000 was raised to meet the unusual distress in London during the winter.[1] A very large part of this was distributed at the Police Courts. Mr. T. Paynter,[2] at that time one of the magistrates at the Westminster Police Court, thus described what took place to a Select Committee of the House of Commons.[3] In December, January, and February, 1860-61, they received at the Court in charitable contributions and expended about £800. 'We had,' he said, 'no knowledge ourselves whether [the applicants] were in distress or not. If you will permit me, I will state in what way we distributed relief before that time. When I came to the Court I found that a practice had grown up of receiving, what were in fact, begging letters ; a very large number of them came to the Court every day. I sometimes had upwards of 50 to open, which is of itself rather a serious encroachment upon the business of a police magistrate. A great number of these letters were written in the same hand, and came from the same lodging-house. We understood (I didn't know it of my own knowledge) that there were persons who made a trade of writing these letters at a penny each, and then there was a penny stamp, so that it cost the person twopence to make the application. We

Payment of rent.

understood that the application was very generally made at the instance of the landlord of the house, and, in fact, was an application to get his rent paid, and that in other cases it was made by certain persons who were interested in the sum obtained by the poor man. I was very desirous of putting a stop to that, but it had grown up and become so inveterate that it was not easy to do so ; and as long as we had a surplus in our poor box, and had no

Distribution of 'cards.'

other means of distributing it, I did not very well see what else to do ; but when the pressure came, the number of letters were so many that it was absolutely necessary to take some other course. I then proposed that we should issue cards, which should be placed in the hands of the clergy, of the district visitors, of the Scripture readers, the City missionaries, the medical men connected with dispensaries, and others, who from their habits of life must almost necessarily be acquainted with the real condition of the poor. One day, when I was absent from the Court, there was a very extraordinary pressure ; a great crowd was about the doors of the Court, and in order to satisfy them at all, without giving them money, a card was given to each. Then, of course, they applied again for cards, but after two or three days we found that it was impossible to go on distributing cards, that it brought as great a number of persons as if we had given money, for

Relief by recommendation.

they seemed to think that the card was a voucher upon which they were to obtain money ; therefore we refused to give any cards at the Court, and sent them through the police to the clergy of all denominations, the Scripture readers and others, who we thought would exercise some discrimination, and only recommend persons who were really entitled to relief. To a certain extent that lessened the pressure on the Court, and

[1] Select Committee on Poor Relief (England). First Report (April 19, 1861) ; Mr. W. Gilbert—Questions 4311 and 4415.

[2] Q. 2841, &c.

[3] Mr. C. P. Villiers was Chairman of the Committee. Among the members were Sir George Bowyer, Mr. Lowe, and Mr. Monckton Milnes.

also remedied the evil of indiscriminate distribution, but only partially. I should be very glad to think that one half of the money which we distributed was really well and properly applied.' The card gave the name and address of the poor person, the cause of his distress, the number of his family, and the name of the person recommending him. There was a notice on the card : ' No donation will be made to persons receiving parish relief, or of intemperate habits. Assistance will be most readily granted in those cases of *temporary* distress, where such assistance is likely to afford *permanent* and *effectual* relief, and especially in cases arising out of, or connected with, the business of the Court.' The clergyman or district visitor filled up the card, and gave it to some person who, in his opinion, deserved relief. 'It was then brought to the magistrate, who, judging as far as he could from the particulars on the card, wrote on the back the sum that should be given to that applicant, and thereupon the officer of the Court charged with distributing the fund gave that sum to the party presenting the card' . . . 'but the person recommending was often just as much unknown to us as the poor person himself, and therefore, unless we made inquiry through the police, the reference was useless.' . . . 'This sort of indiscriminate relief was decidedly calculated' 'to encourage imposture and pauperism, and its tendency is, and its conclusion must be, to make a large portion of the labouring classes of London a mob of mendicants' . . . 'There were occasional complaints' ['against the relieving officer, alleging that he would not give relief'], 'but I do not imagine that the applications at the workhouse became so very numerous, as would otherwise have been the case, because the parties found it much easier to get the 7*s.* and 10*s.* from us than to undergo the test which they must have undergone at the workhouse, and also the more strict inquiry.' . . . 'I think that the district visitors ought to know more of [the poor] than any others, where they have some discretion and judgment, and know how to make the inquiry [as to 'their real condition']; but you never can know the condition of the poor generally in a London district unless you are able to unite a body of inquirers who are administrators of the fund from a variety of classes; our sectarian habits prevent us from forming those agencies which are so useful in France. You cannot get the Roman Catholics, and the Protestants, the Episcopalians and others, to act together; but the district visitors certainly have a greater opportunity, and some of the medical men who practise in these quarters.'

There are, in the Report from which this is quoted, descriptions of the administration of relief, which differ in detail from that given by Mr. Paynter, but show rather greater laxity. Mr. Bowring, the Clerk to the City Guardians, said that [' the circumstance that two magistrates were sitting, distributing relief indiscriminately to all who chose to apply to them '] ' was as if two additional relieving officers were put on, one at the Mansion House and the other at Guildhall—distributing money instead of provisions; and instead of its coming out of the poor rates, it came from public subscription. ['The Poor Law'] did not break down in the City of London; it was never tried.'[1] At the Thames Police Court, ' generally a number of persons, sometimes to the amount of 2,000, collected about the Court . . . there was a large amount of silver, and it was given to the applicants as they passed along, as fast as possible.'[2] Mr. Yardley, one of the magistrates who gave this evidence, was asked how it was that in 1854–55, when the winter was as severe as in 1860–61, £900 was sufficient, whereas in the latter year £4,000 had been distributed by the Court. He replied,[3] 'I

Card or application form, 1860.

Results.

Poor Law not used.

Best means of obtaining information. Body of inquirers from a variety of classes.

Evidence of Clerk to the City Guardians, 1860.

Evidence of Mr. Yardley. Distress in 1854–5 and 1860–61 compared.

[1] Select Committee on Poor Relief (England) : First Report (1861). Q. 97 and 99.
[2] *Id.* Mr. Edward Yardley. Q. 2193.
[3] *Id.* Q. 2271.

will not say ['that there was no necessity for more' in 1854]; that is assuming that all the relief was given which might be given. I will say in favour of this year that there was a marked contrast between the conduct of the people in 1855; there was a great disposition in 1855 to riot and disorder, whereas . . . the people in the district of the Thames Police Court were this year remarkably well behaved.' Mr. H. B. Farnall, the Poor Law Inspector for the Metropolitan District, gave evidence[1] that in the five weeks of frost in 1860-61, the 'extra pauperism' had ranged from 6,648 in the first week to 38,637 in the fourth week, and 28,664 in the fifth.[2]

<small>Extra pauperism caused by distress in 1860.</small>

<small>1860-61 and 1886 compared</small>

The bearing of this reference to the Report of the Select Committee of 1861 upon the question submitted to your Committee will be evident. There was last winter, on various grounds, a similar reluctance to resort to or utilise the Poor Law.[3] There was a similar distribution of forms in some instances,[4] and similar crowds at the offices; and the question of inquiry and the use of references and recommendations on an emergency is opened out.[5] Relief by way of payment of rent, given to the tenant, appears also to have been not infrequently relief to the landlord. On the other hand, it will be evident that progress has been made in many ways.

The resolution of the Select Committee in 1861 was, it should be added, as follows:[6]

<small>Conclusions of Select Committee. 1861</small>

'That, with respect to the extraordinary prevalence of distress in the metropolis in the winter of 1860-61, to which the attention of your Committee was particularly directed, they received strong evidence that such distress could have been relieved by the Poor Law authorities, inasmuch as the legal machinery of administration was sufficient, and the Guardians possessed the requisite powers for raising the necessary funds for the purpose; but the legal charge would have pressed very heavily on some parishes within the metropolis.[7] The regular action, however, of the Poor Law was, to a considerable extent, rendered unnecessary by voluntary contributions; and however desirable it is that in great emergencies destitution should be relieved by spontaneous charity, your Committee find that, on the occasion in question, evils resulted from the want of a sufficient organisation for the investigation of the cases of the persons relieved.'

Other evidence respecting the years 1860-61 and 1878-79 the Committee have utilised in subsequent portions of this Report, but their attention has been mainly directed to the experiences of last winter, and to these they now pass.

II. (1) Charitable Feeling and Non-fulfilment of Local Responsibilities.

<small>The charitable world.'</small>

One most important factor in any scheme of relief is what one witness termed 'the charitable world,'[8] the many thoughtless contributors to relief

---

[1] Select Committee on Poor Relief (England): First Report (1861). Mr. Edward Yardley. Q. 3038.

[2] *Id.* p. 125. With these figures may be compared the returns of pauperism in the metropolis in February and March, 1886. The 'extra pauperism' (*i.e.*, the increase over the previous year, 1885) was in the first week of February last, 2,738; in the third week, 6,136; in the third week of March, 8,848—the highest figure. In making this comparison with 1861, the large increase in the population of the metropolis should be borne in mind.

[3] *Cf.* Evidence, Hayward, 648; Mackay, 1211; Roberts, 1020, &c.; Andrews, 2356, and others.

[4] Acworth, 463; Rev. B. Lambert, 560, &c.

[5] Bramly, 347, &c.; Westbrook, 2015, and others.

[6] Report (printed May 31, 1864), p. 10.

[7] This was before the passing of the Act 34 & 35 Vict., c. 108, s. 8, by which the Metropolitan Common Poor Fund was created.

[8] Hayward, 662.

funds, who have little or no personal knowledge of the work of relief or the conditions under which it can be administered with good results. 'We had rather a sentimental Committee, who were anxious to grant as much as possible,' says one working man. 'That was the great difficulty to contend against. It was thought the public was clamouring for the money to be promptly divided.'[1] Another witness tells how men who were able-bodied and would not work 'are able to live somehow on the public';[2] and 'some of the artisans and labourers preferred to go about with a box, drum, and banner, and get 5s. a day by begging, instead of the 2s. 6d. a day which they might have earned.'[3]

Besides this eager clamour for hasty almsgiving and the lack of knowledge combined with strong opinions, there is a manifest neglect of local duties in many districts. One witness, speaking of a part of South London, allows that 'practically, so far as' they have power to devote their leisure and provide skilful charity, 'the rich and well-to-do who make their money in the district do not make use of it.'[4] He says also, 'a great many men are temporarily dismissed on account of slackness of work. I know a man well who is now out of work, and who had for many years been continuously employed. He had been employed at the docks on a superior class of work. Together with a mate he was discharged in January, the men being told that their services would not be wanted till July. Immediately afterwards the employer subscribed fifty guineas to the fund for the unemployed.'[5] Another witness, an employer, referring to the Guardians, says of another district: 'The Poor Law administration is too much in the hands of the shopkeepers, and working men know very little about it. I don't know whether the vestryman or the guardian is looked upon with the greater contempt.'[6]

Local responsibilities.

(2) NEED OF TRAINING IN ALMSGIVING.

Side by side with this unfortunate and most injurious neglect of local duty and want of confidence in local authorities must be placed the fact that only so far as people are trained to meet ordinary distress, and understand its causes, can they cope with an emergency. This is the more apparent if it is allowed that the problem is to relieve without lowering the status and moral condition of the recipient. The people 'want energy and increase of self-respect,' and relief given upon decisions arrived at 'very fast indeed' 'rather decreased it,' says one witness.[7] Another allows that in a district adjacent to a wealthy suburb their members were not sufficient to make proper inquiries. They could, he thought, 'eliminate the cases' that were 'obviously drunken and dissipated,' but they could not get trained visitors, and could not therefore attempt 'to work to a higher standard.'[8] The administration 'gradually improved,' says another, 'till at last (the fund) was fairly well administered, because the Committee by that time had acquired some experience of that kind of work.'[9] . . . 'A large number of persons entirely unaccustomed to dealing with distress were called together, and forced to administer a large sum of money on a large scheme. If the other plan had been adopted—of using existing associations—you would have had people of some experience.' 'Yes,'[10] says another, 'we were all educated by our experience.' 'The work of relief that has to be undertaken on an emergency should be committed as far as possible,' writes the Fulham Sub-

More and better workers wanted.

---

[1] Andrews, Q. 2330.
[2] Jack, Q. 1035.
[3] Jack, 980, 985; Bramly, 391; Acworth, 473.
[4] Gardiner, 923, 924.
[5] Gardiner, 918; cf. Andrews, 2363, &c.
[6] Roberts, 1096.
[7] Gee, 1411.
[8] Acworth, 434, 497, 498.
[9] Gardiner, 824, 868.
[10] Marchant, 1266.

View of Fulham Sub-Committee of the Mansion House Fund.

Committee of the Mansion House Fund, 'to persons who have had experience in dealing with the poor, and are known to have paid attention to the difficult problems involved. The ordinary volunteer who engages for the first time in work of this description is often full of zeal and animated by the best intentions; but he is as often ignorant of the scope and purpose of the Poor Law, and therefore blind to the importance of keeping its tasks and those of charity distinct. He thinks that if a man drinks, or squanders his earnings in some form of folly or vice, there is at once a sufficient reason for assisting his wife and children, never having grasped the truth that the Poor Law is the only agency that can deal satisfactorily with such cases. His aim is to give; that is what he has come to do, and he will not stay to discriminate, much less to deny.'

(3) DIFFERENT CONDITIONS OF DIFFERENT PARTS OF LONDON.

Another point, frequently overlooked, is the diversity of local conditions in different parts of London. The character of the population differs; the resources of the districts are different; and the administration of the Poor Law is different. Any proposals for the relief of the poor must, therefore, be adjusted to local requirements and must not enfeeble local efforts.

Differences in population.

'The population differs.' At St. George-in-the-East the applicants with whom the almoners had to deal were 'a small number of the lower class of artisans,' but chiefly 'the dock-labouring class, that is, men who have no constant employment, but gain a precarious living in the neighbourhood of the river. This consists of "broken" men, who, by their misfortunes or their vices, have fallen out of regular work, but to a large extent of those who have been born within the demoralising influence of the intermittent and irregular employment given by the Dock Companies, and who have never been able to rise above their circumstances.'[1]

Contrast with this Battersea. That 'district is inhabited by a better class. It has not the real ragged pauper. It has no slums whatever.'[2] And the contrast between Lewisham and Marylebone and St. Giles's is equally great.[3]

Differences in resources.

'The resources of the districts are different.' At Marylebone the Fund was 'only another agency added to the numerous relief agencies in the district'; 'there was nothing to justify such help being offered to Marylebone.'[4] And at Lewisham there was no reason why all necessary relief should not have been raised locally.[5] On the other hand, at Camberwell, Mr. Acworth says, 'I dont know of any local charity, except the Charity Organisation Society, that there would be any use going to.' 'If Camberwell had raised money, it would not have raised £100. One side of Denmark Hill is almost entirely poor, and the other almost entirely rich; and they do not recognise any responsibility. London took up a responsibility which ought to have been discharged locally,' but 'it is fair to remember that the population of Camberwell don't work for the population of Camberwell any more than they work for the population of Grosvenor Square; it is simply a sleeping-place for workers elsewhere.'[6] Here is a recognition of the differences with a reason for combination within certain limits. Yet it must be remembered that what is termed a 'sleeping-place'

---

[1] Report of the St. George-in-the-East and Wapping Committee of the Mansion House Fund, p. 7.
[2] Heale, 1314, &c.
[3] Cf. Fletcher, 69; Valpy, 206, 230; Bramly, 316.
[4] Fletcher, 133, 199.
[5] Bramly, 359, 360; Legge, 1160.
[6] Acworth, 455, 477.

is, after all, the home and the only home of that part of the population of Camberwell to which reference is here made.

'The administration of the Poor Law is different.' To take one point of importance in connection with exceptional distress. Lewisham and St. Saviour's have a labour-yard; Kensington and St. George-in-the-East have none. Differences in Poor Law.

From these references it will be seen (1) that the success of any scheme must largely depend on the education of 'the charitable world' in the distribution of relief. There is evidence of an advance in public opinion, if 1885–86 be compared with 1860–61. It was (*e.g.*) a new thing last year, that at a time of distress relief money should be used to pay up club arrears. (2) The administration of relief will be more or less effectual, according as local duties are honourably performed by those who have local responsibilities. (3) Any scheme of relief should tend to keep alive and stimulate local effort; and it should admit of easy modification according to variations in the administration of the Poor Law, and differences in the character of the population. (4) On the number of persons who have previously acquired knowledge and experience in almsgiving will depend the failure or success of measures adopted on an emergency. (5) This will become more evident as the desire to give relief is superseded by a desire to prevent chronic distress and to raise the condition of the people. General conclusions.

(4) INFORMATION AS TO THE EXISTENCE OR NATURE OF DISTRESS.

A fourth preliminary question is that of obtaining accurate information in regard to distress. In a population such as that in London, there is always a tendency to cry 'Wolf, wolf.' 'The idle, disorderly, and hereditary pauper class' are only too ready to raise the cry. They 'join and make use of numbers of hard-working men for their own benefit, by raising a clamour and exaggerating the distress, in order the more easily to impose on the public, and obtain indiscriminate relief.'[1] The rich, who give without knowledge or on impulse, or because others do, and the almsgivers, to whom the whole problem of charity reduces itself to 'Give, give,' are quick to increase the alarm.[2] Those who trade on charity are always on the alert to 'raise the wind' for their own purposes, and even those interested in *bonâ fide* societies are tempted to appeal for funds on the strength of the outcry.

The Committee have received much written and verbal evidence respecting the best means of ascertaining the facts in regard to alleged destitution. The Poor Law returns are, it would seem, a surer test of widespread distress than is usually allowed.[3] But it is likely that, as the Poor Law is better administered, and as the people are better educated and induced to become more thrifty, there will be a greater reluctance to apply for Poor Law relief. More care has accordingly to be taken to ascertain the actual facts. The inquiries should be made early in the winter, as privately as possible, in order to prevent ungrounded apprehensions and panic;[4] and the tests should be the recognised duty of some public body. The return entitled 'Pauperism and Distress' (March, 1886) shows that the Local Government Board might, with very great advantage to the community, undertake this office, and obtain information, at least, from

---

[1] Letter of the Master of the Wolverhampton Workhouse. Thirteenth Report of the Local Government Board, 1861, p. 39.

[2] 'Those who spoke most strongly as to the unusual distress,' writes a correspondent from a South London District, 'were those who had least experience among the poor.'

[3] Gardiner, 906. *Cf.* Local Government Board Report, 1860–61, p. 15; and subsequently in the Cotton Famine.

[4] *Cf.* Gardiner, 905, 915; Roberts, 1086; Dew, 2086; Mackay, 1194; Heale, 1,366.

various official sources and Government Departments. Apart from this, the Committee would suggest that the work should devolve on the Provisional Committee, which should, in their opinion, be established.

(5) The 'Chronic' or 'Permanent' Poor.

The object of the administrators of relief on an emergency should be to reach those who are in distress owing to exceptional causes, and to pass by those who receive relief habitually and are no worse off than usual. This is a chief difficulty. In spite of rules to the contrary, the latter generally receive the lion's share.

'There are two classes of workmen,' says Canon Legge, 'one regular and thrifty, and the other irregular, which last falls back persistently on to indiscriminate charity.' 'The bulk of the distress is chronic, always coming after the summer and lasting for the winter, year after year.'[2] 'I must admit,' says Mr. Fletcher,[3] speaking of Marylebone, 'that I violated the rule that no part of the funds should be used for the relief of chronic distress, otherwise I should not have got rid of much of the money. Mr. M. Stephany, speaking of the work of the Jewish Board of Guardians, says, 'Practically we exclude no class of case; out-of-work cases come back to us every three or four weeks. They recur every winter.'[4] 'All these people,' Mr. Mackay says of St. George-in-the-East, 'are very poor people. It is a puzzle how they live. I suppose they never earn more than 10s. a week. You say they must of necessity be in distress, and you give them something; but they are not worse off than usual.'[5] 'My experience was,' says Mr. Roberts,[6] 'that the tendency of the Fund was to drift to the relief of the permanent poor. Do what we could to avoid it, we could not help its drifting. And I think it was to some extent owing to the fact that the Committee were composed to a large extent of clergymen and district visitors; and the charity went to their own particular set; it went to the same set as are relieved by churches and chapels. I believe that many of the clergy honestly tried their best to prevent this, but, as the matter was in their hands, these people came. As a rule the mechanic does not go to church or chapel.' 'The better men' 'would not go to a Society which was managed by clergy.'[7] 'They would think themselves bound to return the compliment by going to church or chapel.'[8]

The chronic poor are ready to apply to anyone who will help them, clergy and ministers, local charities, or, if they can obtain out-relief, to the Poor Law. If they are out of work and do not receive their usual relief from these sources, they may, if befriended, be induced to look forward to the future and make some provision for themselves.[9] But when a large distribution of relief is made, the personal care which might help them to do this is not forthcoming. Large numbers have to be attended to. The relief must be given by test or on some principle, and that quickly. And the staff available for the purpose is, more or less, insufficient. If justice is to be done to the better class—for those for whom the funds are intended—the bulk of the 'ablebodied' 'permanent' poor must be excluded, and relief should only be given to them by the Guardians in the labour-yard. It will greatly depend on the administration whether they are still further pauperised (already they are paupers in all but the name), or taught a lesson in self-respect. Mere relief by itself cannot avail. Some chronic distress is due to low wages, but to supplement a low wage is to perpetuate it.

[1] See p. xviii.
[2] Legge, 1145, 1134.
[3] Fletcher, 62, 63.
[4] 2219, 2221, &c.
[5] Mackay, 1216.
[6] 1610.
[7] Dove, 1629. Moss, 2471.
[8] Roberts, 1630, 1681.
[9] See case of a man living on 20s. a week: Gardiner, 888. Cf. Avis, 1551.

(6) The Independent Artisan and Labourer.

There is, of course, every grade of self-reliance and self-respect; but the position of the independent labourer is in the main a marked contrast to that of the chronic poor, and it was generally acknowledged that the distress last winter had, at least in some parts of London, reached the better class.[1]

'The difficulty in that matter,' says an employer of labour, 'is to get one of what we call our good artisans to degrade himself to come and receive charity. I really don't believe that up in our neighbourhood (Islington), in the number that came for relief, there was one thoroughly sterling, honest, straightforward man in the whole lot, judging from examination. Perhaps I am overstating the case; but I could not put my finger upon one.'[2] 'Very few' of the independent artisans 'put themselves on' the Fund, says a working man. 'If I had not pressed them they would not have gone on the Fund. I am afraid [a fund like this] would lower him. That is what I feel myself. I suppose it is human nature.'[3] Another witness says, 'The great bulk of the cases that came at first were parish cases, while the artisans would not come near us. But as time went on, and as the application of the rules became more rigorous and more careful, a better class of men did come, until at last the good cases were, I should say, in a decided majority over the Poor Law cases.'[4]

To reach men of this stamp, and yet to do no injury, charity, it is evident, must do its work most carefully.

The social status of these men has improved with an improvement which has reached also to those of a lower grade than themselves.

'I don't know that [the men] are earning more wages,' says Mr. Vallance, comparing Whitechapel in 1870 with what it is now; 'but the conditions of their life have improved during the last sixteen years.' 'The public-house trade has gone down very much;' there is more sobriety and more thrift, and 'workers among the poor say that rents are paid with great regularity.'[5] Mr. Dove says 'the artisan is now far more respectable. Every man in our shop is rather a gentleman to what he was thirty years ago. It was the rule to find these men keeping Saint Monday and Saint Tuesday too. Such a thing never occurs now, and they go out with their black clothes. They have given up their fustian and corduroy.'[6]

On the other hand, there is evidence of a fall in the wages in some trades, and of a diminution in the amount distributed in wages.

On the former point the evidence of Mr. Nathan Moss in regard to cabinet-making is to the effect that men accustomed only to better-class work are compelled to do inferior work, and thus earn less wages than men engaged all their life on inferior goods, and therefore more skilful in making them. 'People are going in for the cheapest thing they can get.' 'If work different to the ordinary kind is given to nine-tenths of the men, they can't or won't do it.'[7]

On the latter point, Mr. Dove, speaking of his firm in the building trade, says, 'About ten years ago we were paying £1,500 a week for wages: this last winter we only paid £300'; and Mr. Roberts, 'The amount of our wages was two-thirds less than three years ago.'[8] And, says the former, arguing in favour of helping men by opening public works, 'we have always found, as to the artisan, that, if he happens to be out of work for

---

[1] Return, Pauperism and Distress (March 8, 1886): pp. 137, 140, 144. *Cf.* also Dew, 2069, 2077; Powell, 2256, 2253; Westbrook, 1996, 2002; Collie, 1875.
[2] Dove, 1646.
[3] Westbrook, 1961, 1962.
[4] Gardiner, 825; Valpy, 212.
[5] 690 and 726; Avis, 1532, 1533.
[6] Dove, 1671; Roberts, 1672, 1673.
[7] Moss, 2396, &c., 2464, 2455.
[8] Dove, 1585, 1590; *cf.* Bramly, 379.

three months, he is never the same man again. He becomes demoralised. Even supposing we administered a fund like this [the Mansion House Fund] as well as possible, the man would never be the man he was before.'

For these men, then, what courses are possible? For their temporary assistance, relief most carefully distributed or public works under many safeguards;[1] and for their permanent aid, emigration or migration; a revival of trade, or the adoption of some new handicraft. From emigration or migration there is, from a working man's point of view, little to be hoped at present.[2] Of a revival of trade there is a doubtful expectation. In the adoption of new handicrafts, and in such an education as would equip men with a larger stock of faculties available for a time of need, there is more hope.[3] And in those trades which are in their nature periodical, or in which employment is irregular, the only remedy would seem to be that the workman should learn to adapt himself to the changes and be able to turn his hand to more crafts than one. To promote this would seem to be the first duty of charity, rightly understood.

But these are remedies which can only be slowly applied, and which act gradually. In the main, from the point of view of relief, the best safeguard of these men is their thrift, and, apart from other help, the best aid is to keep them in their clubs by paying up arrears or to help them to join clubs. No effort should be spared to save them from falling into the 'chronic' class; and if the ordinary alms-seekers and loafers are kept at bay, it is quite possible to do this. In the North of England, in 1884-85, many of the unemployed, who 'would otherwise have had to be relieved by payments from the poor-rates, were supported by the various trade societies.'[4] And the Secretary of the London Society of Compositors writes, 'that between 1876 and 1885 that Society distributed £41,556. 16s. 7d. to the unemployed, and £1,748. 18s. for emigration. . . . If every workman,' he says, 'in his own particular trade, whether skilled or unskilled, belonged to his trade society,' . . .'. ' he would be able " to tide over " periods of slackness without extraneous assistance, though doubtless in many cases sore pressed.'[5] It is in support of such a view as this that Mr. Powell,[6] as a working man, urges the use of some kind of thrift test at a time of exceptional distress. ' I should not,' he says, ' make any proposal to assist a man unless he had tried to assist himself—anything—if he could only show me an old bank-book. I should let those who had not made any provision go to the Poor Law. It seems formed to meet their case. But I would not do it if he had made the smallest provision for himself. A man must expect to get old; he must provide for that by the superannuation fund. Every man can do something for himself.'

III. AGENCIES FOR RELIEF.

(1) THE POOR LAW; ITS FUNCTIONS GENERALLY.

As is the normal administration of charitable relief, so will its administration be at a time of exceptional distress. And the same may be said of the Poor Law. The function of Charity should be to prevent destitution: that of the Poor Law to relieve it. Between the two there must

---

[1] See below, xiv.

[2] Powell, 2255, 2270, 2271; but cf. Dew, 2094; Westbrook, 2007, &c., 1940.

[3] Powell, 2297, &c.; Westbrook, 2009, &c.; Dove, 1691; Legge, 1149-1158; Roberts, 1662, 1690.

[4] Fourteenth Annual Report of the Local Government Board, p. xxxvi; cf. Dew, 2077; Gardiner, 883-888.

[5] Letter to the President of the Local Government Board, March 2, 1886, p. 142 in Return: Pauperism and Distress.

[6] 2257, 2258, 2266, 2284.

be co-operation. This would imply that volunteers have informed themselves of the functions of the Poor Law, and that the Guardians have come to some understanding with them as to the ways in which they, as Guardians, can turn charitable devotion and liberality to the best account for the poor. But at present the charitable, as a rule, are ignorant of the principles and provisions of the Poor Law, and are inclined to ignore it as hard, arbitrary, and official. The Guardians, in turn, have a not unnatural distrust of the administrators of charitable funds, who seem to them sentimental, wayward, and irresponsible. The consequence is that many societies and individuals are habitually doing what the Poor Law should do, and neglecting to do what the Poor Law cannot do. They distribute a kind of outdoor relief without rule and without method, productive of evils similar to those of outdoor relief under the old Poor Law—a feeling of dependence among the poor and a lively expectation of future largess.[1] On the other hand, the Poor Law Guardians do not feel the need of, nor, as individuals, encourage, any combination of charitable workers with whom they may co-operate to help those whom 'it is undesirable to treat as subjects for pauper relief.'

So great (from the point of view of the Poor Law) are the evils of want of co-operation that the Clerk to the Manchester Board of Guardians writes that 'where the distress is not very severe, or where there is no efficient organisation in existence for the proper distribution of public charity, the Guardians would do well to discourage the formation of a fund. But if a fund is formed there should be interchange of information, and 'the Relief Committee should be strongly urged not to give assistance to anyone in receipt of relief from the Guardians, and the Guardians' allowance should be at once withdrawn in every case in which this recommendation is disregarded.'[2]

Co-operation between the Poor Law and Charity.

Mr. Vallance's evidence illustrates the plan of co-operation at work in some Unions in London. The Committee draw particular attention to this, as without some such system it is hopeless to expect that charitable funds collected on an emergency will be well administered.

'There is,' says Mr. Vallance, 'a perfect understanding between the Guardians and the Charity Organisation Society in Whitechapel. The Guardians have never adopted a "no outdoor relief" policy; but have merely endeavoured to stem the tide of hereditary pauperism by guarding against permanency in Poor Law relief. They have, however, not found it necessary to provide for even the temporary necessities of deserving cases, by reason of the representatives of the Charity Organisation Society on the Board spontaneously undertaking to prevent the first step in pauperism.[3] The poor understand a uniform administration and the application of strict rules, especially when allied with efforts to lift them out of their pauperism.'[4] 'The Poor Law Guardians would not have been able to carry on their work successfully without the sympathy of those outside. When

---

[1] *See* above, *re* Chronic poor. Gardiner. 890, &c.; Vallance, 794; Jack, 1012; Dew, 2057; Mr. W. H. Gurney Salter (Lambeth) writes to the Committee: 'If the distress is no greater next winter, I think such a distribution of alms should not be repeated. Its effect in discouraging providence would be greater the second winter, and after that the poor would be entitled to expect it always—in fact, a second Poor Law system would be established side by side with the first.' The mischief done by want of co-operation between Charity and the Poor Law at a time of distress is no new story. *Cf.* Report by Mr. Andrew Doyle, p. 36; XIIIth Annual Report of the Local Government Board.

[2] 'Poor Relief during Depression of Trade in the Winter of 1878-9, by Mr. Macdonald. Paper read at a Poor Law Conference at Southport, October, 1879.

[3] 683.   [4] 717.

it was found that the ultimate object of the Guardians was to draw a distinction between pauper relief and charitable assistance, definiteness of aim was given both to Poor Law administration and voluntary workers, whilst co-operation between the two agencies was in no small measure promoted. The diminution that has taken place in Whitechapel pauperism is largely attributable to the earnest efforts of voluntary workers to redeem the poor from pauperism and dependence.'[1] This system he thought applicable to other districts, *e.g.*, to one which is in many respects very different, St. James's, Soho,[2] and he felt assured that in Whitechapel with this co-operation the distress of last winter could have been met by existing agencies.[3]

Poor Law Regulations to meet a Time of Distress.[4]

The Out-relief Regulation Order requires ' That every able-bodied male person, if relieved out of the workhouse, shall be set to work by the Guardians, and be kept employed under their direction and superintendence, so long as he continues to receive relief.' It is further provided that ' one half of the relief shall be given in articles of food or fuel, or in other articles of absolute necessity.' The Guardians have authority to take special measures in ' cases of a very exceptional character,' subject to report to the Local Government Board. The Poor Law relief available for the able-bodied consists, accordingly, of relief in the workhouse, and relief by means of work, generally in the labour-yard.

The Workhouse.

To avoid ' the rush ' made ' upon relieving officers ' ' by the improvident poor' ' when it becomes known that the workhouse is full,' Poor Law administrators advocate a reserve of workhouse accommodation.'[5] That may be considered an official view of the question. With it may be compared the opinions expressed by the witnesses. A Wandsworth Guardian said, ' The very worst men, if able-bodied, won't apply to the workhouse.'[6] ' The [' rather undeserving people '] won't accept it,' said a paid visitor of long experience. 'One man [last winter] said he would rather starve; and I said, ' Well, you will have to starve.'

' Was that case relieved ? ' is the next question to the witness ? ' No, sir ; we would not relieve him.'—' And he did not lie down and starve ? ' ' No, he is alive now.'—' When that sort of talk goes on, you are not so frightened as with a quiet person ?' ' No : we know how to deal with them better.'[7] This ' rather undeserving ' class, then, may, at a time of exceptional distress, be safely left to the Poor Law. When, however, there is a wife and family, it is often hard ' to break up the home.' ' It would be as well,' one working man allows, ' that the drinking man should go to the workhouse ; but the difficulty is with his wife and children.'[8] To meet this difficulty in ' no-work cases ' at Whitechapel, ' the Guardians do not require the wife and family to enter the workhouse ; but, conditionally upon the man doing so, voluntary charity undertakes to keep the home together.[9] To this proposal another working man said, ' I think that would have been a fair test. I don't like the idea of breaking up the home.'[10]

The conclusions which the Committee would draw from this evidence and

---

[1] 782. [2] 792. [3] 680.

[4] Return : Pauperism and Distress (March, 1886).

[5] Poor Relief during Depression of Trade,' (1878-9) p. 144 ; *cf.* p. 140, &c.

[6] Heale, 1370, 1371 ; Bramly, 365. In the North in 1884-85, the workhouse test was usefully applied. Comparatively few accepted it : *e.g.*, at Sunderland, 39 out of 104. *See* Fourteenth Annual Report of the Local Government Board.

[7] Mrs. Avis, 1517, 1504, 1505.

[8] Dew, 2068, 2078, 2079.

[9] Vallance, 683.

[10] Andrews, 2357, 2358.

other opinions received by them is, that it is right that the 'house' should be offered in the case of the drunkard and the absolutely thriftless; but that, where there is a decent home, the plan adopted in Whitechapel should be put in force.

The Labour-Yard.

The test of the labour-yard has 'a deterrent effect' 'when properly carried out.' But 'the more indolent of the men are content to bear' with it 'rather than exert themselves to obtain employment involving hard work and longer hours.' The labour-yard 'after a time demoralises' him. And 'the only cure is the offer of an order for the workhouse, which, as experience shows, is rarely accepted.[1]

This is the view of the Poor Law administrator. With it again the evidence taken by the Committee may be compared.

'Stone-breaking is a degrading thing,' says an employer of labour, 'because it is a sort of thing you put the lowest of the low to do. It is like picking oakum. It is in a degree useful; but it is infinitesimal in its use. I am not speaking about loafers. Do what you like with those. Make it as abhorrent as possible to those. I am speaking of carpenters and joiners.'[2] 'It would lower them,' says a working man. 'They would feel it so.'[3] 'But,' he said afterwards, 'I am thinking myself with those dock labourers, if we had had a labour test [in the labour-yard] with them, many of them would have shirked it.'

For the good management, also, of any public works, a division between men sent to the labour-yard and men employed on the works is equally desirable, unless, as at Wandsworth last winter, the works are opened by the Guardians.[4]

The Committee conclude that if labour-yards are opened by the Guardians the administrators of any fund should refer to them all able-bodied applicants of the ordinary labouring class.[5]

[1] 'Poor Relief during Depression of Trade,' 1878-9, p. 141.
[2] Dove, 1659-61.
[3] Westbrook, 1931, 2031, 2032; *cf.* Andrews, 2355 ; Heale, 1374 ; Westbrook, 1999, 2009 ; *cf.* Dove, 1634.
[4] Collie, 1852, 1853, 1848 ; Wilkinson, 1734, 1738 ; Jack, 993, 984, 985.
[5] The following may be quoted as a good scale of labour-yard relief. It is that adopted by the Lewisham Board of Guardians :

'LABOUR-YARD SCALE OF RELIEF.

'The Guardians employ able-bodied and partially able-bodied males, during the whole time they are upon relief, requiring a fixed task of work to be performed by them, and when such task is duly performed, relief is granted on the following scale, which is limited to five days only per week; but it will be discretionary with the Board to alter the character and quality of the relief if, in their judgment, they consider it necessary or expedient to do so.

Total Value of a Week's Relief (5 days)	Class.	
s. d.		
4 4½	A	5 pence, 2lb. bread, ½lb. meat, 2d. grocery per diem— single man.
5 5	B	6 pence, 2lb. bread, ½lb. meat, 2d. grocery per diem— man and wife.
6 3	C	6 pence, 4lb. bread, ½lb. meat, 2d. grocery per diem— man, wife, and child.
7 1	D	8 pence, 4lb. bread, ½lb. meat, 2d. grocery per diem— man, wife, and 2 children.
8 11½	E	10 pence, 4lb. bread, ¾lb. meat, 3d. grocery per diem— man, wife, and 3 children.
10 5	F	10 pence, 6lb. bread, 1lb. meat, 3d. grocery per diem— man, wife, and 4 children.
11 8	G	13 pence, 6lb. bread, 1lb. meat, 3d. grocery per diem— man, wife, and 5 children.

This scale applies to persons WHOLLY destitute.'

xiv

(2) RELIEF BY EMPLOYMENT.

Employment provided at Whitechapel.

Where there is no labour-yard, various expedients have to be adopted.[1] At Whitechapel, last winter,[2] street-sweeping was provided for the ordinary outdoor labourers, by arrangement with the District Board of Works. 'This test was a sore trial' to many of the men; 'the Fund,' they said, 'is a charity, and we are entitled to it without working.' 'The majority did not persist in their application.'

For the employment of a higher class of labourers and men in delicate health, the Guardians gave a contract, which they had before given to a West-End Association, for cleaning the windows of the infirmary, and other work, such as whitewashing, &c., was provided by them. The men so employed 'on the whole gave satisfaction.'

For others, again, e.g., tailors (19) and sempstresses (140), special work was provided, with good results.

Employment provided at Wandsworth.

A word should be added regarding the plan adopted last winter by the Wandsworth Guardians. They were at the time building their workhouse, and determined 'to make the men dig out the sand and put in the foundations, instead of opening a labour-yard.'[3] Under the instruction of the gangers the skilled workmen, who were unused to spade work, soon improved, and the weaker men, or those who had suffered from privation, were put to light work for a week or so. The outlay was £1,402. 15s. 8d. the net loss about £29. The works were open for seven weeks. The average number of men at work ranged from 234 in the first week to 89 in the last. The pay was 2s. 6d. a day for eight hours, slightly in excess of what would have been earned by such a mixed body of men. The several relieving officers took 'great pains in selecting deserving men for the works.' The plan was altogether successful.

At Lewisham, Holloway, and in many suburban districts, road-making could without difficulty be provided by the District Boards.[4]

Conclusions regarding the provision of employment.

On various points of detail the conclusions of the Committee are as follows:

1. The wage should not be a 'charity' wage. 'Men will only put the amount of labour to it,' says one witness who had charge of some road-making, 'you get for charity work'—'not worth 2d. an hour.'[5] The men are inclined to 'loaf,' and the work costs four times as much as it would if done on contract.[6] Last winter the Public Gardens Association paid 4d. an hour for a day of five hours, with sometimes a dinner which cost 4d. in addition; but, in spite of the possible evils of attracting labourers from other places, a larger payment per hour or a longer day's work would seem to be better morally, and for the work's sake.

The best methods of payment appear to be either by contract or by 'measured work,' or by scale.

If payment by contract is adopted, some special arrangement would have to be made that the contractor should take unskilled men.[7]

---

[1] There are strong arguments against the establishment of labour-yards, especially in very poor districts. Cf. Mackay, 1204; Gardiner, 854.

[2] Report of the Whitechapel Union Committee of the Mansion House Fund. Cf. Vallance, 683, 764, 722, 809; and Mackay, 1217.

[3] Heale, 1303; and Report of Mr. Aldwinckle, the Architect to the Board, June, 1886.

[4] Jack, 945, &c.; Dove, 1634; cf. Sir R. Rawlinson's Report in 'Distress and Pauperism.'

[5] Jack, 978, 979, &c., 1022; Wilkinson, 1707, 1708, 1736. Cf. Collie, who gives, on the whole, a good account of the men's work, 1778, 1779, 1819, 1852; Powell, 2296.

[6] Jack, 984; Wilkinson, 1736; Collie, 1820.

[7] Jack, 1019; Roberts, 1643; Dove, 1635; Acworth, 437.

Of payment by 'measured work,' Sir R. Rawlinson wrote in 1866:[1] 'While men were working as a labour test' they had earned '¾ths of a penny per day;' but within two days after the change was made from 'test' to 'measured work,' the same men earned wages exceeding 2s. a day —the work being measured and priced on both occasions, at the same rate. This plan is worthy of special consideration.

If payment be made by scale a minimum (say, 4d. an hour for an eight hours' day) would be settled, and, after proving the men, an additional 1d. or 1½d. or more would be given per hour, according to their ability and industry. In 1864, at Stockport, 'unskilled men' earned 2s. 2d. a day; at Wigan, 'factory operatives' earned 'on an average 2s. 9d. a day, a few of the handiest men 3s. a day, and none less than 2s. 8d. a day for a full day's work.'[2] With regard to wages paid in the winter of 1884-5 at the embankment works on the River Tees, the following extracts of letters from the Clerks of the Middlesborough and Stockton Guardians give particulars:

The former writes: 'The men employed by the contractor on the Embankment works were paid in the first instance according to the work done, and their earnings averaged from 6d. to 8d. per man per hour. The men worked in companies of from 12 to 20, and the work of each company was measured every evening roughly, and accurately at the end of each week, and the amount earned divided equally. As the embankment got nearer the sea, and the work became more difficult and uncertain, in consequence of the action of the water in rough weather, the men grew dissatisfied, and ultimately the contractor agreed to pay each man at the rate of sixpence per hour worked; and this arrangement continued until the worked ceased. The men were nearly all ironworkers, and totally unskilled in the sort of work they had to do, and, as an inducement to the contractor to employ them, the Guardians of this Union provided the plant they required.'

The Clerk to the Stockton Guardians writes: 'The men are employed at the embankment works in digging mud and earth from the bed of the river at low tide, and putting it into small trucks or "bogies," which they run along a tramway to the embankment in course of formation at the mouth of the river. The men are paid by the Contractor 6d. per cubic yard for the earth and mud removed from the bed of the river and conveyed to the embankment, the total weekly earnings of each man averaging from 12s. to 15s. The men are sent to the works by the Relieving Officers, who select them from the applicants for relief; and when employed at the Embankment works they are under the entire control of the contractor.'

5d. an hour for a day of five hours was found satisfactory last year.[3] It is, however, doubtful whether there is any advantage in working the men by shifts and for four or five hours only, in the hope of their using part of the time to look for employment. It seems better that they should work for the eight hours, and take 'a day off' to look for work.[4]

2. To other than works done on contract, men should not be admitted without sufficient inquiry, or a trustworthy recommendation. Unless this precaution is taken, it will be of little use to open such works. There might as well be only a labour-yard.[5]

Recommendations.

[1] Local Government Board Report, 1864-65, p. 58; Jack, 1026.
[2] Cf. Collie, 1847-1849, 1821, 1822; Bramly, 310-312; Heale, 1303; L.G.B. Report, 1864-65, p. 45. The wage paid at Wandsworth is stated above. At Lewisham 2s. 6d. was paid for a day of 7½ hours at road-making. At Chelsea, for wood-paving and the labour connected with it, men had according to their ability, industry, and the kind of work to which they were set, 4d., 5d., and 9d. an hour.
[3] Cf. Wilkinson, 1752; Collie, 1820-21.
[4] Cf. Collie, 1818, and Mr. Aldwinckle's Report. Cf. Powell, 2296. 'This winter we have got very much less work done than the winter before, when we worked eight hours,' Wilkinson, 1711.
[5] Cf. Dr Longstaff, 1754; Collie, 1839, 1768; Vallance, 683; Jack, 1027, 970.

Supervision. 3. The supervision must be strict.[1] The employment may be an opportunity of improving the character and physique of the men, and even teaching them a new trade. There should be a division and subdivision of the works. The men should be employed in small gangs, and those unaccustomed to rough labour mixed with the more skilled workmen.[2] And the manager must have the power of summary dismissal, and receive the support of his Committee in a reasonable use of the power.[3]

Wages in kind. 4. As a rule it is not well to give part of the wage in kind—*e.g.*, in a meal. In this and other respects the position of employment by contract should be assumed as far as possible. Many of those who want such help will be labour-yard men. If it is required by others, it is better that it should be given independently by a Relief Committee.[4]

Kind of work. 5. Though it requires some time to habituate men to the use of the spade and shovel, and the value of their work may be at first small, it is clear that earth-work is suitable practically for all classes. If, *e.g.*, road making is provided, it will not be necessary to give any other kinds of employment, except possibly in the case of weaker men, and of a few others who belong to one or two trades for which such labour would unfit them.[5] Suitable work may, by a little ingenuity, be found in all parts of London.

6. It is very important that works should not be opened unless there is a clear necessity for them. They should not be allowed to become the ordinary resource of the labouring poor. Many men will prefer to do 'charity work,' especially if the supervision is not strict, 'at 4*d.* per hour' than 'contract work at 6*d.*'[6] It is nothing but harmful to supply work for men who 'can hardly be got to work at all;' who begin by smoking, and will not come 'at 7 o'clock in the morning.'[7]

(3) Charitable Relief.

In regard to charitable relief, the Committee would draw attention to one or two of the difficulties which a large fund tends to create.

There is likely to be an immediate rush of applicants to the Relief Centres.

At St. Marylebone, at first, 'the scrimmage was so fearful sometimes that I feared,' says one witness, 'that I should have to call in the police to keep order.'[8] The news of it 'spread like wildfire,' says another.[9] 'The applications came in by hundreds.' 'We had such a crowd of applicants that we were obliged to have, I think, four policemen to keep order.'[10] 'The Mansion House Fund might do a deal of good if properly managed, but this one was a general scramble.'[11]

Publicity and Advertisement stimulate applications.

'If you go into the street with your pockets full of sovereigns,' says Mr. Mackay, 'and have it advertised that you are going to give them away, there is no end to the applications you will have to deal with. As an

---

[1] Jack, 1019, 1031, 1014.
[2] Local Government Board Report, 1864-65, p. 37 ; Collie, 1844.
[3] Collie, 1777.
[4] *Cf.* Local Government Board Report, 1864-65, p. 38 ; 1862-63, p. 40 ; Wilkinson, 1729, 1730 ; Collie, 1813 ; Jack, 1024.
[5] Vallance, 808 ; Heale, 1305, 1306, 1317 ; Jack, 1003 ; Dove, 1647, 1648 ; Collie, 1790-1792. *Cf.* Powell, 2294.
[6] Jack, 1002.
[7] Wilkinson, 1712, 1713.
[8] Fletcher, 195.
[9] Bramly, 296.
[10] Mackay, 1184-1181.
[11] Jack, 969

instance in point, just round the corner, from our office in St. George's, there is a little court, by no means the poorest in St. George's—I believe almost every single inhabitant applied. They are all very poor, but a great many of them were no poorer than they always are. This shews how an advertisement brought in applications.'[1] 'Large numbers of men were,' says Mr. Vallance, 'making their way towards London in the hope of securing a share of what was regarded as an inexhaustible fund.' In Hertfordshire the master of a workhouse 'told me that he was overwhelmed with tramps who were making their way to London.' 'Lodging-houses were overcrowded; whereas not long before some were scarcely paying at all, they then got more applications for admission than they could accommodate.'[2]

It is impossible to follow rules in such a tumult, however good the rules may be.

'No sufficient inquiry can be made,' says another witness. 'We had to do it quickly, and we got the best information we could, and the only ones we cut straight off were the drunkards.'[3] 'I don't agree with a fund administered as it was last time.' Says another: 'Pressure makes sufficient inquiry impossible. The rush is too great. When you get 300 or 400 rushing into a room every day, it is impossible. You could not do much in two or three hours.'[4] Yet it is at such a time that inquiry is most necessary, for there is every temptation to imposture.' 'I was so thoroughly deceived by them,' says a working man, 'I could not believe them.'[5] 'There was evidence of great imposture.' 'At the latter end, he was satisfied with the administration of the Fund.'

Men are tempted away from honest labour.

'The fund,' says Mr. Valpy, 'acted as a direct inducement to many to remain idle.'[6] 'Expectations were raised that people would get as much as £10 or £15 each.'[7]

In their alarm people are inclined to give relief without any principle or method.

'All were in distress,' says Mr. Roberts, 'and that was considered sufficient ground, whether they came within the Mansion House lines or not.' If anyone made a remark, the answer was, 'The man was in trouble.'[8] 'The Committee,' says another, 'would occasionally relieve the family of a man who was a known drinker, and, when remonstrated with, said they must think of the wife and family.' 'When some of these gentlemen tackled an applicant, they did not know what questions to ask

---

[1] Mackay, 1209; cf. Marchant, 1244, 1245.
[2] Vallance, 671, 673. In any attempt to deal with distress in London, this initial difficulty has to be considered. There has been a tendency in late years to migrate into London, where the conditions of life are more cheerful. There is a general impression that work is always to be found in the metropolis. If we allow people to believe that, failing work, London is the best place for the unemployed, because large funds are raised in any time of exceptional distress, we shall increase this tendency to seek refuge in London on the occasion of any trade dispute, or temporary pressure. It should be the first endeavour of relief committees to induce applicants to return to the country. Emigration, which is held out as a remedy, will, as a rule, only introduce the successful applicant to a life of toil in country districts in the colonies, where he will miss the companionship and the allurements which make London so attractive.
[3] Bramly, 375.
[4] Heale, 1334, 1333, 1326.
[5] Westbrook, 1955, 1892, 1958.
[6] Valpy, 206.
[7] Evidence 206, 263; cf. Dew, 2057, 2110.
[8] Roberts, 1620.

B 2

him. On the first day a man came in who was a thorough soaker, and had sixteen shillings given him there and then. I protested. A member of Committee said, "Yes, no doubt he drank, but the weather was cold, and he had a large family, and we must relieve the distress."[1]

General conclusions as to a Fund and its desirability.

The conclusions that the Committee draw are:—

1. That the creation of a Central Relief Fund should, if possible, be avoided.
2. That whether there be such a fund or not, it is desirable that the outlines of local and central administration, and all important details should be pre-arranged.
3. That this work should be entrusted to some conjoint body, which should be entitled to public confidence, and be held publicly responsible.
4. That this body should avoid all unnecessary publicity, both in making its arrangements and in obtaining information.
5. That if the question of opening a fund arises, such a step should not be taken without the fullest and most definite information as to the existence and extent of the distress, nor without previous consultation with the chief relief agencies in the Metropolis.
6. That if a fund be opened—
   - (a) The money should be dispensed through local agencies only.
   - (b) No grants should be made to such agencies until the central body is satisfied that their organisation is sufficiently complete, and that money placed in their hands will be distributed according to methods which it approves.
   - (c) That the rules adopted for the guidance of the local administrators of the fund should be published in the general press, advertised in the local papers, and made known to applicants who come to the offices.[2]

CHARITABLE AGENCIES NOW AVAILABLE.

It is the duty of your Committee to report 'on the best means of *dealing with* exceptional distress.' They have therefore, in the above conclusions, made special reference to the formation of a Central Relief Fund which may, under conditions of comparatively rare occurrence, become necessary. They feel, however, that no opinion can be formed on such a question, except by those who have some knowledge of the very large provision already made for the relief of the poor in London, and of the existing agencies, which by combination and adjustment, and by co-operation between class and class, might be expanded so as to withstand the pressure even of times of unusual impoverishment. In 1885 the relief dispensed to the poor in London by the Poor Law Authorities amounted to £2,418,049. Of this £181,581 was given in out-door relief, while the maintenance of indoor paupers, apart from the relief of pauper children, the relief of the insane poor, and of vagrants, and apart from all medical relief and all salaries and office expenses, was £235,450.

The gifts of 'charity' also are very large. How large, only those who are in frequent contact with the poor are aware. There are pensioners of local charities, and of charities administered by the City Companies; there are local philanthropic, and friendly aid societies; there are the parochial charities of the clergy, and the congregational gifts and

---

[1] Gardiner, 858, 861; *cf.* as to good results of Fund, Acworth, 398, 413, 433.
[2] *Cf.* the Report of the Mansion House Fund Committee for St. George in-the-East. Mackay, 1208; Fletcher, 171; Avis, 1570; Marchant, 1244; Heale, 1301.

contributions of churches and chapels; there are the collections made in West-end churches for poor parishes in other parts of London, and the—sometimes considerable—sums spent by individual donors in connection with parishes in which they take an interest; there is the help that artisans give to artisans from the benevolent fund of the trade society or benefit club, or by a 'friendly load' in the workshop; there is also the casual relief, which constantly passes from 'mate' to 'mate,' and from one poor neighbour to another; for the charities of the poor might, in the spirit in which they are bestowed, and in their relative value, often put to shame the charities of the rich.

The following metropolitan societies (besides one or two others) are general relief societies, and they and their members, assisted so far as possible by additional helpers and colleagues, should, the Committee consider, bear the brunt of any exceptional pressure.

The Metropolitan Visiting and Relief Association, 46 Pall Mall, S.W. This makes grants to the clergy, who distribute the money mostly in small sums, tickets, &c., on condition that the recipients are visited. These grants amounted to £4,495 in 1884-5.

The Society for the Relief of Distress, 28 King Street, St. James's, had an income of £2,547 in 1884–85. This is distributed in relief of all kinds through upwards of a hundred almoners. The expenses of the Society are met by a private guarantee fund.

The Jewish Board of Guardians, 13 Devonshire Square, E., is ready to deal with all applications from Jews. Its income in 1885 was £15,491.

The Society of St. Vincent de Paul, 31 Queen Square, W.C., is a Roman Catholic Society. It has 31 Conferences or Committees in London. Its income in 1885 was £1,480.

The Charity Organisation Society[1] has 40 District Committees. Through its agency £20,972 was raised and expended in relief in 1884-85.[2]

The Public Gardens Association should also be mentioned. In the department of supplying employment, it would naturally be the ally of any societies that might join forces to deal with exceptional distress.

THE CENTRAL AGENCY AT A TIME OF EXCEPTIONAL DISTRESS.

The evidence before the Committee points to this alternative: either to create a new Central Society, or to federate and develop existing societies.[3]

The Committee do not approve of the former course, for the following reasons. Among the clergy of all denominations and their helpers, and in connection with such charitable agencies as are mentioned above, are probably a very large proportion of those who have had experience in relief work, or who would prove capable assistants on an emergency. A new society, or permanent committee with paid officials, would in a measure displace these, would probably have to look for its support from yet another section of the public, and would entail increased expense. For local work it would have to create new machinery, as was done last winter, with every chance of failure. The local organisations of the various societies could not abandon their own proper work to join the new Committees, the management of which would thus, in many instances, fall into new and untried hands.

[1] *Cf.* Roberts, 1615, 1631, 1632; Dew, 2111; Powell, 2277.
[2] This does not include £14,543, the expenditure on central and local organisation and other branches of work.
[3] *Cf.* Fletcher, 174; Valpy, 227, 229, 243; Stephany, 2206, and others.

RECOMMENDA-
TIONS.

A Central Provisional Committee.

The Committee propose to proceed on the lines of developing existing agencies.

They would propose the establishment of a Provisional Committee. It should be convened, they think, at as early a date as possible, by Rev. M. S. A. Walrond, one of the Hon. Secretaries of the recent Mansion House Fund; by Mr. Albert Pell, the Chairman of the Council of the Charity Organisation Society; and, should he consent thereto, by Mr. Francis Peek, who has proposed the formation of a Committee similar to that here suggested. It should consist of representatives of the above societies, of the Guardians, of the working classes, and of influential persons who are specially interested in the condition of the poor or have special experience in the work of relief. It should be comparatively small, but thoroughly representative. To this Committee would be entrusted the following duties:

I. To ascertain privately, from trustworthy sources, the actual state of affairs in different parts of London, and, if there be unusual distress, the classes and trades which it more particularly affects and the districts in which it is prevalent.

II. To summon, if necessary, special and influential meetings (which might be private), and to submit to them the result of their inquiries.

III. To obtain funds, if they be required for the relief of distress, at these meetings, privately and unostentatiously, but with due public safeguards.

IV. To forward to the press such statements of information as would show that satisfactory steps were being taken by them to meet whatever distress might arise, and to advise as to the necessity of making a public appeal in the last resort.

V. It should further be the duty of the Committee to consider, in conjunction with persons well acquainted with the locality, the best means of extending local machinery to meet increased pressure. In all districts there would have to be trustworthy local Committees. In some, new Committees would have to be formed. In others, a local Society or Committee already in existence might be expanded and throw out Sub-Committees. In others, again, other special combinations would have to be made. In this way the existing machinery would be utilised and improved instead of being set aside and injured. Some districts, well able to cope with local distress, might not require grants from a central fund, but would make, through their local organisations, whatever local appeals might be necessary.

The importance of a careful selection of the members of local Committees cannot be too strongly insisted on.

Considering the very great importance of co-operation with the Guardians, the districts of the local Committees should be co-terminous with Poor Law Parishes or Unions or form sections of such Unions.

VI. Monies received by the Provisional Committee would be paid by way of grants to the Local Committees or other agencies, only under such conditions and such control or inspection as would ensure careful almsgiving, so far as may be possible.

The Provisional Committee would publish a report of their methods of administration, together with an account, approved and signed by a public auditor, showing what money they had received, and where and how it was spent.

VII. The Committee hope that the Provisional Committee would adopt, and require the Local Committees to adopt (subject to necessary local modifications) the suggestions for dealing with exceptional distress appended to his Report.

NOTE.—*This Section of the Report is printed as an Appendix, in order that it may be reprinted by itself. It necessarily repeats some of the statements made in the Report.*

APPENDIX.—LOCAL COMMITTEES AND THEIR RULES.

SUGGESTIONS AND SUGGESTED RULES FOR DEALING WITH EXCEPTIONAL DISTRESS BY LOCAL COMMITTEES.

I. GENERAL POLICY OF RELIEF.

It has now been repeatedly proved that the only way to meet widespread and exceptional distress, without doing permanent injury to the mass of the poor, is to adhere to certain general principles and fixed lines of action which they will readily understand. Indecision and vacillation at such a time produce grave mischief.[1]

The creation of a large relief fund tends to occasion additional difficulties and perplexities. Confusion and waste can only be avoided by taking careful measures for the administration of relief beforehand, quietly and without panic.

To deal with large numbers of people quickly and effectually 'tests' are necessary, no less than inquiry. *'Tests' and inquiry.*

Roughly speaking, applications come from three classes: *Classes requiring relief.*
(1) Thrifty and careful men;
(2) Men of different grades of respectability, with a decent home;
(3) The idle, loafing class, or those brought low by drink or vice.

To the first of these, relief should be given; but if public works are opened they should be recommended to take such work, not as a test, but as temporary employment.

To the second class (according to the character of the case) relief should be offered (1) conditionally on employment in public or other works; or (2) the applicant should be referred to the Poor Law labour-yard; or (3) admitted to the workhouse, while the wife and family are supported by charitable relief outside.

The third class should be left to the Poor Law. Relief by way of alms only maintains them in their evil habits, discourages the thrifty and striving, and leads to still further neglect of wife and family.

Public works should not be undertaken unless there is clear evidence that the want of employment is so great that some such temporary measures are absolutely necessary to prevent better-class working men from living in semi-starvation. Their tendency must be to keep labour in the same grooves. If the distress is occasioned by some temporary and definite cause, after a short period there will be an improvement in the labour market. If the distress is occasioned by deeper and more permanent causes, public works *Public and charitable 'works.'*

---

[1] *See* 'Suggestions for Dealing with Exceptional Distress,' published by the Charity Organisation Society, 1884 and 1885.

In a time of 'commercial embarrassment' 'an ill-regulated distribution of charitable donations may not only fail to relieve the class for whose benefit the funds were collected, but further diminish the resources they would otherwise have obtained by their own exertions.'—Dr. KAY, Third Annual Report of the Poor Law Commissioners.

'It is the stoutest, not the kindest, heart that is wanted' 'in times of scarcity or unusual stagnation'; and 'all we have to do is to weather the storm as well as we are able, taking additional care to be vigilant and strict in keeping all members of the community within the bounds of duty.'—Quoted by Mr Longley in his 'Report to the Local Government Board on Poor Law Administration in London,' 1874.

will act merely as a palliative which may divert attention from the source of the evil and tend to become as chronic as the shortness of work.

If public or other works are opened—

(1) Men should only be admitted to them after inquiry or on satistory recommendation.

(2) The wages and the hours should be as nearly as possible according to contract rates.

(3) Care should be taken to supply sufficient overlookers, and to group the men according to character and ability.

(4) If a meal is wanted, or clothing, it is better that this should be supplied separately from a relief fund. The employment should be given, as far as possible, in accordance with ordinary business contracts, and not as 'charity work,' which tends to be as ill-done as it is ill-paid, and to degrade men instead of improving them.

(5) Public and other relief works should be of a local character, planned according to estimates drawn by the local authorities, and conducted under local superintendence. This will be some guarantee against waste and irresponsibility. Such works only should be undertaken as are likely to create the least disturbance in the labour market.

Labour-yards. Poor Law Labour-yards are sometimes the only test available, but they have a tendency to become permanent institutions for the supply of cheaply-paid and practically useless labour to casual and idle labourers of all kinds.

The modified workhouse test. The plan of applying a modified form of the workhouse test in certain cases, by which the man is maintained in the workhouse while the wife and family are supported by voluntary charity, is suggested for the following reasons:

(1) The assistance is adequate; no homes are broken up, and the relief is so given as to meet the wants of the family—the wife and children as well as the husband.

(2) It will act as an education in provident habits.

(3) The burden of sacrifice will be thrown on the man; whereas in all other schemes for dealing with this class, it is liable to be thrown on the woman.

II. THE LOCAL COMMITTEES.

Co-operation with guardians indispensable. It is clear that none of the three classes mentioned above, except the first and part of the second, can be properly dealt with, unless there is co-operation between the administrators of charitable funds and the Poor Law Guardians. This co-operation is indispensable.

Of whom they should consist. That there may be agencies for this co-operation and for the direct distribution of relief, local Relief Committees are necessary. These should include representatives[1]—

(a) Of the Principal Land and House Owners,
(b) Of Employers of Labour,
(c) Of Working Men[2]—including representatives of trade societies and benefit clubs.
(d) Of Charitable Agencies,
(e) Of Poor Law Guardians and of the Vestry,
(f) Of School Teachers and Visitors,
(g) Of Clergy of all Denominations.

Committees should be comparatively small and composed of members well acquainted with the district.[3] To such persons the street or neighbourhood in which a man lives may be a rough test of some value. So far as possible, people of judgment, who have had some experience, and

---

[1] Gardiner, 849, 899, 900.   [2] Powell, 2260, 2288, 2290; Andrews, 2367.
[3] Gardiner, 892.

have already interested themselves in the work of charity, should be chosen. Members, *e.g.*, ought to know what questions to ask and how to take down an application.[1] The Clergy should act as advisers to the Committee, rather than as almoners or honorary officials.[2] Their knowledge of the district, of the persons who apply, is often very valuable.

The area covered by the Committee should be comparatively small.[3] <small>Area of Committee.</small>

To avoid a rush of cases— <small>How to avoid a rush.</small>

(1) Unnecessary publicity should, in the earlier stages, be avoided.

(2) The rules which the Committee propose to follow should subsequently be advertised in local papers, and given to all applicants. These rules should show in general terms, but clearly, whom the Committee wish to relieve and whom they intend to leave to the Poor Law. (*See* below IV.)

(3) It should be clearly stated that relief will only be given after inquiry, or with a labour test.

(4) Trustworthy persons, who have been selected for the purpose by the Committee, and who are well acquainted with the district, should refer to the Committee cases which they believe they can thoroughly recommend. A number of suitable cases may thus be brought to light, and the multitude of personal applications in part avoided.

III. INQUIRY.

Applications should in all cases be made by the head of the family only. <small>Application on recommendations.</small>

Application forms (*see* Form A), or forms of reference, should be given to members of Committee, selected employers and foremen, the officers of trade and benefit societies, and to clergymen and district visitors of experience.[4]

These forms should be given by them to applicants whom they recommend as suitable, according to the rules. (*See* above.)

The applicant should be required to attend at the office, and bring with him the application or reference form, duly filled up and signed; and, if the person who sends the case is not an employer or foreman, a recommendation from the employer or foreman will be necessary.

In all these cases the home will be visited and the reference or recommendation verified, if the pressure is too great to do more. If not, other points in the case may be taken up with a view to a more thorough treatment of it.

If there is no reference of the applicant to the Committee, he will attend at the office, the application form will be filled up, and such inquiries made as the time allows. <small>Direct application.</small>

Two things should never be omitted:—

(*a*) *The home should be visited.*

(*b*) *An employer or local reference should be communicated with.*

---

[1] *Cf.* Gardiner, 868, 832, and others.

[2] Bramly, 304, 339; Mackay, 1186.

[3] Roberts, 1655; Powell, 2305-2308, and others. 'I venture to say,' writes Mr. Salter, that, as an active member of the Kensington and Lambeth Charity Organisation Committees for ten years or more, I was struck by the advantage of the small Local Committees, and the system of assigning certain streets to certain members of Committee. A small Local Committee is more likely to secure the services of the clergy and others immediately concerned than a Charity Organisation Committee which deals with a large district. The knowledge, the interest, and the responsibility of its members are greater.'

[4] Valpy, 206; Bramly, 346, &c. *Cf.* Acworth, 426, &c.; Westbrook, 2014, 2017. *Cf.* Powell, 2288. It is best not to use the application form as the paper of reference. The details to be filled up in the application form can, as a rule, be entered with less trouble and more accurately when the applicant is seen at the office of the Committee.

Who should make the inquiry.

The inquiry should be made by members of Committees and others who have had some experience in relief work. They may in many instances require the assistance of one or more paid officers. It was found last year that much time was saved by the use of a form (*see* Form B) for corresponding with references or employers.[1]

Enquiry of Relieving Officers.

To ensure co-operation with the Guardians,[2] it will be well to ascertain from them whether cases are known to them; and the Guardians might be asked to supply a list of the names of persons in receipt of parochial assistance. Similarly lists of those relieved by the Committee should be sent to the Guardians from time to time.

IV. DECISION.

Sifting of cases. Decisions.

To prevent delay and haphazard and unjust decisions, it will be found convenient to come to an understanding with regard to groups of cases; with this object it is suggested that the following rules should be adopted by the Committee, and only deviated from by vote on any special case.

1. That persons known to be drunkards, 'loafers,' or persons of bad character, should not be assisted.[3]
2. That no one in receipt of Poor Law relief should be assisted, except by the payment of club arrears.
3. That no cases of chronic distress, in which the head of the family is habitually out of work in the winter or never in regular work, be assisted.
4. That no cases of chronic distress occasioned by long-continued illness, or by old age, be assisted.[4]
5. That no persons living in common lodging-houses should be assisted.
6. That relief should not be given to persons who have not resided in the district of the Poor Law Union for less than six months, unless there be special reason to the contrary.
7. That those who have made any provision for the future should be assisted.[5]

It should be remembered that for several of the above classes it will be best to apply some form of labour test, *e.g.*, the labour-yard, &c.; they would then obtain relief conditionally. But no applicants should be sent to public works, or works set on foot by any relief association, except on recommendation from some trustworthy source or after inquiry.

Decisions upon cases should be made by Committee, and not left to individual almoners.[6]

Meetings.

The Committee should meet daily, if possible. At least half the meetings should be held in the evening, so that working men may be able to attend.

---

[1] Bramly, 376; Acworth, 405, 458; Westbrook, 1952, and others. Mr. Edgcombe (Kensington) writes: 'Employers and references were almost always communicated with, usually by letter; it was observed that employers replied with singular readiness.'

[2] *Cf.* Fletcher, 73; Bramly, 369; Acworth, 461; Westbrook, 1957; Roberts, 1612.

[3] *Cf.* Gardiner, 858. This rule should be adhered to even when there is a wife and family. Otherwise the husband is encouraged to neglect them. Few persons realise how strong a feeling self-reliant working men have as to the waste and injustice of the relief, thoughtlessly given to this class.

[4] These would naturally be dealt with by the more permanent relief agencies.

[5] Tests of this provision would be membership of a club or benefit society, membership of a trade society, savings as shown by bank book, &c. *Cf.* Valpy, 211; Bramly, 354; Legge, 1137, &c., as to need of thrift; as to possibility, *cf.* Dew, 2077, 2114, &c.; Moss, 2472; and Powell, 2255, 2256, 2266, 2284.

[6] Fletcher, 43; *cf.* Bramly, 370.

V. Relief.

Relief can be varied and adjusted to the actual wants of an applicant, only if the inquiry is sufficient or the person who recommends the case has a real knowledge of it. To minimise friction and delay and promote effective relief, these two means of discrimination—recommendation, and inquiry should be worked together. *Suitable relief only possible if there is sufficient inquiry with trustworthy recommendation.*

Relief should not be given at the office, but taken to the homes by members of Committee, almoners, or others. Valuable information is frequently obtained in this way, and crowding at the offices is still further prevented. *Relief not given at office.*

The visitor also may find that the relief ordered should be withheld for further instructions.

A receipt should be required in all cases upon the Application Form (see back of the Form).

If, owing to the number of applications, it is not possible to adjust the relief to the wants of each case, the following scale, the sufficiency of which has been tested by experience, should be adopted as a minimum: *Scale of relief.*

    Weekly Scale for Food and Fuel exclusive of Rent.
    An adult living alone, 3s. 6d.
    Two or more adults living together, 2s. 6d. each.
    Children under 4 years, 6d. each.
        ,,   from 4 to 12 years, 1s. each.
        ,,   from 12 to 16 years, 1s. 6d. each.

Not more than 10s. in one week should, as a rule, be given to any family, as there are generally in large families earnings or income (other than charity) available.

Relief in kind is not recommended.[1] It is no safeguard to give such relief in doubtful cases, cases in which the head of the family is a drunkard, or where the inquiry is defective. Knowledge of the case is the only real safeguard. *Relief in kind.*

If, however, relief is given in kind, it should be by orders on any respectable tradesman in the neighbourhood.[2] (*See* Form U.) An arbitrary and injurious interference with the custom of the smaller and poorer shopkeepers in the district will thus be avoided.

Soup-kitchens tend to bring masses of the poor together to be relieved wholesale. The chronic poor may be accustomed to this method of relief. Those of a better type, whom it is the problem of charity to relieve as far as possible, privately and without lowering their self-respect, will shrink from such distributions.

In special cases it may be found desirable to assist by providing meals. Orders upon cook and coffee shops, or coffee taverns, should then be given. It may be necessary to provide food for children in this way.

If clothing or boots are required, these too may be provided, after strict inquiry, and when there is definite promise of work.

If boots are given for children, inquiry should always be made of the schoolmaster or mistress in the first instance, and they should be informed of the gift.

As a rule it is best to take a view of the whole case, and to estimate its wants, with a view to its ultimate requirements; and then to give to the applicant in money what is necessary for his adequate assistance. If this be a temporary allowance, it will be given weekly.

If money is given for any special purpose, the visitor or almoner who has taken it should be required to report that it has been expended in the manner agreed upon with the applicant. He should see the receipts. *Report of visitor as to use of money.*

---

[1] Fletcher, 180; Gardiner, 864, and others.
[2] *Cf.* Valpy, 262, 208; Westbrook, 1940, &c. Another form for orders on coffee taverns for meals for a fixed period was drawn up by Mr. Valpy and found useful in checking sale of tickets, &c.

Payment of rent.

It is not desirable to pay the applicant's rent, if it can be avoided. But if, as is often the case, a portion of the relief will be used for the rent, it is better to recognise the fact and pay a week's current rent.

Back rent[1] *should under no circumstances be paid.*

The following further forms of relief are suggested:

(1) Payment of club arrears, after consultation with workmen upon the Committee, and reference to the Secretary of the Club, to whom the money should be paid.

(2) Taking tools and necessaries out of pawn. The money should in this case be paid to the pawnbroker direct.

(3) Medical relief.

(4) Migration.

(5) The emigration of carefully chosen emigrants to colonies in which it has been ascertained that there is a definite opening for them.

Cases after pressure is over.

It has been found that many of the most distressing cases occur after a period of distress, and as the result of the privation and sickness which it causes. However large the fund, therefore, there should be no over-haste in distributing it. The money will be hardly less wanted some weeks after than at the actual time of the greatest pressure of applications. And it will be easier then to do justice to the work.

[1] Fletcher, 156; Valpy, 206; Gardiner, 874. *Cf.* Mackay, 1215; Hayward, 654, &c.

EVIDENCE.

LIST OF WITNESSES.

Friday, June 4, 1886.
Mr. A. P. FLETCHER. | Mr. R. A. VALPY.

Friday, June 11, 1886.
Mr. J. R. J. BRAMLY. | Mr. W. M. ACWORTH.

Friday, June 18, 1886.
Rev. W. CURTIS HAYWARD. | Mr. W. VALLANCE.

Friday, June 25, 1886.
Mr. T. GAGE GARDINER. | Mr. W. H. O. JACK.

Friday, July 2, 1886.
Hon. and Rev. Canon LEGGE.

Friday, July 9, 1886.
Mr. T. MACKAY. | Mr. W. HEALE.
Mr. T. W. MARCHANT. | Miss M. M. GEE.

Friday, July 16, 1886.
Mrs. AVIS. | Mr. R. ROBERTS.
Mr. F. J. DOVE. | Miss F. R. WILKINSON.

Friday, July 23, 1886.
Mr. G. COLLIE. | Mr. G. T. WESTBROOK.
Mr. G. DEW.

Tuesday, July 27, 1886.
Mr. M. STEPHANY. | Mr. J. D. POWELL.
Mr. A. S. ANDREWS.

Friday, July 30, 1886.
Mr. N. MOSS.

MINUTES OF EVIDENCE.

Special Committee
OF THE
CHARITY ORGANISATION SOCIETY,
To consider the best means of dealing with
EXCEPTIONAL DISTRESS.

FRIDAY, JUNE 4TH, 1886, 11.30 A.M

Present—MR. A. PELL, in the Chair.

Mr. J. H. ALLEN,
Rev. W. CURTIS HAYWARD,
Mr. J. R. HOLLOND,
Mr. F. J. S. EDGCOMBE,
Hon. and Rev. Canon LEGGE,
Dr. G. B. LONGSTAFF.

Mr. R. HEDLEY, attending on behalf of the Local Government Board.

Mr. C. S. LOCH, *Secretary*.

MR. A. P. FLETCHER, examined.

Mr. A. P. FLETCHER
June 4, 1886.

1. (*Chairman*): Mr. Fletcher, would you kindly give me your address?— 7 Abercorn Place, N.W.
2. You have been good enough to come here as a witness. What do you represent?—I am one of the honorary secretaries of the St. Marylebone Committee.
3. Of the Mansion House Fund?—Of the Charity Organisation Society. I was for a time, as representing the real almoner for the Society for the Relief of Distress for Marylebone, General Gardiner, acting as almoner of the Mansion House Fund, before the local Mansion House Committee was appointed.
4. Did you take any part in the distribution of the funds of the Mansion House Committee?—Yes; for about three or four weeks.
5. Who appointed you?—I was appointed by Mr. Allen, as representing the Metropolitan Visiting and Relief Association.
6. Who appointed Mr. Allen to appoint you?—The Committee of the Mansion House Fund, I take it.
7. You considered you were entrusted with certain duties by the Mansion House Committee?—By the Association, as acting for the Mansion House Committee.
8. That is to say, the Mansion House Committee delegated their function to another Association?—Yes.
9. What association?—The Metropolitan Visiting and Relief Association, and the Society for the Relief of Distress.
10. The Mansion House Fund Committee delegated their functions to these two Associations?—Yes.
11. One of these Associations invited you to act?—Yes; perhaps it would be more correct to say that the two Associations agreed to ask me, as one of the almoners of the Society for the Relief of Distress, to act. They acted conjointly in the matter.

Mr. A. P. FLETCHER.
June 4, 1886.

12. Did they consult you at all, or merely ask you to distribute certain funds?—They asked me to distribute their funds. And they gave me immediately some directions as to the manner in which the funds were to be distributed.
13. Were those directions given in writing?—In writing. I am sorry it did not occur to me to bring them.
14. They gave you certain printed instructions?—At first they were written.
15. Did you act upon these?—Yes.
16. What were the first steps you took in consequence of the instructions you received?—Well, at first I took up a merely passive attitude. The applicants came in such large numbers that it was not necessary to take any active steps.
17. What do you mean by a passive attitude?—There was neither the time, nor did I see the necessity, to take active steps for the administration of the fund, the applicants came in such large numbers.
18. How did they find you out?—The Mansion House Committee, I believe, issued instructions right and left indicating where the different channels were through which the fund would be distributed. I think I have evidence of that.
19. You think that the Mansion House Committee issued instructions right and left, denoting where the carcasses were—where applicants might go for relief?—That is my impression.
(*Dr. Longstaff*): They certainly advertised it in the papers. I have seen circulars in which the names of the different offices were printed.
20. We have this stated by Mr. Fletcher. He says he believes that there were notices issued telling these applicants where they could go to ask for the money. That is how they came to him. We have not got a copy of one of these notices that were put about?
(*Mr. Loch*): I have got some of those.
21. We want to trace how the people came to you?—Besides the issue of these printed forms, the applicants went in great numbers to the Mansion House, and were no doubt sent on to the different districts.
22. Well, then, have we got a copy of the paper that the Mansion House Committee sent you?—That is a copy of the first communication I received from the Metropolitan Visiting and Relief Association. The letter is as follows:—

METROPOLITAN VISITING AND RELIEF ASSOCIATION,
46A PALL MALL, S.W., *Feb. 11th*, 1886.

DEAR SIR,—You will have seen that the Lord Mayor is raising a Fund for the Temporary Relief of the Unemployed in London. At a meeting held at the Mansion House yesterday, four Sub-Committees were appointed to supervise the distribution of this Fund, and our Committee takes charge of the north and west of London north of the Thames.

We have the pleasure of enclosing you a cheque for the sum of £   , to be distributed by you on the following conditions:—

(1) That relief be given, as far as possible, in kind to deserving working-men thrown out of employment through the present depression of trade, and not to the ordinary chronic cases of sick and aged, or the class who never are in work.

(2) That when relief is given, in order to prevent overlapping, communications be interchanged with the Parish Authorities, the Almoner of the Society for the Relief of Distress, and the Local Committee of the Charity Organisation Society.

(3) That a return of all cases assisted from this Special Fund be forwarded to this office as often as possible, and kept separate from the ordinary cases of distress.

We are, Sir,
Yours truly,
CHARLES BRUCE.
HY. HARDCASTLE.
F. C. TREVOR
J. H. ALLEN.

23. It is signed by Lord Charles Bruce, H. Hardcastle, General Trevor, and yourself, Mr. Allen ?—(*Mr. Allen*): Yes.

24. Four members of the Committee ? (*Mr. Allen*): The whole of the Committee.

25. Having received this—it is dated the 11th February. It is not from the Mansion House ?—(*Mr. Allen*): No ; we were a Sub-Committee of the Mansion House Committee for the north and north-west of London.

26. How much money was sent you ?—£10 was the first sum I received. I got it on the same day as the instructions.

27. What did you do with it ? Did you bank it ?—Yes ; I passed it into my own private account. I did not open a separate account, or mix it with the funds of the Charity Organisation Society.

28. And then you remained passive ? What was it that interrupted you ?—The first thing I found it necessary to do, besides dealing with the cases as they appeared, was to appoint sub-almoners throughout Marylebone.

29. What first disturbed you ? What stimulated you into activity ?—The press of the applicants.

30. Did they come in large numbers and knock at your door ?—Yes.

31. Were you surprised at that ?—I was at first. The people came knocking at the door of the Charity Organisation Society Office.

32. I want to know whether the office at which the funds were distributed was the office of the Charity Organisation Society ?—Yes.

33. When you found that the applicants came to the office, you appointed other almoners ?—Yes ; by degrees.

34. You and a special Committee of the Charity Organisation Society, I suppose ?—Well, the Committee of the Charity Organisation Society took no active part. They did not desire to be identified with the fund. They gave the use of their offices, and allowed me to devote my time to it, and gave me the use of the entire staff, and even employed additional agents for inquiries. The whole strength of the Marylebone Charity Organisation Office was turned on.

35. How many almoners did you appoint ?—By degrees nearly all the clergy throughout Marylebone—about twenty in number.

36. Every clergyman, and ministers of other denominations ?—Yes ; Catholics and Nonconformists as well. Three parishes I was not able to deal with up to the time of the Committee being formed. One was Christ Church, of which the Rev. Llewellyn Davies is Vicar.

37. Did he act with you ?—No ; he resolutely declined to have anything to do with it. I pressed him very much. I was very anxious that he should help me ; but he would not.

38. He did not agree with the principle of the fund ?—No ; he had the courage of his convictions, and would not have anything to do with it.

39. Did you endeavour to find an almoner as a substitute for Mr. Davies ?—Yes ; one was eventually found—a Mr. Physick, a sculptor, a Nonconformist, connected with a Visiting and Relief Society in the parish.

40. Having taken all the gentlemen connected with spiritual matters in the parish, did you get any other class as almoners ?—The Committee in Pall Mall appointed a Mr. Blennerhassett, a layman ; and besides Mr. Physick I appointed a Mr. Fraser, who worked amongst the poor in St. Thomas's parish, and Mr. A. K. Connell, who undertook the district of Portland Town. These were all laymen.

41. Generally, as a rule, your almoners consisted of the clergy and Dissenting ministers ?—Chiefly the clergy.

42. These almoners being appointed, had they any voice in the settlement of the principles upon which the fund was to be distributed ? Were they called together at the offices of the Charity Organisation Society ?—No ; they were left to do as they liked in the places which got grants from the fund.

43. The Mansion House Fund was the heart, and you were the great vein, and these were the subsidiary veins through which the money passed ?—Not strictly so ; nominally so. In reality, I always regarded the other almoners as quite independent of me. My connection with their appointment was the recommendation of their appointment to the Sub-Committee in Pall Mall.

44. The almoners having been appointed, the distribution of the grants they

Mr. A. P. FLETCHER

June 4, 1883.

Mr. A. P. FLETCHER.

received was in their own judgment?—Yes; I had nothing further to do with it. When they were once appointed, they rendered their accounts direct to the Committee in Pall Mall.

45. Did they receive money direct from Pall Mall?—Yes.

46. As soon as you sent their names in?—Yes; as quickly as the circumstances of the case would allow. It took time.

47. Did you receive more than £10?—Yes; £40 in all.

48. Could you say what the other almoners received?—Not without reference to my papers. Not a very large sum.

49. About £100 or £200?—Up to the time of the appointment of the Committee, I should think something like £500.

50. Did the other almoners use the Charity Organisation Society Office?—No; scarcely at all.

51. Did you take any further part in the proceedings after the other almoners were appointed?—None, except as regards the three parishes which I was not able to get almoners for—Christ Church, and two others. They were three of the poorest parishes in Marylebone—one sent hundreds of applicants. Up to the appointment of the Committee, I was the almoner of these three parishes.

52. I thought this £10 was the first money that came into your district from the Mansion House?—It was.

53. How could you have been an almoner before you got any money?—It was with my appointment I received this £10.

54. Do you mean that you distributed some of that before you appointed the other almoners?

(*Dr. Longstaff*): Mr. Fletcher refers to the appointment of the Committee. The almoners were appointed by the Committee. (*Mr. Fletcher*): The Committee retained the whole of the organisation I had made. They did not disturb the organisation I had made.

55. You were invited by this Sub-Committee of the Mansion House Fund, a Sub-Committee acting for your district, to accept the £10, which you were to distribute upon certain conditions set forth in this letter. That was the commencement of the whole thing. Upon the receipt of the £10 you, after remaining passive for a little time, and finding the applicants pressing at the Charity Organisation Society Office, appointed more almoners? You did not give away any of the £10 yourself?—Yes; I gave it myself. It was naturally spent very quickly. I never handed any part of my £10 to the other almoners; I administered what grants I received myself.

56. You got almoners appointed, and they received other money—something like £500 direct from the Mansion House Fund—which they distributed in a way about which you knew nothing?—In a way about which I had no official knowledge.

57. Would you tell us what you did with the £10?—I acted upon the methods of the Charity Organisation Society: I did not give any money away without a certain amount of inquiry. As we had the cases inquired into, I distributed the money, and the £10 was quickly spent.

58. And thereupon you applied for a further grant—that was at the same time as you were making arrangements for subdividing the district?—I made application for a further grant for myself as an almoner, and it was sent me. The amount which came into my hands in all was £40. I distributed that individually.

59. You tell us you received £40; would the distribution of that relieve the funds of the Charity Organisation Society very much?—I am not sure that I understand the question.

60. Did you take up cases that would otherwise have had to be dealt with by Charity Organisation Society money?—I think that extremely little of the money would have been granted by the Charity Organisation Society.

61. Is that your judgment? Do you think that if the Charity Organisation Society had had the £40 in their hands, they would not have distributed the money as you did?—Undoubtedly, as to a great part of it. I think the majority of the cases were more or less chronic cases. We should have had difficulty in finding anybody to participate if we had excluded chronic cases altogether.

The rules issued by the fund were produced. They were as follows:—

Mr. A. P. FLETCHER.
June 1, 1886.

MANSION HOUSE RELIEF FUND FOR THE UNEMPLOYED.
LOCAL COMMITTEES.
Constitution of Committees.

THE Committees should include representatives—

(a) Of Clergy of all denominations,
(b) Of Charitable Agencies,
(c) Of Working Men,
(d) Of Poor Law Guardians.
(e) Of Employers of Labour.

The Central Council reserves the right of nominating Members on the Local Committees.

The area of each Local Committee shall be, if possible, conterminous with that of the Poor Law Union in which it is formed. Such Local Committees may be divided into Divisional Committees, the boundaries of which should be clearly defined, and, further, into Sectional Committees, if thought expedient.

The Sectional Committees (when such exist) shall report daily all cases relieved, and the expenditure upon each case, to the Divisional Committee.

The Divisional Committees shall report all cases in their divisions, and the expenditure on each case, to the Local Committees, who shall be responsible to the Central Committee at the Mansion House, and send in returns of all cases relieved, and the expenditure on each case, as often as may be required by the Central Committee.

Rules for Distribution of Relief.

1. That no part of the funds be used for the relief of cases of chronic distress.
2. That, as a general rule, no relief be given to able-bodied single men with no one dependent upon them, except as a means of enabling them to obtain employment.
3. That no part of the funds be used for the payment of back rent.
4. That relief be not given to any persons who have come into their respective parishes since January 1st, 1886, except after rigid inquiry.
5. That money may be paid to keep a man on his club, or to reinstate him when his membership has recently run out.
6. That in respectable cases, after strict inquiry, necessary articles that have been pawned may be redeemed.
7. That the relief given should never exceed 3s. to 4s. for an adult, and 1s. for each child; nor more than 10s. weekly for the family.
8. That money grants should be made only in approved cases.
9. That no money should be given to those in receipt of out-door relief, except where the applicants belong to clubs, in which cases their club arrears may be paid up.

62. The first rule of the fund is, 'That no part of the funds be used for the relief of cases of chronic distress.' You admit that you violated that rule?—I am afraid I must.

63. I want to know whether, if you had not violated that rule, would you have got rid of the money?—Not of much of it.

64. You were obliged to pursue what you think a bad and a mischievous practice because you could not get rid of the money in any other way?—You know, sir, that it is only by practical experience in the administration of a fund of this kind that you can positively say whether you are relieving proper cases and at the same time acting in accordance with the instructions of the donors or not. I can only say that in nearly every case I was in doubt.

65. You violated the rule, or were in doubt about it. As a member of the Charity Organisation Society, would you be opposed to the giving of money to such cases as you relieved?—As regards a great number. Yes.

66. You would not relieve them? Why?—Because it is a cardinal principle of the Charity Organisation Society that they will not give relief which is inadequate, or which will not permanently benefit the recipient.

67. In your own judgment would you have done it?—If I had been free from all the restraints cast upon me by acting with the Charity Organisation Society, I think in many cases I should not.

68. (*Dr. Longstaff*): What was your reason for giving to these cases? Did

c

Mr. A. P. FLETCHER.
June 4, 1886.

you feel a sort of pressure upon you from the number of the applicants, and, in consequence, did not like to refuse? Did that lead you to break the rule? - No; if that was so—if it was mere pressure—I could have given the amount 100 times, and more.

69. (*Mr. Edgcombe*): Were you influenced by the fact that in a long time of frost the Charity Organisation Society would relax its practice?—No doubt that had something to do with the consideration of the question in many cases, but, generally speaking, I did not find that the cases that came before me were different in any appreciable degree from the ordinary cases applying for relief. I have no doubt that in the East End and other parts of London there were cases of the kind contemplated by the fund, but in Marylebone the poor consist very much of the classes that hang upon the rich.

70. (*Chairman*): After all, is their condition now different from last year?—I often put the question to them, and I am sorry to say it was rather in the nature of a trap, because, generally, thinking to strengthen their claim, they said 'No; their condition was very much the same'; I then told them, that being so, they were not intended to be recipients of the money received from the Mansion House Committee.

71. Still you relieved them?—Not much. I only distributed £40 in all.

72. Now, Mr. Fletcher, the next instruction was that in order to prevent overlapping you were to enter into communication with the parish authorities, the almoner of the Society for the Relief of Distress, and the Local Committee of the Charity Organisation Society. Who were the parish authorities?—The relieving officers, I take it. I won't say we went to them in every case. We were not able to make the usual Charity Organisation Society inquiries. There was no time. We did make some inquiry, but had to limit it to verifying the applicants' statements as to addresses, last employers, and so forth.

73. You did communicate with the relieving officers?—I should not like to pledge myself to that in every case.

74. Did you communicate with them at all?—I am not able to answer the question. I hope we did in some cases.

75. You did not apply to the relieving officer for any lists of the cases on his books?—No; I think not.

76. Does not the relieving officer come to the Charity Organisation Society's office to see?—No; we only send round. We come into touch with the relieving officer on certain individual cases.

77. What was the nature of your inquiry of the relieving officer?—I am afraid the inquiry was not made as much as it was intended to have been.

78. In fact, very little was done with the relieving officer?—I think there was.

79. Did he ever come to you saying you were doing harm?—No; he would not be likely to do that. He would be rather pleased, because cases would be likely to be taken off his hands.

80. Did any guardian ever say a word to you on the subject with reference to individual cases?—No; I think not.

81. (*Mr. Edgcombe*): Is the stoneyard open in Marylebone?—I do not know.

82. (*Chairman*): You were also to communicate with the Local Committee of the Charity Organisation Society. That of course you did?—Yes; I was in constant communication with them.

83. Did you make any return of the cases assisted by you?—Yes; I was bound to do that. The rule was, when applying for a further grant, to send in a statement of the cases relieved, merely giving the heads of the cases, the names, and so forth.

84. What were the heads? Did you set forth whether the relieved person was a married man or a single man, a married woman or a single woman? Did the particulars go in upon any form?—Yes; they gave us a form. At first, a simple form; afterwards, a more elaborate one.

85. (*Rev. W. C. Hayward*): The first form was from the Society for the Relief of Distress.

86. (*Chairman*): That came to you shortly after you received the letter?—At the same time, I think.

Mr A. P. Fletcher,
June 4, 1886.

87. This was the return you filled up—afterwards there was a more elaborate return?—I have not got a copy.

88. This return set forth, in different columns, first the name, then the address, then the occupation, then the weekly wages, then the number of the family, ages of children, and circumstances of distress; how long in London, date, and amount of relief?—That is the more elaborate form.

89. No; the first form? (*Mr. Allen*): The first form was exactly the same as the Society for the Relief of Distress sent round.

90. The first form left out the circumstances of distress. Did it give how long in London?—I think not.

91. Did it give the number of the family and age of the children? (*Rev. W. C. Hayward*): The circumstances under which relief was given is in the first form.

92. How much money did you distribute with the first form before you, and how much with the second?—As far as I was individually concerned, I only used the first form. I never used the more elaborate form.

93. You yourself only used the first form?—Yes.

94. How did you proceed when an applicant came before you? Did you have this sheet before you?—No; I never used that until afterwards. I only entered down the cases that were relieved. The applicants were admitted one by one into one of the waiting-rooms of the Charity Organisation Society. Their story was heard. If I thought it was a case which would be certain not to be entertained, I dismissed it at once. I never took down any written particulars unless of a case which there was a chance of my relieving.

95. Did you have many cases that were manifestly improper cases?—A very large number—at least 50 per cent.

96. You rejected, without inquiry, about 50 per cent.?—Yes.

97. Fifty per cent. were beggars, in fact?—No; but obviously cases not intended to be relieved by the fund.

98. Not cases that could be dragged within the meaning of the fund? They were destitute cases, were they not?—Probably many were pronounced chronic cases, and not good cases of their class.

99. Did you exclude these cases—where they were manifestly chronic cases?—If they were manifestly chronic cases, I dismissed them.

100. Did many of this 50 per cent. come to you for payments of back rent?—The majority of them were in that position. There must have been a stronger reason for dismissing them than that. The plea was always out of work, of course. I cannot say the number. I am sorry to say I did not keep a list.

101. (*Mr. Hollond*): Would you give us an instance of a case you would reject after making the ordinary inquiry?—Of course of these a great many were known to the Charity Organisation Committee. They had already been before us, and had been proved to be cases which were not of a remediable character. A considerable number were of the class of servants. In Marylebone there is a great number of domestic servants, especially of the male sex, out of place. I rejected these applications.

102. (*Chairman*): Do you think they came to you while they were in service?—No; when they were out of place. I did not consider that they came within the rules.

103. You took down the names and addresses of all cases when you went further into them, asked the occupation, the weekly wage—filled up this paper, in fact?—We filled up the Charity Organisation Society paper, and made inquiry by one of the inquiry officers of the Society.

104. Ultimately, you recommended the man for relief?—This paper had to be filled up only if I had given relief.

105. In making the inquiry, at what point did the cases you thought might possibly be fitting for relief—at what point did they generally fail? Did they give false addresses?—No.

106. False name?—No; probably on the ground of character.

107. False statement as to wages, or as to number of family and age of children?—We should not regard these statements so much. The poor often misstate their circumstances.

108. (*Mr. Hollond*): There is no exclusion on account of character in the

c 2

Mr. A. P. FLETCHER.

June 4, 1886.

rules; nothing to exclude a drunken man, for instance, from relief?—I never gave money to a man I knew to be a drunkard. I should regard him as inadmissible. I did make character a condition.

109. There is nothing said about it in the rules?—No.

110. (*Chairman*): You had this money placed in your hands for the relief of destitution—character is not mentioned at all in the rules; it was for the relief of unemployed persons? You did take character into account?—Yes; certainly.

111. (*Mr. Allen*): My first letter from the Metropolitan Visiting and Relief Association stated that it was for the relief of deserving working-men out of employment.

112. (*Chairman*): When you did relieve, you filled up this paper and sent it in?—One point, I think, you are forgetting. It was not for the relief of the poor, but for the class thrown out of employment *by the present exceptional state of trade*. That was one of the directions we received from the Mansion House Fund, and I kept it before me as a guiding principle.

113. May we take it, as a rule, that the persons with respect to whose cases you filled up the form were really working people?—Yes.

114. Did you assist such people as clerks?—We had very few. I would not have refused a clerk if I had ascertained that he was thrown out of employment by the depression of trade, though I don't think the fund was intended for him.

115. With respect to depression of trade, what evidence had you of the depression of trade in your district?—Not much.

116. Was there any, apart from what usually accompanies winter, when plasterers, of course, cannot plaster, harvest people cannot cut corn, gardeners cannot plant out annuals, apart from the ordinary suspension of trade which accompanies frost, and which everybody may calculate upon? What can you tell us of exceptional depression of trade?—The trade of the country being depressed—it may be admitted that there is some depression in trade—of course affects the richer classes, who are not so well able to spend money; and the working men of Marylebone depend very much upon the prosperity of the rich.

117. (*Dr. Longstaff*): Did you get evidence with regard to trades influenced by season? Did you get evidence that it had been an unusually bad summer the year before, and the people were not so well off?—Yes; they were further behind; their unemployed time had been longer.

118. They had not been able to lay by a reserve?—That is the cause of all the distress with these classes; they spend the wages they earn while they are in employment.

119. (*Chairman*): Did they tell you that wages had come down?—take a bricklayer, for instance.—I am not able to say.

120. I know, and with respect to your district, too, that they have not come down; they never did come down—9*d*. per hour is the price that bricklayers have been paid in your district the whole of last summer, and since about the year 1870.

121. Can you tell us of any trade of any working man who satisfied you that his rate of wages had been less in the summer of 1885?—No; I have no recollection of that particular point being discussed.

It is a particular point in this inquiry.

122. Did you ask any of these people whether they had been out of work in the summer?—Yes; always.

123. And the length of time?—Yes.

124. Did they tell you why they were out of work?—They would say it was the state of trade, or the state of the country.

125. Did you ask 'Who did you work for?'—Yes; always.

126. Did you ask the rate of wages they received in the summer? Did they differ from the wages he usually received?—That I did not go into.

127. Did you ask him how long he had been out of work?—Yes; always.

128. And the cause?—I never got anything but slackness.

129. You never in any one case tested that? You were satisfied with the general expression of slackness?—Yes.

130. Slackness might have been originated by a strike?—Yes; possibly.

131. It might have originated from a man not doing the work in the way the

contractors liked it do ●, and fresh men being introduced from the north to supersede and supplant men who did not fulfil what was required of them. You never entered into that part of the inquiry?—No.

132. (*Mr. Hollond*): As a matter of fact, you had to relieve with your fund cases which would, under ordinary circumstances, be relieved by the ordinary relief agencies?—Undoubtedly.

133. Your fund was only another added to the numerous relief agencies in the district, clerical and otherwise?—Undoubtedly.

134. In point of fact, the only effect upon your district was that the appeal for the fund simply made the number of applications to the other charitable agencies smaller?—One effect, certainly.

135. Your general view would be that, so far as Marylebone was concerned, the appeal of a special fund stimulated applications for relief?—Yes; I am strongly of that opinion.

136. Can you state your opinion as to the general policy of these special appeals, whether such appeals should be made, or the money distributed through the ordinary relief agencies?—I have jotted down very briefly answers to the questions on the agenda, but I don't know whether you care to read them. My general views would perhaps be gathered from the notes I have made by way of answers to these questions. I do not know whether it would be possible for me to answer your question without making a very long statement.

137. I think you assented to this proposition, that, as far as Marylebone is concerned, the appeal for the Mansion House Fund was not particularly wanted; that the relief that was required could have been got from the ordinary relief agencies; that, as a matter of fact, the class relieved was just the class that would have been brought in due course before the ordinary relief agencies?—Undoubtedly; that is not only my own opinion, but also the opinion of members of my Committee. So far as I have had an opportunity of ascertaining, there was no doubt about it at the Charity Organisation Society Committee.

138. Do you mean the Charity Organisation Society Committee, or the almoners?—I am speaking of the Charity Organisation Society Committee.

139. I gather that the almoners did not meet with you?—There were no meetings of the almoners?—Not until after the appointment of the General Committee, when my functions as almoner ceased.

140. Other almoners may have had a different experience to yourself You have not exchanged experiences with them?—That is so.

141. (*Hon. and Rev. Canon Legge*): You said there were a large number of servants out of place?—A considerable number—yes.

142. Men-servants, coachmen, butlers, and the like. It has been stated that the number of men-servants employed is much smaller than usual. Do you suppose that is the case?—Yes; probably. I fancy the rich are not quite so well off, and are not employing so many men-servants.

143. An unusually large number are now out of employment?—Yes.

144. These would be rather a large class, would they not?—I am speaking merely from the number of cases that came before me at the time of the distribution of the Mansion House Fund.

145. It is the result of the experience you gained in administering the relief.

146. Did you go to registry offices, and so forth, to ascertain this?—No; it was my impression.

147. (*Chairman*): Did you ever write to a master to know whether the story was true?—No; I don't know that I relieved any.

148. (*Hon. and Rev. Canon Legge*): If they were out of employment in consequence of the depression of trade, would not they be cases contemplated by the fund?—We did not think so. We regarded the fund as more especially for artisans thrown out of employment by the state of trade. I think that was what the Mansion House Fund was for, though in time it degenerated into something very different.

149. You did not include coachmen and domestic servants under the head of working men?—No.

150. (*Chairman*): More the handicraft people?—Yes.

Mr. A. P. FLETCHER.

June 4, 1886.

Mr. A. P.
FLETCHER.

June 4, 1886.

151. (*Hon. and Rev. Canon Legge*): I think you said you had the parish of Christ Church specially under your supervision ?—Yes.

152. I suppose that the principles of the Charity Organisation Society are adopted by Mr. Davies, the Vicar ?—Yes ; and he relieves all his own poor. He uses our machinery of inquiry and for obtaining accommodation for convalescent cases, but he never asks us for funds for the assistance of his cases. He does that all himself.

153. His action did not result in a smaller number of cases being received from his parish than from others? The temptation was too great ?—Yes.

154. (*Chairman*): If you relieved his cases, you defeated Mr. Davies?—Possibly.

155. (*Mr. Allen*): In the event of next winter being a severe winter, would you recommend the establishment of another Mansion House Fund ?—No ; I should not.

156. (*Dr. Longstaff*): Did you have experience of the poor filling up forms ?—I had no occasion to supply forms. They found them themselves very easily. A certain Mr. Kenny distributed little printed forms in every court in Marylebone, and, I suppose, all over London. I received in one day a batch of 12 or 20 of these little forms all filled up in the same handwriting, which I heard was the landlord's—all Irish cases applying for back rent.

157. Do you think that there is any particular advantage attaching to the forms being filled up by the people themselves ?—It adds to the facility of applying.

158. But, on the contrary, do you think it adds facility to your considering the cases ?—Yes ; I think it does.

159. (*Mr. Loch*): How does it add to the facility of checking cases ?—If a man sends in the form, we might probably be able to deal with the case without troubling him to come to the office. It gives us notice of the name, and so on.

160. (*Dr. Longstaff*): Did you have any cases in which the addresses on the form were false ?—If I had, they were rare instances. I always verified the address, and saw the last employer. These were the two essential inquiries. We ought always to have gone to the relieving officer, as we do in Charity Organisation Society inquiries, but there was no time for thorough inquiry.

161. (*Mr. Loch*): Does not the distribution of the form stimulate applications ?— Yes ; it is probably a drawback for that reason.

162. (*Mr. Hedley*): You first had to do with the fund through Mr. Allen's letter ?—I received that letter because I was one of the almoners of the Society for the Relief of Distress. In that capacity they wrote to me. I was acting for General Gardiner.

163. You obtained the co-operation of the clergy of the parish in the distribution ?—Yes.

164. Did you communicate to the clergy the conditions laid down in the letter as to the persons to whom the Mansion House Fund was to be distributed ?—I think I left that for the people in Pall Mall.

165. They did not know at all the conditions ?—I did not supply them with the forms and instructions.

166. Did the people in Pall Mall know ?—(*Mr. Allen*): We did. Whenever we made a grant, we always sent out the rules at the same time to the almoner.

167. (*Mr. Hedley*): Did you comply with the conditions laid down in the letter ?—I endeavoured to do so, but cannot say I strictly did it. I kept them in view.

168. With regard to what has been said about men-servants in Marylebone, is it within your knowledge that a large number of people in the parish of Marylebone employ foreigners as servants instead of Englishmen ?—We had a good many applications from foreigners ; I think it is not unlikely. I have no particular knowledge upon the point. We have had at the Charity Organisation Society Office several applications from domestic servants—Germans, Swiss, and others. I should not wonder if such was the case.

169. (*Mr. Loch*): It seems to me from the evidence you have given that there was a considerable want of clearness in the rules for the distribution of the fund. Do you think that the policy of the fund should have been more clearly stated ?—Yes, certainly ; all the five points entered in the rough draft of

agenda ought to be set forth in the policy of the administration of any future fund.

170. That would have helped you considerably?—Yes.

171. (*Chairman*): Have you got a copy of the rough draft agenda of the Committee sitting here to-day?—Mr. Loch is now referring to the five divisions on the 4th sub-section on the bottom of the first page.

    4. Should those who appeal state what will be their policy of administration? Thus: (1) The classes they wish to reach or exclude.
          (2) The machinery they intend to use.
          (3) Their policy as to the Poor Law.
          (4) Their co-operation with charities.
          (5) Their co-operation with working-class societies.

172. (*Mr. Loch*): Would you say it would be necessary?—I do say so, emphatically.

173. Take these five heads. Would you add anything to them, or exclude anything from them?—The heads are so comprehensive that I don't think I can suggest anything.

174. Take the question of machinery. If there is a special fund, would you say you ought to have special machinery, or would you utilise the machinery as it stood, much as you did in the first few weeks when the Society for the Relief of Distress came to the front?—I think it is better to use the ordinary machinery.

175. (*Chairman*): A member of the Committee, who has been obliged to leave, has left this question, whether cases were always considered on the individual judgment of each almoner?—I had no one to advise me, and was obliged to act upon my own judgment in giving relief.

176. You gave without seeing the applicants?—Oh! never.

177. Did you consult the guardians as to the out-of-work cases?—I am afraid not.

178. There is a point here upon the agenda—point No. 7 upon the second page—did you keep yourself in touch upon the question of the amount of distress by getting any reports from the other parts of London as to what the Sub-Committees were doing there?—I did not.

179. Or by any inquiry as to what was going on in other parts of London?—I made no such inquiry.

180. Are you quite satisfied, with the information on your paper, that the cases relieved by you might not also have been relieved by another Sub-Committee?—The clergy limited themselves strictly to their own districts. The clergy were the almoners, with one or two laymen.

181. Do you say that the clergy would have made inquiries whether a person was getting relief from another part? How did you know?—The clergy would not relieve cases out of their own district.

182. But supposing a man worked in the City, and slept in Marylebone, and went into the City, and said he had been at work on large works at the Bank of England, which had been stopped, and he was thrown out of work; are you satisfied that the man would not have got relief upon the spot, and afterwards from you?—I think it would have been very careless if it had happened.

183. You did not interchange information with the Mansion House Committees?—I think it might be safely assumed that a man would not be relieved except in his own particular district—the district in which he resided.

184. (*Dr. Longstaff*): It was a general principle that the people should be relieved in their own particular district?—Yes.

185. I take it that you did not hear of any cases where a man was relieved in two districts?—No.

186. (*Chairman*): You were told that relief was to be chiefly in kind. Did you relieve in kind?—Very little. I was advised by those who were experts in the matter, and they told me that the poor could always make much more of the money than of the ticket. In one or two cases, I made arrangements with the different tradespeople, but I found it better to give the money. We tried to limit the relief to people who could be trusted. The tickets could be sold, you know.

Mr. A. P. FLETCHER.
June 4, 1886.

187. (*Mr. Allen*): You did not have anything to do with the money given to Lord Brabazon's Society* ? £150 was spent in Marylebone ?—Yes; I believe there was. I had no official knowledge of it.

188. (*Mr. Hedley*): Didn't you have the general feeling in distributing the Mansion House Fund that the money was there, and you must get rid of it somehow ?—Well, I should not like to say that no good was done. I was very glad when I had done with it.

189. You would not have liked to have sent back the money because there was no one to receive it ?—The unsatisfactory part of it was that one seldom felt sure that one was right in giving.

190. (*Chairman*): Did you ever find out what were the habits of life of the recipients by observing afterwards the business of the public-houses? Was there any depression in that particular industry? Have you seen a publican and asked him ?—No ; I have not.

191. Or a butcher ?—No.

192. Or a baker ?—No ; my evidence would be worthless upon this question.

193. Upon the point of food you cannot give evidence as to whether the 'run of teeth' was less ?—No.

194. (*Dr. Longstaff*): Did you inquire of the pawnbrokers ?—No ; I did not. There was such a hurry-skurry.

195. The people came in such crowds that you were not able to do justice to the work ?—It was impossible. The scrimmage was so fearful sometimes, that I feared that I should have to call in the police to keep order.

196. You had to make the best of a bad job ?—Yes ; as somebody put it, we tried to minimise the evils of the Mansion House Fund.

197. (*Chairman*): You tried to do as little mischief as possible ?—We were the almoners of certain moneys, and we tried to administer them with the least injury to the poor. I think I should decline it if I were asked next year, unless with the same object. As the Committee knows, it is always a difficult thing to benefit the poor without running the risk of injuring them. The Mansion House Fund was only a little worse than many other relief agencies.

198. You don't think there was, in connection with the district, depression in trade—the term they made use of—to justify the appeal from the Mansion House ?—No depression calling for exceptional measures.

199. Nothing to justify the municipal authority of the greatest city in the world offering to help the people at Marylebone ?—Most certainly not, as regards Marylebone.

MR. R. A. VALPY, examined :

Mr. R. A. VALPY.

Mr. Loch produced a letter received by him in April last, as Secretary of the Charity Organisation Society, from Mr. Valpy, giving a sketch of his proceedings with regard to the administration of the Mansion House Fund.

200. (*Chairman*) : Mr. Valpy, you are a barrister ? We have your address— 1 Hare Court, Temple ? You have been in the room the whole of the time during which Mr. Fletcher has been examined? (*Mr. Valpy*: Part of the time.) Do you generally agree with the observations he has made as to the usefulness, or the contrary, of the Mansion House Fund ?—Generally, I agree with what Mr. Fletcher has stated.

201. And as to the necessity of it ?—Speaking generally, I agree with what he has said.

202. Did you have some of the forms put in your hands that Mr. Fletcher has referred to ?—We did.

203. Any others ?—I have got most of the forms I had given me.

204. Mr. Valpy, are you a member of any Committee ?—I am a member of the St. Giles's Committee of the Charity Organisation Society, and have been for many years past.

205. Were you a member of any of the Sub-Committees of the Mansion House Relief Fund ?—As almoner of the Society for the Relief of Distress, I received a preliminary grant of £10.

206. You were not on the Committee of the Mansion House Fund ?—No ; not

* The Metropolitan Public Gardens Association.

on the Committee itself. I was appointed treasurer for the district of St. Giles's by the Committee in Pall Mall. That is a Sub-Committee of the Mansion House Fund.

The Chairman here read the letter referred to by Mr. Loch, which was as follows:—

1 HARE COURT, TEMPLE :
April, 4 1886.

DEAR MR. LOCH,—According to my promise, I send you a short account of the mode of distribution of the Mansion House Grant in my district, that of St. Giles, St. George's Bloomsbury, St. Clement Danes, and Clare Market. You are doubtless aware of the peculiar nature of the inhabitants, who consist largely of casual labourers about Covent Garden Market, people employed in the various jam and pickle manufactories, seed warehouses, and such like, an employment necessarily precarious, and depending upon the supplies sent to the market. There are also a large number of the lowest class of Irish, builders' and paviours' labourers, painters, and others, who are never regularly employed throughout the year, but who depend on what they make in the busy time for their maintenance during the rest of the year.

My first intimation of a grant from the fund was, as almoner for the Society for the Relief of Distress, when I received a preliminary grant, with little or no instruction as to dealing with it. I at once communicated with the recipients of other grants in the district, numbering in all seven, and established friendly co-operation with them, with one exception, that of the Rector of St. Clement Danes. The others sent in from time to time lists of cases relieved by them, and thus to a certain extent prevented overlapping. Seeing the great danger of this which existed, I placed the matter before the Sub-Committee at 46A Pall Mall, who asked if I would act as treasurer of the whole grant for my district ; this post I accepted on the condition (which was adhered to) that no other grant should be given to any person except myself, and that they would recognise the Committee which I should form as the only one for the district. I proceeded to form a Committee by simply expanding the Local Charity Organisation Society Committee, adding to it such persons as were thought reliable. This Committee numbered 30, but only 16 or 18 actually gave their services, and of these, 13 were members of the Charity Organisation Society. There were representatives of the clergy of different denominations, of employers of labour, of the Metropolitan Association for Befriending Young Servants, of the Local Sanitary Aid Committee. I failed to obtain the services of any representative of the Board of Guardians, though I requested it, or of any working men. Several district visitors, and visitors of the Strangers' Friendly Society, and others were associated with the Committee as visitors, but it was thought undesirable to accept them as members of the Committee. This was fortunate as it turned out, as I had strong reason to believe that politics somewhat influenced the anxiety to assist us shown by one or two. The inquiry work undertaken by them proved, as a rule, of little value, and much had to be done over again. I employed, in addition to our own, three extra inquiry agents at salaries of from 25s. to 30s. a week. Two of them will, I think, be of use to the Charity Organisation Society, should their services be required. A Sub-Committee was formed at 28 Betterton Street, where rooms were kindly placed at our disposal by Mr. E. C. Grey for the purpose of dealing with applicants residing south of Great Queen Street, and east of Drury Lane. The Committee at 27 Duke Street dealt with all other applications in the district, and the work thus appeared to be very equally divided.

In order to relieve the Committees as much as possible, I made an offer to each of the ministers of religion that he should come to me from time to time with a list of cases personally known to him, and vouched for by him as within the object of the fund ; that I should go over such lists with him, and with him consider each case and decide on the amount of relief to be given, and then give him a cheque for the amount required in order that he might personally distribute it. Only four of the clergy availed themselves of this offer, and I have every reason to believe that those so recommended by them were good cases. No investigation by the Charity Organisation Society was made in these cases. All other cases, with a few exceptions, dealt with by myself personally, were disposed of by the ordinary machinery of the Charity Organisation Society, whose principles for the purpose of administering this fund were somewhat relaxed.

Relief was given *in money* where thought desirable—for weekly relief, adopting the scale used in administering the relief in East London in 1881 ; for redeeming tools, clothes, &c. required for work ; for buying clothes required for service ; for stock ; for advertising for situations.

It was as far as possible ascertained that the relief given for the last four purposes was so applied, but in some cases the landlords or the publicans secured the grants.

In *kind*—
By orders for food on coffee-taverns and dinner kitchens ;

Mr. R. A. VALPY.
June 4, 1886.

Mr. R. A. VALPY.
June 4, 1886.

By orders for soup, bread, and coals;
By penny dinners at the Coal Yard Board School; and
By boots and shoes for children at school.

We had between 3,000 and 4,000 applications at the office in Duke Street. Many, obviously ineligible, were dismissed at once; others residing out of the district were referred to the proper quarter.

About 850 cases were taken down and investigated; of these, about half were refused, and the rest relieved as above.

I shall have received altogether about £465 for the relief of them. Five of the clergy received grants amounting to £130, so that probably £600 has been expended in the district.

I am not able to state at present the number of cases relieved by the clergy, or the mode in which they have distributed their grants; but, so far as I have been able to ascertain, most have simply given out doles of from 5s. to £1 each, without much regard to the circumstances of each case.

It was the opinion of workers in the district that no exceptional distress prevailed till after the first week in March, when, owing to the prolonged severity of the weather retarding building operations and the arrival of flowers and vegetables at the market, great distress did undoubtedly occur. Some good has been done by enabling a certain number of deserving people to tide over this bad time, by payment of club arrears, by providing the elder girls of families with clothes for, and procuring them, situations, and by providing boots and dinners at school for the younger children; but very few have been helped in this way. Many families have been kept from semi-starvation by orders for food.

On the other hand, many evils were apparent. The fund acted as a direct inducement to many to remain idle. Expectations were raised in many instances of receiving grants of £10 or £15 each, and the expectation of similar appeals to the public in the future necessarily engenders unthrift. There were some cases of men in good employment leaving their work for several hours in order to obtain relief (? by false pretences). One of them is being prosecuted at Bow Street. Complaints were made by employers of labour that men refused work in order to pose as unemployed.

It is needless to mention, besides, the large amount of imposture and fraud resorted to. Great pressure was put on tenants by landlords for back rent. The plan of distribution adopted has, I think, worked well and easily, but one or two other Sub-Committees would have lightened the work, which has practically been done by about ten or twelve members, working often from 10 A.M. till 7 or 8 P.M. The greatest difficulty would have been found in obtaining suitable offices, and, had it not been for Mr. Grey's kindness in lending us two rooms at his Club, I do not know what we should have done.

It was remarkable how little the clergy or the relieving officers knew of the great majority of the applicants. Much valuable information would appear to be derivable from the masters and visitors of elementary schools. The cases sent by the Roman Catholic clergy were mostly ineligible. There was a manifest want of co-operation between the local charities, which are numerous, and I fear do much to pauperise.

I am, however, hopeful of much good in the future by the friendly relations which have been established between some of them and the Charity Organisation Society.

I have somewhat hurriedly put these remarks together, but if suggestions as to the future would be of service, I shall be glad to make them on another occasion.

Yours very truly,
R. A. VALPY.

207. (*Mr. Hedley*): I have only one question. When dealing with a case that came before you, did you make any particular length of residence in the district a condition?—As a rule, we refused to relieve any unless they had resided at least six or eight weeks in the district—two months, as a rule.

208. A person living in a common lodging-house would have been treated as eligible?—As a rule, no. A few cases of people living in common lodging-houses we relieved under very exceptional circumstances. As a rule, we refused to relieve any living in common lodging-houses.

209. (*Dr. Longstaff*): Did you find cases vouched for by people, in whose word ordinarily you would have perfect confidence, thoroughly deserving good cases or not?—I cannot answer that question, as you put it, in the affirmative. It depended very much upon who the people were. Some people, who could most thoroughly be trusted ordinarily, are on these occasions most unreliable.

210. There was a statement in one of the letters to the Press at the time that a Committee in some part of London did its work admirably, because no case was relieved except upon the personal recommendation of a clergyman,

district visitor, or city missionary. Would your experience lead you—all other things put on one side—to consider that the strong recommendation of the clergyman, district visitor, or city missionary was sufficient ground to go upon?—Certainly not.

211. Another point. Have you found that any considerable proportion of the cases relieved were members of clubs?—I have been endeavouring to get statistics upon that point, but have not been able to do so yet. Very few of them belonged to thoroughly good clubs—very few, indeed. There was a singular want of evidence of thrift in that way. A great number of them, especially the Irish, belonged to burial clubs.

212. Had you any other distinct evidence that you came into contact with a superior class of working-men, who were vouched for by superior members of their own class?—I cannot say I had. The only superior working-men I came across I found out myself with very great difficulty; also by going to the clergy, and getting an account of what they needed, and going myself to see them. They would not come forward on account of the crowd of ragamuffins assembled round the office every day.

213. Did you relieve many people known to be, and to have been, for a long time total abstainers?—We relieved a certain number of these. We always took that as evidence in their favour.

214. Did you accept the man's statement that he was a total abstainer?—Not necessarily. We came across a few. They generally brought their cards, or some book; or we found out from references, as a rule, whether they were total abstainers.

215. Did you relieve much in kind?—As far as my recollection serves me, I spent about £110 or £120 in kind. I received myself £450, and expended about one-third in kind.

216. (*Mr. Allen*): In your district the chief people, I think, are general labourers and people employed in Covent Garden?—Yes.

217. Not skilled labourers?—No; there are very few skilled labourers, so far as I know. (The map was here referred to, to show the position and extent of the district, and Mr. Valpy explained that last year the St. Giles's Charity Organisation Committee took over, as part of their area, part of the Strand Union, viz., the parish of St. Clement Danes and the district of Clare Market.) Now we come right down to the river, I don't think we had any cases south of the Strand. A large proportion of our cases came from Clare Market.

218. These fellows were dependent upon work in Covent Garden?—A large number of the people in the district are dependent upon Covent Garden.

219. And are always out of work at that time of year?—Not necessarily. They hang about the market and pick up, perhaps, one or two shillings a day. The supply of vegetables of course depends upon the weather.

220. Did you inquire from pawnbrokers as to the amount of distress?—No; judging from the pawntickets, those individuals who applied to us had largely pawned.

221. Do you know whether there was an exceptional amount of pawning?—I don't know.

222. (*Dr. Longstaff*): Have you any general impression that the pawning was recent—when the pinch came?—It appeared to me, from the tickets I saw, that the pawning had been general all through the winter. There is a class of people who are habitually pawning.

223. Did you verify the pawntickets?—No; we did not.

224. They might easily have been passed from one applicant to another?—That is quite possible. We did not verify them, except in a few cases where we thought it necessary to redeem tools and clothing from pawn. The agent went to see that the things were in pawn, and the cases all proved right.

225. Were you in communication with the relieving officer?—Yes; in daily communication with the relieving officer. I was away in South Wales part of the time, and whenever I came back to the office and found the agents were not in communication with the relieving officer, I insisted upon it.

226. Would you recommend another Mansion House Fund being raised another winter?—Not in the form it was put before the public this year.

Mr. R. A. VALPY.

June 4, 1886.

Mr. R. A. VALPY.
June 4, 1886.

227. (*Chairman*): In what form?—I have an idea that a permanent relief committee might very well be formed. The Mansion House would naturally be selected, and the Lord Mayor, for the time being, might be the head of it.

228. (*Mr. Allen*): Do you think a relief fund necessary?—It may or may not be necessary. I should have a permanent committee, to be in touch with everybody all over London. I should leave the appeal to be made on their recommendation only; and not at the instance of the Lord Mayor himself.

229. (*Hon. and Rev. Canon Legge*): Would you propose that the Committee should employ its own organisation or existing organisations in the distribution?—I think it should very largely employ existing organisations. There is no better organisation than the Charity Organisation Society.

230. You said that most of the applicants were unknown to the clergy and relieving officers. Did the cases come from the class not in the habit of seeking relief, or not under regular visitation?—It is a peculiar district in this way. There are a large number of places of entertainment, eating-houses, and those sort of places, and these people exist very largely upon the broken victuals from these places in times of distress. They rely upon this, and do not apply to the guardians. They came to us in large numbers.

231. Do the St. Giles's Guardians issue lists of persons in receipt of relief?—I don't know. The Rector of St. Clement Danes did not co-operate.

232. Did he give any reason?—No; he received a grant, I think, of £50. He gave out doles of 5s. to 10s. each to different people. We used to send down to him begging for lists of the people he relieved, in order that we might not relieve the same individuals; but he never gave a list.

233. It was not the relief he objected to, but the organisation?—I don't know what he objected to. He gave some relief. He had money for the purpose.

234. (*Mr. Hollond*): Did you take any steps to get working men upon the Committee?—I tried to get working men on the Committee. One or two promised. There was a working man engaged at the British Museum—an excellent man, whom I knew a good deal about from Mrs. Poole—but he could not attend.

235. Did you try to get any members of friendly societies?—I am not aware that any friendly society has its headquarters in our district.

236. But there are branches?—I went to so many people to get co-operation; I meant to have gone to them, but did not do so.

237. I rather gather from you that the machinery of the Charity Organisation Society, when strengthened as you strengthened it, is sufficient for the purpose of investigating cases?—In a district like ours, I think it is. It would have to be very largely strengthened in a large district—in a district like Clapham or Wandsworth.

238. You had three more inquiry officers, who dealt with these 3,000 or 4,000 applications that you received?—No; 850 cases were taken down and investigated, the rest were rejected. They were simply cases that were obviously ineligible. A great number resided in other districts. A great number came from St. Pancras.

239. Did you find the rules issued by the Mansion House Fund of any use in the distribution?—I drew up a set of rules very similar myself. I did not receive those rules until a week or ten days after the distribution began.

240. Did they go pretty well on all fours with those rules?—I think they did.

241. I gather that you consider that the fund was of use in touching cases that would not have been touched by the ordinary relief agencies?—I think it was. I have found from experience that the ordinary relief agencies are not available when there is a pressure of cases.

242. (*Mr. Hedley*): You don't include the Poor Law?—No; my opinion of the Poor Law is, that it should deal with a different class of people—people who are already paupers. The ordinary charities ought to try to deal with a different class of people, to prevent them becoming paupers. I remember, I think it was two or three years ago, when the demolition of buildings first began for the new street, Shaftesbury Avenue—the part towards Endell Street is in my district—the demolitions for the purpose of making the Avenue caused very great hardship to several of the small shopkeepers, who depended for their living upon the people inhabiting the old slums, and a good many came for relief.

Several of the cases were thought very desirable to be relieved out of the funds of the Society for the Relief of Distress. I applied for a further grant—my first grant being expended—and they told me that they had no further funds at their disposal. We met these cases through private friends of mine.

Mr. R. A. Valpy.

June 4, 1886.

243. Might not these cases have been met by the various relief agencies, in a time of pressure, issuing their own appeals to get their hands strengthened ì Is it necessary to have a central appeal bringing applications from all quarters ?— If you can secure the harmonious co-operation of all the different agencies, which is impossible. They are generally antagonistic, and will not work together. Each wants to go its own way, and has its own faith, and from this you have overlapping.

244. You are accepting the principle of a central appeal. Do you think there should be a particular fund ? Don't you think it would be enough, if the appeal came from the Mansion House, to strengthen the ordinary charities ?— I think one or two of the charities—the Charity Organisation Society, the Society for the Relief of Distress, and the Metropolitan Visiting and Relief Association—take these three, and strengthen their hands, and, I think, it would be perfectly possible to deal with any ordinary exceptional distress, unless there is any very great distress indeed—something much greater than last year.

245. (*Chairman*): Was inquiry made as to whether there was any need for the fund—on the score of exceptional distress ?—Canon Nisbet called a meeting of all those receiving grants from the fund and others at the vestry. I explained to the meeting that I had been appointed treasurer and sole representative of the fund in the district, and that no other grants would be made there, except to me. At the close of the meeting, Canon Nisbet asked the opinion of everybody round the room as to whether there was any exceptional distress, and, I think, everyone said there was no exceptional distress.

246. Were the persons in the room employers of labour ? Did they refer to their books and see what they were paying weekly as wages ? Were the bulk of them employers ?—The bulk of them, I think, were clergymen and churchwardens. There were two or three guardians.

247. Did you, or anybody on your behalf, go to the employers of labour in your district, and ask them to give you this simple information—How much are you paying out a week now for wages ?—No ; I did not do that. I went to several employers of labour and asked their opinion.

248. You never put the question—Would you look at your labour account and tell me how much you paid away in labour last week, or this week, and compare it with what you have paid at other times ?—I did not.

249. Does not that appear to you obviously the best test ?—I think it would be.

250. If you got hold of the large employers.

251. (*Mr. Hedley*): You would not get hold of the small shopkeepers.

252. (*Chairman*): We have got out in evidence that the fund was for handicraft people.

253. (*Witness*): That was only Mr. Fletcher's view. My view is different.

254. There was mention in your letter of a society that distributed some money, the Strangers' Friend Society, and that you thought that their politics entered into it ?—My remark did not apply to them. There were various people who came forward ; some were very keen, indeed, to help us ; they were very anxious to sack me, and to get hold of money if they could. From conversations I had with some of the unemployed, I had strong reason to believe that they wished to favour especially some of their own supporters. I made inquiries afterwards, and found that these people were very active political partisans in the district.

255. You said you did communicate with the relieving officers. Did you with the vestry clerks, or the persons who distributed the City Parochial Charities in the district ?—I am not aware of any City Parochial Charities in the district.

256. You are not aware that in St. Clement Danes there is a considerable fund for the assistance of deserving servants out of employment ?—No.

257. Did it never occur to you to see what public money there was in the

Mr. R. A. VALPY.
June 4, 1886.

district?—I have here a list of all the charities of the district, so far as I was able to ascertain them.

258. You did communicate with the Poor Law people, but not with the parochial charities? Of course you would not be within the City there?—I communicated with the local charities—with those who had the distribution of them.

259. You did communicate with them?—Yes, as far as possible.

260. Did you ever assist any cases that were being relieved by the Poor Law?—Not that I am aware of. The cases being relieved by the Poor Law are mostly cases of thoroughly chronic distress, which it would have been perfectly useless to try to assist. The relieving officer sent up two or three cases, but we refused to help them.

261. (*Mr. Hedley*): Did you relieve chronic cases?—No; we did not; we referred them as much as possible to the clergy. No doubt, we did relieve a few chronic cases, but not purposely. We discovered them afterwards.

262. (*Chairman*): Did you take the word 'deserving' into account, or did you think that the requirements of the case were satisfied if a man in distress could prove that he was unemployed, though his character might be anything but satisfactory? Did you inquire into character?—A man of that kind I should be inclined to help unless he was a notorious character—a regular thief. If I had reason to believe that he would apply the money to the support of his family, I would relieve him, certainly. I would rather relieve him in kind.

263. Do you think that the establishment of the fund, and its continuance for the length of time it was in existence, disturbed the labour market, and discouraged people from seeking for work? Did it interfere with the relations between master and servant?—I have no doubt about it. It acted as an inducement to a large number of people to remain out of work. Expectations were raised that the people would get as much as £10 or £15 each.

264. People purposely remained out of work? More people would have been at work if the fund had not been established? It withdrew people from the labour market?—To a certain degree. I did hear that tradesmen were complaining that people would not come and work.

265. You don't employ any hands yourself? You didn't find it affect any person you paid, so that they, or any of their relations, had to work for less money?—No; I know nothing of that kind.

266. Did you have any statements from masters and employers that you were interfering with the relations between labour and the employer?—I had no communication with them myself on this point. Some members of the Committee did communicate with employers of labour, who stated that they had great difficulty in getting hands.

267. Could you give us the name of any large employer of labour in the district who would come and give evidence?—I will make inquiries.

268. (*Mr. Loch*): I think you said you relieved by tickets in certain instances?—They were given on the Windmill Street Soup Kitchen and Canon Nisbet's Soup Kitchen in Endell Street. In cases of extreme poverty and distress, I gave interim relief in the shape of dinner-tickets. To those cases which it was undesirable to relieve in money, I gave these dinner-tickets and soup-tickets. I found that the tickets were being sold in the public-houses. Tickets worth 7*d*. apiece, providing sufficient food for two grown-up people, were being sold at the rate of three for a shilling. A friend of mine saw in a shop in the district, 'Mansion House Tickets Bought Here,' and inducements were held out by small shopkeepers and the publicans to get the people to sell these tickets. I adopted this card (produced and read by the Chairman). I largely employed the Coffee-Tavern Company; I was told that the tradesmen were unreliable, and that they gave money to the people in exchange for the tickets instead of food. We found that they could not sell the ticket I had adopted.

269. (*Chairman*): You found the little shopkeepers combining with the holder of the ticket to defraud?—I have no direct evidence of that. I think I can bring evidence as to the sale of the tickets in the public-houses.

270. (*Mr. Loch*): Did you say you referred chronic cases to the clergy? Did they deal with them out of the moneys they received as grants from the Mansion

House Fund?—I found some of the clergy strongly inclined to do so, and I represented to them that it was not the object of the fund.

271. While you were refusing to relieve them, you referred them to the clergy who did it?—I cannot say that I found the clergy had been relieving numerous chronic cases. I did leave some chronic cases to two or three of the clergy with whom I was in friendly co-operation, and they said, 'We will not relieve the cases out of the Mansion House Fund, but out of the parochial funds.'

272. (*Mr. Hedley*): Did you give weekly allowances when you had decided to grant money to an applicant?—Sometimes we gave a lump sum to buy stock, and sometimes weekly allowances, as stated in my letter to Mr. Loch.

(*The Committee then adjourned.*)

Mr. R. A. VALPY.
June 4, 1886.

FRIDAY, JUNE 11TH, 1886.

Present—MR. F. J. S. EDGCOMBE, and subsequently MR. ALBERT PELL, in the Chair.

Sir JOHN TILLEY,
Dr. G. B. LONGSTAFF,
Mr. E. PETERS.

Rev. W. CURTIS HAYWARD,
Mr. J. H. ALLEN,

Mr. R. HEDLEY, attending on behalf of the Local Government Board.

Mr. C. S. LOCH, *Secretary*.

MR. J. R. J. BRAMLY, examined.

273. (*Chairman*): What district do you represent, Mr. Bramly?—Lewisham civil parish.

274. Is that the whole parish?—No; the parish is a very large one; it extends up to the Crystal Palace. We go up to Catford.

275. About what population?—I could ascertain and let you have that, but I do not know.

276. You have some defined limit to your district?—The parish is divided into six distinct poor groups.

277. Your district is that of the Society for Relief of Distress, or the civil parish? (The *Secretary* here referred witness to a map.)—*Witness* (pointing to map): Our district is practically from here to Catford.

278. (*Chairman*): When you talk of your district to-day, you speak as representing the Mansion House Fund?—Yes.

279. Now, who set out that district?—We did, with the consent of the Central Committee at Greenwich.

280. You were a sub-division of the Mansion House Fund?—Yes; we sent to say that we could not cover the whole of it.

281. Had you any previous experience?—No special experience. I am the Hon. Secretary to the Lewisham Charity Organisation Committee.

282. You are not a guardian of the poor?—No.

283. What first moved you to act? Who first introduced you to the Mansion House Fund?—We had summoned a special Committee of the Charity Organisation Society to consider what steps we should take to meet the distress.

284. Did you communicate with the Mansion House Fund first?—No; the Rev. Brooke Lambert came up from Greenwich and produced a telegram from the Lord Mayor, asking him to form a Committee for the district, and he moved that we should form ourselves into a Committee. The clergy refused to be almoners.

285. What date?—February 13.

286. On February 1, or thereabouts, had any circumstances come under your notice to lead you to believe that there was exceptional distress?—No.

287. Between February 1 and February 13? I am not talking of rumours; but, from your own experience and observation in that part of London, did you come to the opinion that there was an exceptional state of distress?—

Mr. J. R. J. BRAMLY.
June 11 1886.

Mr. J. R. J. BRAMLY.
June 11, 1886.

No; there was more distress, but not so exceptional as the newspapers made out.

288. More than usual in winter?—Yes.

289. But winter has, or ought to have, come to a conclusion?—Yes; but it has been a very long winter.

290. But you thought that during the winter there had been more distress than usual?—Yes.

291. Do you think there was enough to justify an appeal to the public?—Not in Lewisham. We summoned this Committee to see how it best could be met. We thought that we ourselves, *plus* existing Church agencies, or the parochial authorities, could meet it.

292. I will just go through this letter.* You had application forms printed, which were issued to members of the Committee to distribute?—We did not print those forms. A Sub-Committee was formed by the Central Mansion House Committee at Greenwich.

293. How were they issued?—They were sent in large bundles to the clergy.

294. But I think that you said that the clergy refused to be almoners?—Yes; but they issued the application forms through the district visitors.

295. Did you see anything of advertisements in the local papers—did you see any advertisements?—No.

296. Did you issue any advertisements?—No; it spread like wildfire, before the application forms went out. On the Saturday night, at the meeting of the Charity Organisation Society, which subsequently became the Relief Committee, when the meeting had practically broken up, a member got up and proposed that he should have £50 put at his command—£50 or £25, I forget which—for immediate distribution. I opposed that as strongly as I could. The irregular motion was however agreed to, with some dissentients, of whom I was one.

297. That was £50 of the Mansion House money?—Yes; part of that was distributed unwisely.

298. Did he get the money?—He spent it before he got it.

299. But it was refunded?—In all £25 was spent before the formation of the

* A letter from Mr. Bramly to the Secretary of the Charity Organisation Society, which was submitted to the Committee, is referred to. It was as follows:—

LEWISHAM COMMITTEE,
HIGH STREET, LEWISHAM, S.E.:
17th March, 1886.

DEAR MR. LOCH,—As the Lewisham Branch of the Mansion House Fund closes its doors on the 24th inst., after an existence of thirty-four days, and as no new experience is likely to be gained during the next and last week, it may be well to send you a short account of its work to date.

You are aware that the Rev. Brooke Lambert attended a special meeting of this Committee on Saturday the 13th ult., with a request that a Committee should be formed in Lewisham to deal with the Mansion House Fund. The persons present were thereupon formed into such a Committee, with power to add to their number. Mr. Cleeve, a Guardian, and myself were opposed to the proposal, as the need did not seem sufficiently pressing—our idea being that existing local agencies should receive from the Greenwich Committee such sums as they might deem necessary to meet the distress, which, though much exaggerated, is certainly greater than during several previous winters.

1. *Composition of Committee:*
    (a) Ministers of all denominations,
    (b) Leading persons interested in charitable works,
    (c) Working men,
    (d) Employers of labour,
    (e) Two foremen of Messrs. Penn's,
        One small coal dealer,
        One working shoemaker,
and these attended very regularly.

In one part of the district a Working Men's Committee was formed under the Vicar, Rev. W. A. Moberly, and every application from that district was submitted to it previous to decision by Executive Committee. A Working Men's Committee was also formed in one part of St. Mary's, but speedily dissolved.

The Hon. Secs. (two) are both Charity Organisation Society folk, and I have attended the greater part of every day.

Mr. J. R. C. BRAMLY.

June 11, 1886.

Committee which commenced work on February 19—that is between February 13 and February 19—but this irregular expenditure was stopped after February 17—great dissatisfaction having arisen, as was foreseen, through relief being given in one portion of the district, while none was obtainable in the other portions. The homes of the clergy were besieged and much annoyance experienced by them.

300. As soon as these forms got out, the eagles began to flock to the carcass?— Yes; on the 19th was the first meeting—the forms were sent out on the 17th. There was a direction exhibited to put them into a large box at the gate of the house. We did not want them to come trooping up to the Committee-room.

301. What was done with the forms? Did you ever appoint any staff of almoners?—Yes.

302. Did you appoint them? Who undertook the office?—The names of a few are given in the Mansion House Committee's Report. One was a head-gardener. But we were very short of almoners.

303. (Rev. W Curtis Hayward): Did the clergy refuse to act? Only as almoners.

304. (Chairman): The clergy took no part in the distribution of the alms?— No; but they took a very leading part in the Committee meetings. We had two Committee meetings a day, and it rarely happened that one or more of the clergy did not attend. They would not become the channels for giving the money, but they knew the people who were their parishioners, and we got a great deal of valuable information from them.

305. These gentlemen you got to act as almoners were, as I gather from what you have said, rather below the middle station in society?—Only two of them.

306. What were the others—manufacturers, builders, and so forth?—No; ladies and gentlemen.

307. Is it not more correct to say that they were ladies with only two exceptions?—No. The female almoners were ladies, without exception.

308. I have only the names of two gentlemen—Mr. Bates and Mr. Kenward?—But there were several others.

309. Well, then, the labour test was first of all adopted. That broke down because it barred the man getting relief who had gone into the workhouse.

The Executive met twice a day, the first meeting, by order from Greenwich, being held on the morning of February 19.

2. *District:*
    Lewisham civil parish, less Sydenham and Forest Hill. A glance at the map will shew how much ground had to be covered in inquiry and relief—Catford, Brockley, Loats Pits, Loampit Vale, Hither Green, and Lewisham proper.

3. *Procedure:*
    Application forms (drafted at Greenwich—copy enclosed) were issued to the various ministers, and were also to be had at the office, Court Hill Road. Those from Loats Pits were sent to the Working Men's Committee; the others were taken by members of Committee, verified as far as possible, and brought up for decision at the next meeting. Local references have been referred to, and, in some cases, those at a distance.

The Rules were only received after some days, and we commenced to work on those (copy included) a rough draft of which I showed you at the Mansion House, and which were read to and tacitly approved of by the Central Committee, Greenwich, on the 16th February

The issue of the Mansion House Rules landed us in one difficulty—*i.e.*, that we had made the labour-yard a test, offering to supplement wages according to family. Several men on this had gone in, and the Rules cut them off from participation in the Fund. The Committee felt the injustice of this, and finally decided to take deserving men out of the yard and maintain them until work presented itself. On two occasions a considerable crowd of men at work in labour-yard came to the office to complain of the injustice of treating them worse than those who were standing about with their hands in their pockets. A deputation of three were sent up to the Lord Mayor to plead their own cause, and the result was, practically, a free hand to us to treat them as we liked. Our decision was to take the best men out as detailed above.

By arrangement with the Lewisham Board of Works a labour test was started last week. A selected list of men was sent to the Surveyor for work, which would be no

D

22

Mr. J. R. J.
BRAMLY.
June 11, 1886.

Then there was another labour test—seven hours' work for 2s. 6d.?—Yes; only about £75 was expended on it. It was useful to a certain extent, because some refused the 2s. 6d.

310. There were 144 offered this relief upon test, and only 50 accepted. Was there room for more than 50?—No; but the 50 men were only reached when we had offered it to 144. We had to offer it to 144 before we could get the 50. Two-thirds refused it. We could not have taken more than 50, but there were a good many more than 144 to be asked.

311. Is this the case, that the labour test proved that a great many persons were applying for relief who really did not want it?—Did not want it so badly as to be content to accept 2s. 6d. a day.

312. As to be content to accept it on the terms of 2s. 6d. a day?—When it was offered to them, they went out grumbling 'Half-a-crown a day! Washerwomen's pay!'

313. Do you think the Mansion House Fund got into these people's hands in any other way? Could they get at it except through you?—Quite impossible.

314. With the exception of the clergyman, whose case was referred to, you say there was no other mode?—No.

315. The applicants, you say in your letter, consisted of bricklayers and plasterers and gardeners—what I call non-winter men. I suppose they were not exclusively of those classes?—The report gave an analysis.

316. (After reading a clause in the report.) So that 50 per cent. were distinctly connected with the building trade.* Then 34 per cent. were labourers.

relief of the rates, to be paid at the rate of 2s. 6d. per day of seven hours. To date, 144 men have been offered this, and 50 have accepted. No more can be taken on.

The Committee, feeling that many of the applicants were not suited to such work, passed a resolution to offer it to every man, but not to press the test home in cases of skilled workmen who had *not* been in the labour-yard.

£75 has been granted for this work. The almoning has been done by Committee and by volunteers—the clergy have taken no part in it.

Intending emigrants have been maintained, as the Colonial agents refuse those families any member of which have received parish relief.

Relief has been according to scale, and given for seven days.

'Renewed application' forms have been issued.

No fresh application has been received since March 6, inclusive.

I sent you in some weeks ago a sketch of distress in this neighbourhood, as far as could hastily be obtained, and I do not think the results of the Fund have falsified it.

The applicants, as a rule, have been those who have generally little or no employment during winter months—bricklayers, plasterers, painters, jobbing gardeners; but the work that those connected with the building trade have had during last summer has at the best been intermittent, and the pawnbrokers' testimony that the people have not been able to take out the things they put in last winter, 1884–5, is confirmed by the evidence of the application forms. We find pawn-tickets to the value of several pounds in nearly every case.

We deferred dealing with these until the applicants were in work, but our funds will evidently not allow us to take out even a very small proportion of clothing and tools. We have redeemed in a very few cases tools on written evidence of employment, and in a very few others, difficult to help in other ways, clothing.

Arrears of clubs have been paid, and boots (over 200 pairs) have been given to children whose parents are not in receipt of parish relief, on the recommendation of teachers. On the whole the fund has been fairly administered, and few glaring cases been relieved. Still some, no doubt, have received relief who were not entitled to it as far as character is concerned. We have of course heard the usual tale of the wrong persons getting it, and have tried to fix the informant, so as to verify the statement, but little has come of it. We hear of much dissatisfaction; but that is inevitable, and from some quarters it implies compliment. Our Agent has devoted himself from early morning to late at night to the work—we have been admirably served by him and by his brother.
I am, yours truly,
J. R. J. BRAMLY.

* The analysis is as follows:—Labourers, 93; carpenters, 30; painters, plumbers, paper-hangers, &c., 52; gas-fitters, 4; gardeners, 18; clerks, 6; plasterers, 19; bricklayers and brickmakers, 36; carmen, 9; stonemasons, 3; sawyer, 1; drillers, 2; stoker, 1; shoemakers, 3; engine-fitters, 6; other occupations not included in foregoing trades, 38. Total 321. No. of applications, 474.

May I not take it that half of these were dependent on the building trade? — Yes; ground-men they call them.

317. Then, gardeners—of course they were frozen out? Have you yourself any knowledge of what is paid to the excavator?—A few years ago it was 6½d. an hour, but now a painter does not get much more than that.

318. This is a very curious thing; these are all engaged in one trade where men must fairly calculate on not being able to work in winter; and even among the other classes, there are, for instance, stonemasons. Was the distress greater amongst artisans than amongst gardeners, ground-men, etc., whose usual pay would be less than 5s. a day?—No. I think there was more distress amongst the class earning 5s. a day than the others, though the analysis scarcely shows this, I admit. You must consider that in our neighbourhood, besides the silk mills and a cigar factory, there is practically nothing else but building.

319. You refer in your letter to pawn-tickets? You had the sanction of the Mansion House Fund for getting out of pawn some tools? Do you take it as one of the circumstances of life in your neighbourhood that the people should be intimately acquainted with pawn-shops?—I think so in ours.

320. Do you think it natural for men, whose pay is 9d. an hour, or an excavator, whose pay is 6d. an hour, natural that they should have their tools in pawn?—But they don't get those wages now.

321. Men are working for me at the West-end of London, and the builder, under whom they work, and whom I employ, assures me that he has to pay men 9d. an hour. If you can correct me, if you can tell me that that was not the pay in 1885, I should be glad to put that down?—We have one very large builder down there.

322. Have you heard, or did your Committee make any inquiries, among the employers of labour as to the cases? Did you ask them whether they had been paying a less amount of money during the year, or less per hour? Was any inquiry of that sort made?—No, not directly. There was no time for all these things. The public cried out for immediate distribution.

323. Don't you think, upon reflection, it would have been doing better service to the public if you had resisted acceptance of this money from the Mansion House Fund until you had satisfied yourselves that you could distribute it without doing injury to society, as you find it around you? Am I right in considering that you distributed it without time for inquiry?—No, not exactly. The meeting of the Charity Organisation Society was held for the purpose of dealing with the extra, though not exceptional, distress, but we did not think that the Mansion House Fund was the best way of dealing with it. We could not help taking it, for it was forced upon us.

324. You thought you could make it as little mischievous as possible?—Yes.

325. You have told us that, until the Mansion House Fund was discharged upon you, you did not know of the exceptional distress?—Not to the extent reported in the papers.

326. Do you think that the Mansion House Fund was the cause of the declaration of distress?—Yes; many who would not otherwise have applied for relief came for it then.

327. Would you yourself expect that bricklayers and plasterers, and the men dependent upon them, should be at work in the winter?—No; unless the winter was more or less open, as it is sometimes.

328. As a fact, frost coming would prevent building?—Yes.

329. It is not quite as certain that a plasterer should fail of work as that a haymaker should fail of work?—I don't think it is so certain as regards plasterers; a certain amount of work has been carried on all this winter.

330. Did you make any inquiry at the savings banks as to the withdrawal of funds?—No; but when I sent in a report before the Mansion House Fund, I said I had seen the relieving officers and other people, from whom I learned that there was nothing indicating exceptional distress. Provident societies and savings banks were increasing their members; and the same with building societies.

331. Did you go to the savings bank?—Excepting those managed by the

Mr. J. R. J. BRAMLY.
June 11, 1886.

clergy, we have no independent savings bank—no savings bank beyond the Post Office Savings Bank.

332. Should you be in favour of any preparation against the recurrence of distress?—I have hoped that something would be done to meet it. The ragamuffin section fully expect another Mansion House Fund next winter. For the last few weeks of winter they paraded the streets with boxes, and levied blackmail on the public. An attempt was made to stop the proceeding. The question was asked in the House of Commons, but Government declined to interfere.

333. Were they threatening?—No; but it was just after the smashing of windows in London, and people gave their money to prevent that.

334. Would you tell the Committee what steps you would suggest should be taken with reference to a distress that you might anticipate to appear again—whether real or feigned?

335. (*Mr. Hedley*): Beyond the existence of the Poor Law?—If the money-giving public get it into their head that there is distress, they will not be satisfied with the Charity Organisation Society.

336. That is putting it hypothetically. I want to know whether you have any suggestion to make? Do you think you ought in October to endeavour to make inquiries?—I think it would be a wise thing to do, but it is still more important to know what we shall do when we know that there is distress.

337. (*Rev. W. C. Hayward*): Have you any almoners of the Society for the Relief of Distress?—No; we have not.

338. (*Chairman*): You have no definite scheme that you would like to submit to the Committee?—No; I came up for light more than anything else.

339. Do you feel that you can rely upon the Poor Law machinery as sufficient to prevent anything serious—anything that could be fairly entitled to be called human suffering?—No; I think we shall very likely have more than the Poor Law can deal with, and I don't know that extra funds entrusted to parochial agency would be wise. I mean the distribution of charity through the clergy. I don't know that it would be wise for the district visitors to have it.

340. Was any reference made in the pulpits to this terrible state of destitution?—No, nothing, as far as I am aware; there were appeals for money, but not for personal service, as far as I am aware.

341. Do you know of any instance in the Lewisham district in which one or more persons really themselves distributed, and went among their neighbours to render assistance, apart from any society?—In regard to exceptional help, no; our ground is not like London; there is not a dense population. I do not think it necessary.

342. Did you ever receive any letters from any parishioner saying, 'I hope you will look up the case of So-and-So, in such a place, where I know there is serious suffering existing, and who ought to be assisted, apart from the question of character?'—No; not as far as my memory serves me.

343. Then it was a general claim for help by the members of a special trade, met by a portion of the Mansion House Fund?

344. (*Mr. J. H. Allen*): You said that these clergymen, as members of the Mansion House Committee, were useful in giving information, stating that So-and-So was in great distress. Did you find cases so authorised that proved on inquiry not to be deserving?—Yes; one or two. An almoner was entrusted to take some money where there was said to be urgent distress, and, when he got there, the father and mother were both out. The father, who was in employment, had not come home from his work, and the mother was out also. But it turned out, on further inquiries, that it was a house of ill-fame. This case, however, was one to be relieved out of the £50 voted irregularly as I have described.

345. (*Chairman*): But that is a very valuable case—that the clergyman really recommended to you. I know a case in which a friend of mine was actually subsidised for years to the extent of several hundred pounds for such a house as that, which was kept by an old servant.

346. (*Mr. Allen*): On the whole, you found that the information was trustworthy?—Yes.

347. Did you find any instances of people sending in a list of persons they knew to be deserving people in great distress that any were not deserving or in great distress?—Yes, several.

348. I mean persons who had been recommended?—There were some, but not a large proportion.

349. In other words, you consider in any similar state of affairs in the future that it would be desirable to confirm the recommendation of anybody, however strong?—It would depend on whether I knew the recommender.

350. But you would not accept it unreservedly?—No.

351. Would you consider that inquiry was necessary?—Not in every case, but, as a rule, I should.

352. Among the people you found generally speaking to be deserving and really in distress, did you find much evidence of thrift?—I may say that we paid arrears of clubs to the amount of some £32.

353. How many people? Do you know?—No; I am not prepared with that because I have come at short notice.

354. Was one man in ten in a club, do you think?—I should say nearer one in five.

355. Then you think that there really were men, who had shown some knowledge of thrift, who were absolutely in distress?—Yes; I went into several cases of people I had never heard of before, but who, I feel certain, were respectable people.

356. (*Mr. Hadley*): I understand that you would not wish to see a Mansion House Fund raised again?—No.

357. And you have no scheme to suggest to the Committee?—It is rather a difficult question

358. I think you should know. Has your Committee any scheme or plan? You did not go into the question?—My own private opinion is that if it is real, or the public believe it to be real, then some central body would have to be formed—a Committee of leading people and guardians, and so on, but I don't think that we, as a Committee of the Charity Organisation Society, would quite have the public confidence.

359. (*Chairman*): Would the primary object of this Central Committee be to supplement the Mansion House Committee?—No; to distribute a local fund, I think. I don't see why it should not be raised locally.

360. (*Chairman*): You think it ought to be raised locally?—Yes.

361. (*Mr. E. Peters*): Were the persons to whom you say you think you did good—were they of a class above those who apply as a rule to the Poor Law? Do you see any reason why they should not have applied to the Poor Law?—Yes; many of them. I remember a gardener who had been up from the country only for a year or two; he would not have liked to go before the Poor Law Guardians.

362. Was that the only case you remember—speaking generally?—You will see by their trades that we did not go above the artisan. We did not go to poor gentlefolks. I certainly came across many respectable people.

363. (*Rev. W. C. Hayward*): Was the distress the means of breaking up many homes – to go to the workhouse? Or, rather, was the scale of relief sufficient to make it probable that they would be enabled to keep out of the workhouse?—Yes, undoubtedly.

364. (*Chairman*): You think that these people would have really gone through a great deal of suffering sooner than apply for relief?—Rather than go to the workhouse.

365. Do you think that these persons whom you had in your mind had feelings that would have prevented their going to the parish?—It would have hurt them.

366. Would you have been exceedingly surprised if they had?—I should not have been surprised if they applied to the labour-yard at Lewisham. A large proportion of the men there was from the artisan, as well as from the labouring, class. The Lewisham Committee wished to supplement labour-yard pay, for that reason. But to this Mr. Brooke Lambert did not agree. He was judging from the Greenwich labour-yard, which, he said, was the annual resort of the scum of the population there. We think that those who will work in the yard are more entitled to relief than those who stand about with their hands in their pockets.

367. (*Sir John Tilley*): You are not sure that you did better than the

Mr. J. R. J. BRAMLY.
June 11, 1886

guardians could have done by a well-considered plan of outdoor relief?—The guardians already give so much outdoor relief.

368. (*Mr. Hedley*): Did you give them lump sums, or money by the week?—By the week.

369. (*Chairman*): How did you satisfy yourselves that they were not getting relief from the relieving officer?—We had the fortnightly out-relief lists made up to the previous evening, and the list of men in the labour-yard corrected to the previous day; we kept a careful watch upon that.

370. (*Mr. Peters*): Besides clergymen, had the almoners any discretion, or were they limited by the orders of the Committee?—Strictly limited by orders. They had so much money and vouchers, and brought back receipts for what they had paid.

371. (*Mr. Edgcombe*): You said that you could hardly call the distress exceptional, but that it was great?—Yes; owing to the intermittent work in the summer.

372. Is the distress more than you are in the habit of seeing—more than during the continuance of a long frost?—Yes; than there has been since 1881.

373. You said a number of persons applied who never would have applied if it had not been for the Mansion House Fund?—I think so.

374. May it not have been that there were many of them whom it was well to relieve?—A small portion of them; but there were cadgers among them.

375. Did you make the ordinary inquiries—the Charity Organisation Society inquiries?—We had to do it quickly, and we got the best information we could, and the only ones we cut straight off were the drunkards.

376. Was the last employer communicated with?—There was no time for that; but local references were applied to.

377. You say that one-fifth of the applicants belonged to clubs? Yes; of all sorts.

378. Good clubs and bad clubs?—Yes.

379. (*Chairman*): Now, Mr. Bramly, I ask you if you will do a thing for the Committee. Would you ask the builder you have referred to, to have his books out before you, and get on paper the sum of money he paid in 1885 for labour, and the same in 1884? We will also take a bad year—1880; and if he would give you the money he paid in 1879 and 1880, we will compare the scale of payment in 1884 and 1885 with that in 1879 and 1880.—It would not be a true test, because our population is annually increasing.*

380. (*Chairman*): We can check that with the census. If your population is increasing, it is an evidence you are doing well?—They are building all over the place.

381. (*Mr. Hedley*): You are talking of the Lewisham parish?—Yes.

382. You have no such thing as a slum in Lewisham?—Not one like Mill Lane, Deptford; but then the population comes up to us.

---

* From evidence kindly furnished by Mr. J. R. S. Bramly, it appeared that, comparing 1880 with 1884 and 1885, there had been no great decline in the amount of wages distributed by large firms in the district. In the case of one firm of builders, indeed, the amount expended in wages had increased from £18,832 in 1880 to £40,062 in 1884, and £35,972 in 1885. The rate of wages of some firms for average workmen in the building trade was as follows:—groundmen, 6½d. the hour; bricklayers, 9d.; bricklayers' labourers, 6d.; carpenters and joiners, 8½d.; masons, 8½d.; plasterers, 9d.; painters, 7½d. Three others gave ½d. more to carpenters and masons. Two other firms and several smaller builders gave ½d. and 1d. less per hour in all branches. 'The wages were not bad if a man had constant work, but there was so much time lost between finishing one job and getting another.' Speculating builders frequently let the work out by the piece, and some at a very *grinding* rate. Comparing 1880 and 1884 and 1885 in a large nursery garden the total amount of money paid in wages was £2,620, £2,378, and £2,528. Men in each of those years earned 18s. to 30s., and boys 6s. to 10s. In another garden the amount of wages for the above three years was £700, £600, and £600; and the scale of wage was, in 1880, 20s., 22s., 24s., up to 30s.; in 1884, 20s., 22s., up to 27s.; and in 1885 the same. 'Wages the last two years had tended downwards,' said one informant. Mr. Bramly sums up: 'My impression, therefore, that though the distress last winter was greater, it was not as severe as stated, is, I think, fairly borne out. In fact, many men had opportunities of bettering their position last summer which I was not aware of. That they did not take advantage of them is their own fault.'

383. (*Chairman*): Have you no large gardeners in the district—market gardeners?—Several large nursery gardeners.

384. Do you think some of these gentlemen would give you the same figures?—Oh, yes.

385. I have one other question just to ask you. I should like to know whether you are more uncomfortable about the chance of a Mansion House Fund next winter, or the chance of distress among the population—which is the more uncomfortable consideration?—I think that there will be more distress probably than when the Mansion House Fund was raised—more real distress but I should certainly view with apprehension the establishment of another Mansion House Fund.

386. You fear that more than the distress—or rather, that it would be more difficult to deal with a Mansion House Fund than with the distress?

387. (*Mr. Edgcombe*): You don't think the Mansion House Fund will help you?—No; these men that carried the boxes were great drunkards. One man who carried a large box was so drunk that he could scarcely get down the hill.

388. (*Dr. Longstaff*): Did you notice any unusual begging when the Mansion House Fund was going on?—That is difficult to judge. The Deptford and Greenwich beggars come up to Lewisham and Lee.

389. Were you troubled at your own house?—No; they know I belong to the Charity Organisation Society. There was more begging last winter.

390. Did you hear complaints of servant girls being frightened by beggars coming to the doors?—No; but I have heard of ladies being followed in the streets and frightened.

391. My point is, whether among the multitude there has been increased begging?—They begged with more persistence, perhaps, and perhaps a little threatening was done. They thought that the public hand was open.

392. (*Chairman*): There is no depression in the public-house trade, I suppose?—No; I think not. Some of them, a few years ago, were shifting their ground, I believe, because the trade was not so good.

Mr. J. R. *Bramly*, June 11, 1885.

Mr. W. M. ACWORTH, examined.

393. (*Chairman*): You, Mr. Acworth, represent the Camberwell district of the Mansion House Fund?—Well, I was honorary secretary for the whole district, but I had very little to do with the distribution.

394. Now, were you first brought into connection with the Mansion House Fund about February 13?—I cannot tell you the exact date. There was a meeting at the Mansion House at which Committees for the South of London were constituted.

395. Before then, had you had any scheme coming under your notice to lead you to believe that there was exceptional distress?—We had inquiries sent down to us from this office about the last week of January. We discussed it at considerable length, and myself and another member of the Committee overruled the secretary that there was not exceptional distress.

396. You live in that district?—Just out of it.

397. From what you know—your own knowledge—do you think there was exceptional distress at the end of January?—Yes; now I do; but not until the Mansion House Fund commenced. I am now convinced that there was.

398. What happened to convince you?—I thought there was not, because the people who came to us were the ordinary people who came, who are a little above the Poor Law; but, as soon as the Mansion House Fund came on, I saw a number of people who came to us, and said that they had never in all their lives applied for charity before. I saw them personally; and had their cases inquired into.

399. Now, you say personally; did you personally inquire into the cases yourself?—No; I caused inquiries to be made by the Charity Organisation Society's agent.

400. Yes; who is an expert. Now, in the case of these persons you had never seen before, the Charity Organisation Society officer went and inquired? What was his report? Did he say they were in want of food?—Oh, I think there was no doubt of that.

Mr. W. M. *Acworth*.

Mr. W. M.
Acworth.
June 11, 1886.

401. Do you remember the nature of the report? Were they in want of food, clothing, or fuel? You did not personally inquire, but saw that somebody else did; and, I ask, what was the character of his report, what were the classes?—Clerks, artisans, warehousemen in the city.

402. Taking warehousemen, can you call to mind any of those cases?—I could mention clerks. I remember a man who came to me, who was a clerk of mine, almost the other day, and his wife told me she was absolutely starving. The man was a most respectable man in every way.

403. Where had he been serving?—He came up from Brighton. His last employer had in some way rendered himself liable to the criminal law, and so he lost his place. We had a great many clerks.

404. And you are quite satisfied yourself about it that there were many clerks?—Yes.

405. Now, in regard to these clerks who had lost their situations, was any inquiry made of their employers as to how they lost them?—I don't think, practically, any were made at the time; but, subsequently, I picked out forty, and sent letters to the employers. I think they were all cases that had been helped. I believe I took fifty cases, and we got answers from forty, and thirty-eight of them were entirely satisfactory.

406. That is to say, enough to justify the relief?—'Good man.' 'Slackness of trade; leaving on that account.' 'Glad to employ him again.' That was the kind of answer. They were not selected at all; they may have been labourers, or any class.

407. Until the Mansion House Fund was created, you had not an idea that there was so much distress, but you satisfied yourself that there was exceptional distress?—That I cannot say, because I do not know what it was in former years. A great many of them were builders' people.

408. How did you distribute the fund? What almoners did you employ?—Well, we divided ourselves. We had Sub-Committees in different parts of the parish, and each Sub-Committee distributed all its money—professed always to distribute it—through its own members. One particular member visited the case, and reported on it on the application form; he brought the report up to the Committee, and the Committee voted the money.

409. Was it given in money or in kind?—We made a rule that it should be money only. It was transgressed in one or two cases.

410. You had printed forms of application?—Yes; very much like those of the Mansion House Fund.

411. Did you adhere pretty strictly to the rules as to able-bodied men that the Mansion House Committee referred to?—We considered ourselves at liberty to help some in the stone-yard.

412. Was there any advertisement that appeared in the local papers?—One of the Sub-Committees put up notices, 'Applications for the Mansion House Fund may be made here at certain hours.' We had a discussion whether it should be done in other places, and it was generally disapproved.

413. Do you believe that the Mansion House Fund did more good than harm?—I cannot say what harm it did: Of physical good, I think it did a great deal; but as to the higher side, I don't know.

414. (Sir J. Tilley): You are a Poor Law Guardian?—Not in Camberwell.

415. Do you think the Poor Law might fairly have been left to deal with these cases?—Well, I think to many it would be a terrible degradation. They will not apply to the Charity Organisation Society.

416. Was there any great difference in the money to be obtained from the Mansion House Fund and that under the Poor Law?

417. (Mr. Edgcombe, who had temporarily taken the place of the Chairman): You mean as to the feeling of the people?—I believe a great many of them would have suffered much greater straits than they did before going to the Poor Law.

418. (Rev. W. C. Hayward): They would rather have received help from the Mansion House Fund?—Yes.

419. (Dr. Longstaff): Did you notice any evidence of the people in your district considering that they had a right to this money from the Mansion House?—Yes; but very little. One man made a row, and said there was £70,000, and he did not see why he should not have some of it.

420. Was your method criticised? Were you threatened or bullied?—I think it gave every satisfaction.

421. You say that the Committee voted upon cases, and intrusted a certain sum to the almoner?—Yes; a member of the Committee.

422. Did any almoner return the money without giving it?—Oh, certainly.

423. Did that happen frequently?—The money was given for four weeks; 5 per cent. for the second and third weeks, and 10 per cent. for the fourth week, dropped out, because, mostly, they had got work, and partly because we found out their characters.

424. Did you find that the Committeemen had a fairly reasonable desire to withhold the money from the people who were undeserving?—Some took a great deal of trouble, and some took none.

425. Money was sometimes refused which had been granted?—Yes.

426. Then you made use of forms of application? Now that the whole thing is over, do you think that it was a wise thing to have them?—I don't think it would have been possible to have worked the district in any other way.

427. In what did the advantage consist? What would have been the alternative?—We must put the particulars in writing.

428. Did you put the particulars in writing yourselves, or did the applicant?—We tried to get them taken down by members of the Committee as far as possible.

429. From the applicants that came themselves?—Yes. If any members of the Sub-Committees were there to do it, they took down applications. But if the applicants got too numerous, they were given forms, and told to fill them up.

430. Did you find that the facts filled up by the applicants themselves were correct?—They erred rather by deficiency than error. Our relief was taken to the man's house.

431. Do you think that the system of having papers enabled you to give the bad cases a chance of getting at you?—No; my opinion was that by the use of these papers respectable people in real distress came to us.

432. Who distributed them?—As a rule, School Board visitors and district visitors, who went about among them. They sent us in many cases a list of names of persons in distress, who were deserving of assistance, and we sent back the list and asked them to put the particulars on a printed form, and add their own name as reference. I think it reached everybody we wanted to reach.

433. (*Mr. J. H. Allen*): Should you be in favour of another Mansion House Fund being raised?—I should be in favour of nothing of the kind if, without it, you could prevent other people raising funds, but I think the Mansion House Fund was a great deal better than a great many things we had. The *Daily News* sent down a commissioner to inquire, and then rained down money that did a great deal of harm.

434. Were your Committee in favour of any other scheme or plan? Did they talk over any alternative scheme?—We tried very hard to get some work set going. We urged the Metropolitan Board of Works to lay out Dulwich Park.

435. You would prefer giving them work of a local character?—Yes; we quite made up our minds to that.

436. You have no alternative scheme?—I should say that it would be very much better if distress occurs next winter for plans to be got out for some of the squares to be turned into gardens.

437. (*Chairman*): By special local funds for that purpose?—I should like them done as a purely local and commercial transaction. Whether it is done by the vestry or a charitable organisation, I don't think would matter.

438. (*Mr. Allen*): You are in favour of giving work instead of money?—Yes.

439. (*Rev. W. C. Hayward*): That would not meet all the cases. You could not employ a clerk about work of that kind?—No; but you tend to ease the market all round.

440. (*Mr. Hedley*): Did the Committee deal with the whole parish of Camberwell?—Yes.

441. The Camberwell population consists of 200,000?—We spent £3,700.

442. On a population of 200,000?—We spent a little over £1 a head of those we helped. We had 4,000 cases, and we helped 3,000 of them.

Mr. W. M. Acworth.

June 11, 1886.

Mr. W. M.
ACWORTH.

June 11, 1886.

443. Yours was the Mansion House Fund. That first week you had great distress?—Yes; I said that from my experience of the Charity Organisation Society I had not seen exceptional distress. Everybody had heard that there was exceptional distress, but I thought it exaggerated.

444. Then it was in consequence of the applications that were made to you that you became aware of the exceptional distress?—They were a different class of people. It was that that drew my attention to it. One man who applied told me distinctly that he had been 25 years in one house, and never had applied for relief.

445. (*Sir J. Tilley*): Were you well acquainted with the people by visiting them?—No. I cannot claim to have visited much.

446. A great deal of distress may surround you without your knowing it?—Oh, certainly.

447. Is it not a very surprising thing that you did not know if there was exceptional distress?—No; I don't see that.

448. (*Chairman, Mr. Pell*): In Camberwell, does a man never know of distress incidentally except through the Charity Organisation Society or the Mansion House Fund? Have you never in your life heard of distress among people incidentally, as your neighbours, or being connected with you in some industry, or from their working in your house? It seems so extraordinary that distress should only be heard of through some official channel. You have not told us whether you knew of distress of brothers or sisters of your servants, or connections of workmen in your house?—I have heard of people being out of work.

449. Did you know more of that in January this year than in other years?—Yes; from talking to a workman, who told me.

450. Yes; a man may come and say, 'I worked for you so and so, and I am very badly off now.' Many things of that kind will crop up without going to the clergyman. Did you have more of that connected with your private life than what you knew from your connection with the Charity Organisation Society or Mansion House Fund?—I only remember one case of a man asking me for work; but that was not in the parish of Camberwell.

451. Did you have more of that sort of call upon you this winter in your life?—I will say, at once, that I did not.

452. (*Rev. C. Hayward*): Does that apply to London or the country, or both?—(No answer.)

453. (*Mr. Edgcombe*): I think you said that after the Mansion House Fund was started you became aware of exceptional distress—clerks, and so on, applying for relief, who would not apply otherwise?—Yes.

454. If the Mansion House Fund had never existed, would it never have come to your knowledge? What would they have done?—Some would have got through, and some would have gone to the workhouse.

455. Would they not rather have come to the Charity Organisation Society than to the Poor Law or a local charity?—I don't know any local charity except the Charity Organisation Society that there would be any use going to.

456. So that by the existence of this fund you had an opportunity of becoming aware of this distress. Was there much rent due?—Yes; there were a good many weeks in arrear.

457. What inquiries did you make into these applications?—Each case was visited by a member of the Committee, and the report was put on the back of the form; there was a reference at the bottom of the form. If the scheme was properly carried out the referee was visited, and asked what he had to say. Then the case was visited once a week, when the money was taken to the house.

458. Was the employer communicated with?—No; it was not possible.

459. (*Chairman*): Was the house agent, or rent-collector, asked whether there was a large amount of unpaid rent on their books? Was there a test applied to ask rent-collectors or collectors of parish rates?—I could not give it you at first hand, but I have heard it again and again.

460. That the agent had been asked?—I heard it from active members of the Committee. I could not say that I had asked any individual rent or rate-collector.

461. Were any of your Committee guardians?—A great many. The relief-sheets were, as far as possible, submitted to the relieving officer of the district

in which the applicants lived. Out of 2,000, they were able to tell us, in five or six cases, that they were in receipt of outdoor relief.

462. (*Mr. Loch, Secretary*): The Camberwell Mansion House Report, signed by yourself, says: 'The Committee desire to draw special attention to the number of duplicate and triplicate applications, &c.' You would wish to manage these details in a future year quite locally, not worked from a District Committee? You would have the application form used solely by the Ward Committee?—I think the Mansion House Fund ought not to do it, and I don't see why the Local Committee should do it, except that no one really knows what a ward is. Most people know whether they are in the parish of Camberwell or not, but not the wards. Then I think that School Board officers and rent-collectors in model buildings should have some.

463. (*Reading*) 'Hundreds of forms were received.' Do you think that the eagerness was due to the fact that the question of relief was in the wind, or that the distress was very pressing? Was it starvation that goaded them to application, or that the Mansion House Fund was there with its hand open? Do you think there was actual starvation from your own inquiry? No doubt; but personally I cannot say.

464. But cases were visited by members?—Yes.

465. Then if there was starvation, the members would have seen it?—I think so. I wrote to you that the best person to give that information is the Chairman of one of the Sub-Committees.

466. (*Mr. Edgcombe*): The Central Committee did not get these details?—They never got anything after the Sub-Committees were appointed.

467. Did you get any applications by way of letter?—Very many.

468. How did people come to send them? Was it simply the noise, so to speak, that there was a Relief Committee?—They heard there was relief to be had, and they wanted relief; it was advertised that there was a place to apply at.

469. (*Mr. Loch*): When they came in large numbers, did you find it help you most to take the applications in the office?—Far better that they should be taken in the office, because you got a good many more particulars.

470. Don't you think it was difficult to work the plan side by side with the reference function?—It was.

471. Can you suggest any way in which that could be arranged with a crowd?—I cannot, except by suggesting that we got far more people to do the work than we had.

472. Could you suggest any means of reducing the number by saying what people you could help, and what you could not?—We helped three out of four of those who applied, so that you could only get rid of about 25 per cent.

473. Suppose you had a labour-yard supported by charity, could you have said, We will not take cases of able-bodied men unless *e.g.*, they go to these works?—I don't think I can answer that. It seems to me it is a question of what the public will stand.

474. A fund is established, a crowd is got together, you cannot work properly without more helpers unless you can reduce your crowd? How is it to be done? Would you establish a labour-yard?—I would not give relief to anyone who would not go to the labour-yard.

475. (*Mr. Hedley*): Would you not refuse relief to those who had not been one year in residence?—I don't think it would be fair in a changing population, as in London.

476. (*Chairman*): Would not you gain something by taking one acknowledged rule? Mr. Hedley wants to know whether you can distribute public funds without some such rule?

477. (*Mr. Hedley*): There is always the Poor Law behind you?—This was not a local charity. If Camberwell had raised money, it would not have raised £100. One side of Denmark Hill is almost entirely poor, and the other is almost entirely rich; and they do not recognise any responsibility.

478. So that London took up a responsibility which ought to have been locally discharged?—No doubt it is a fact. It is fair to remember that the population of Camberwell don't work for the population of Camberwell any more than they work for the population of Grosvenor Square; it is simply a sleeping place for workers elsewhere.

479. Do you look forward to getting larger personal help for the distribution

Mr. W. M.
ACWORTH.

June 11, 1886

of the fund?—We really did get a great deal; not enough during the day in taking down cases, but enough to decide them.

480. Assuming that they had been taken down properly?—Yes.

481. (*Mr Loch*): You could not go to employers? They lived in other parts of London, in most cases. It implies correspondence arrangements with people in other parts of London. We should have had fifty people writing to Mowlem and Burt.

482. The organisation for inquiry was wanting?—Yes.

483. And then, as regards visiting, you depended upon the personal visits of members?—Yes.

484. And yet these members were not sufficiently numerous to do it properly?—No.

485. How many cases was a person expected to visit in a day?—I don't think I could tell you.

486. (*Reading*) 'The Committee regret that it was not found possible to open public works, &c.' Is it proposed to start anything this year? Are the local authorities doing anything?—I have heard of nothing.

487. Then, in that case, may I take it for granted that nothing is being done?—I think you might.

488. Is it your impression that you will be in the same difficulty next year, that the remedy is wanted and won't be applied?—I think so.

489. What would you propose to do then, as a member of our Society, or as interested in Camberwell?—I don't see that a private individual can do anything.

490. Would you suggest any public action in Camberwell, for example? I think the Board of Guardians might be moved perhaps to set some form of works on foot, or the vestry might lay out public places; a large number might be employed at Dulwich Park.

491. (*Chairman*): Is not that communism?—No, I think not. I don't think it is a worse thing for the vestry to find work for people in the winter time, than it is for you or me to find work for a carpenter. All I understand by the proposal is that works—to be done sooner or later—should be done not in the busy time of year, but at the slack time.

492. (*Chairman*): How would that suit me as a person building in another part of London? Should the builder come to me and propose deferring my building until the winter, when work was slack?—I didn't say building, but laying out a park.

493. (*Mr. Edgcombe*): You said the guardians might undertake certain works?—The Wandsworth Guardians did that.

494. (*Dr. Longstaff*): That was anticipating building. I heard that the contract was not concluded for the casual ward, and they thought they might have the excavations done.

495. (*Mr. Hedley*): Yes; and they dug out a great deal of valuable sand?—That was exactly the kind of thing that was in my mind.

496. The circumstance was entirely exceptional?—Yes.

497. (*Mr. Loch*): Weekly visitation—do you think you could count in another year on getting such number of persons to visit weekly as would ensure a proper sifting of cases, and better than you had this year?—I think we are capable of eliminating cases that are ineligible under our rules—cases that are obviously drunken and dissipated.

498. But suppose you tried to work to a higher standard, do you think you could get sufficient visitors for the purpose?—I don't think we should get trained visitors.

499. (*Mr. Edgcombe*): This visiting requires some practice?—And a considerable gift to start with.

500. (*Mr. Loch*): Then, would you be able, for instance, to get visitors to ascertain the facts as to thrift, and to adopt a higher standard of relief work by taking the amount of thrift as, in some degree, a test?—The question of thrift would hardly be a question for a visitor at all. You would require the production of a savings bank book; and you would see the pawn-tickets.

501. (*Mr. Peters*): You come to this, then, that if there is a thrift test, there are so many means of testing it that you could do it without increasing the visitors?—Yes.

(*The Committee then adjourned.*)

FRIDAY, 18TH JUNE, 1886.

Present—Mr. ALBERT PELL, in the chair.

Hon. and Rev. Canon LEGGE,
Rev. BROOKE LAMBERT,
Dr. G. B. LONGSTAFF,
Mr. F. J. S. EDGCOMBE,

Hon. C. W. FREMANTLE,
Rev. W. CURTIS HAYWARD,
Mr. J. H. ALLEN,
Mr. E. PETERS.

REV. W. CURTIS HAYWARD, examined.

502. (*Chairman*): Do you believe that there was much exceptional distress—distress that you would not have had in other years ?—I believe that there was. I speak chiefly of St. James's and Soho.

Rev. W. CURTIS HAYWARD.
June 18, 1886.

503. Was that a general distress, or more remarkable in particular industries—in some industries more than in others?—The population is chiefly composed of poor: tailors, shoemakers, a certain number of people in the building trade, decorators, and a good many silversmiths.

504. Among all those industries you found distress?—I did.

505. You have a great many foreigners in Soho ?—Yes, a good number.

506. Did the distress affect them as well as the others?—I think it did.

507. Did any of the French people come to you ?—There were one or two Italians.

508. Had they been in the habit of coming for relief in other winters?—Sometimes.

509. But you found more this last winter?—At least, they were in greater distress last winter. They had been longer out of work.

510. Which came under your notice first, the exceptional distress or the Mansion House Fund ?—The exceptional distress.

511. The date of the Fund was the 11th February; when did the exceptional distress begin to strike you ?—I should say the whole winter.

512. No; but when did it first strike you?—Oh, all through the winter.

513. When do you take to be the commencement of the winter?—The beginning of November.

514. Then in the beginning of November you were first struck with the presence of unusual distress ?—Yes, I think so.

515. And the causes of that distress must have been before November—during the summer probably ?—Yes.

516. During the summer was there anything to lead you to believe that distress might come upon you in the winter ?—No, I think not. I found that they had less work than usual during the summer.

517. Then you think the people were not well employed in the summer ?—I do.

518. What definite evidence was there of the existence of distress in Soho in November ?—I am only connected with that district as almoner for the Society for the Relief of Distress; and I am a member of the Charity Organisation Committee. I am not connected with Soho otherwise. The clergy brought cases of distress before the Charity Organisation Committee. If they brought the cases of people who were out of work to us we said we were not allowed to help out-of-work people.

519. Then it was the clergy who first brought it before you ?—Yes, and other charitable persons.

520. Persons distributing bounty ?—Tradespeople.

521. Can you tell us anybody else ?—It was the general impression.

522. I want to get rid of general impression.—I can show you how we ascertained that the distress was real. When I say it struck me first in November, I think it had been in existence a considerable time previously, and if I had been the clergyman of the district it would have come more under my notice. My daughter and I visit a good deal among the poor, and we are thoroughly convinced that there was more distress than usual.

Rev. W. Curtis
Hayward.
June 18, 1886.

523. Then there was something more than the statements of the clergy. What was the circumstance that led you to believe that there was exceptional distress in Soho in November?—I don't say it commenced in November; I say it had been gradually increasing.

524. But there had been something—we won't be nice about it—what was there besides the statements of the clergy that led you to believe that? Are you a landowner or a householder in Soho?—Oh no; and I do not live there.

525. What was there beside the statements of the clergy that led you to believe there was distress in November?—There were a number of people who said, 'Would you look to such and such a case?' and I said in reply that we had no fund to do it with.

526. Who was it?—Some of the people we visited told us of the distress of others. I don't say they came to me, but in visiting among them I got to know.

527. Did you go to look out for distress?—No, I never do that; but when a case is brought to me and I am asked whether I can go I do so, and I make a point of visiting every one whom I relieve; and I am convinced that there was exceptional distress at that time among the class of tailors, shoemakers, and other mechanics.

528. Well now, when this distress became apparent to you and statements were made by tailors and shoemakers that they were in distress, what did they say that the money was wanted for—was it to pay rent, or were they in want of food?—Yes.

529. Did you check those statements by inquiring of the persons for whom they worked?—I did.

530. I will pass these questions by till we come to the Mansion House Fund. Well now, what in your mind was the cause of this distress as you believed it to exist—want of employment?—Yes, I think it was chiefly owing to a want of employment; they had not had employment for a sufficient time to enable them to prepare for the winter.

531. Do you think that that want of employment was caused by demanding higher wages than the employers were prepared to give?—No, I think not.

532. You don't trace anything to the weather?—No.

533. Had there been in Soho any transfer of industries to other places?—No. I should say they ought to be better off than formerly, because many of the smaller houses had been pulled down.

534. I think the shoemakers in Soho work upon ladies' goods chiefly?—They work chiefly for the shops.

535. Is not the trade of the shops and factories for which they work in ladies' goods?—No; I think they work for all the firms about there.

536. Has rent been raised in Soho?—I think not.

537. Are the necessaries of life dearer?—No.

538. Is education more costly for the poor?—No.

539. Has this distress at all subsided?—Oh, very much.

540. When did it begin to subside?—As soon as people began to leave off their overcoats.

541. If this distress has been so long coming on, how could they so suddenly find the means of escaping it at the end of a long and severe winter? Did they get credit?—Oh yes; as soon as people began to leave off their overcoats, people began to get their summer clothes.

542. Oh, they got work then? Do you think the amount of work distributed in Soho is larger than it was last year?—No.

543. Do you think the causes of distress are beginning for next winter?—Yes. Well I think that depends on how soon work ceases; they are pretty well at work now; people are getting their spring clothes.

544. But what is there in this year that would lead you to believe that there will not be distress?—Oh, I very much fear there will.

545. Have you taken any energetic means to raise another fund?—I should very much deprecate another Mansion House Fund. It did some good, but a great deal of harm.

546. Now, with reference to the Mansion House Fund, were you the chairman of a Relief Committee?—Yes. We commenced with the Mansion House money

being sent to all the almoners for the Society for the Relief of Distress. Soho happens to be pretty well covered by almoners.

547. But it first came to the Society for the Relief of Distress. Was a Committee formed then?—Yes.

548. And you were chairman?—I was.

549. (*Mr. Hedley*): Was that about February 20?

550. (*Chairman*): Why was the Committee formed? Was not that Society equal to the distribution of the money?—I think it was; but an order came to us to form a Committee and we formed one.

551. Of the old instruments really? Had you an office?—Yes.

552. Have you published any reports since?—No.

553. Did you take a room?—Yes.

554. Was there a placard outside?—We commenced by using the room of the Charity Organisation Society, but this interfered with their work so much that we took another.

555. Was there anything outside to indicate that you were sitting there?—The people knew it well enough. Several things were sent round, such as these (*producing two papers*).

556. (*Mr. Hedley*): The room was not taken, I think, till the Mansion House Fund was nearly at an end?—About three weeks before.

557. Were these papers issued by delegates of the Mansion House Fund?—These (*indicating*) were issued from the Mansion House Fund. These others we issued.

558. (*Chairman*): How were they issued? Did people go about with them?—No; there was a notice put at the door of the room of the Charity Organisation Society that these forms could be had there.

559. I am very anxious to know how those papers were distributed. There is a statement that money was to be got on application. How was it distributed?

560. (*Rev. B. Lambert*): People came to the Mansion House knowing that relief was given there. That paper was sent to you by post from the Mansion House. They were sent out in packets. I had hundreds sent to me as chairman of the Committee.

561. (*Chairman*): What we have got is this—that there was a sheet issued by the Mansion House Central Relief Fund, containing upon the back of it the addresses of the Sub-Committees in London, and on the other side an application form; that this application form was filled up by persons applying at the Mansion House, and then were sent to the Committee acting in the district to which the applicant said he belonged. Now, having got the room and formed the Committee, what were your proceedings? Who constituted the Committee?—About eight, I should say. I was chairman, and there were five other almoners—Miss Tillard, Hon. Secretary Charity Organisation Society, who was on the Committee, and two or three ladies. Mr. Watson, inspector of nuisances, was put on by the Mansion House Committee.

562. But he belonged to Soho?—I do not know.

563. The Committee consisted of eight persons and one who was added by the Mansion House Fund?—Yes.

564. Then you met daily?—No, twice a week.

565. Did you see the applicants?—Yes.

566. They came to the Committee-room?—No, they sent their papers. We gave them papers; the Secretary asked them questions and filled in their answers.

567. Did you see the people?—I saw them at their homes. I did not relieve a single case in which I did not go to the house, at all events the first time. I afterwards sometimes sent.

568. Was any almoner acting under you who helped you?—Yes, two ladies, who were a great help.

569. Did the almoners verify the statements before any money was given?—Almost in every case. I could not always go myself. For instance, here on an application form is 'Where was your last employ?' I either went or sent to the employer to say, 'Is this true? Do you think that there is any reason why he

Rev. W. Curtis Hayward.
June 18, 1886.

should be in exceptional distress?' And in almost every case he said 'Yes.' I might mention one case—a cabinet-maker who had at one time received high wages, a first-rate man, who worked for Shoolbred. Some years ago he had 50s. a week, and he assured me when I was there that he had never for the last three years received more than 25s. a week. A great part of that time he had been out of work. That was a case I thought for relief, and I relieved it very substantially. I sent to Shoolbred's foreman. He said, 'He is a most respectable man; we have very little work, owing to want of trade, but I should be very glad to employ him as soon as I have work to give him; there is no doubt his wages would not average more than 25s. a week.'

570. (*Dr. Longstaff*): Did Shoolbreds get a good deal of work from the country?—He said he got a good deal from Germany.

571. (*Dr. Longstaff*): I happen to know one in the West of England who makes for a great many London firms.

572. (*Chairman*): Now for the Poor Law officers—did you see a relieving officer and ask him?—I did not. There did not seem any necessity for it.

573. Did any Poor Law cases come to you, do you think? Do you think that these people who came to you had been in the habit of asking relief from the Poor Law?—No; it is a different class of people, and they would scarcely in any case have got out-door relief, because they would have been sold up.

574. We don't take the cabinet-maker as a type of the class. A man having 25s. a week you would not give relief to for the reason that he once had 50s.?—No; but he said he had not had a stroke of work since October, I think.

575. Did you make any inquiries of the pawnbrokers?—They said that the distress was so great that they could not advance money upon tools.

576. Did you make any inquiries of the benefit or provident societies to know whether the payments into these societies had abated at all?—No; I inquired of the applicants themselves whether they were in benefit societies.

577. You are a good deal among the poor of Soho; did you see any indications of the trade of the publican abating?—No.

578. Have any public-houses been shut up? It is a question that just arises from my own knowledge of these places of business—it has been an unusually good winter for them in the east of London?—I feel pretty well convinced that none, or a very small part, of the money I gave went to the public-houses.

579. You have a very large number of French people in Soho?—I did not come across many.

580. Church Street is in the district, and Gerrard Street. Is not the population almost all French—at least one house in three?—I did come across one French baker, but there are very few.

581. Did you find that these foreigners had met with exceptional distress?—There are a good many that come to the Charity Organisation Society.

582. (*Chairman*): More applications from women than from men?—No.

583. Were the young as much affected as the old? Did it strike you that many middle-aged men and women came?—Oh, as a rule I did not relieve the old if they were past work.

584. (*The Rev. B. Lambert*): You went as in other years and you found more distress. Was there a gradual increase after the Mansion House Fund was raised, or was there a jump?—I cannot say that; I was not enough amongst them to notice that. In talking it over we have said it is very easy to say that there is not exceptional distress.

585. I understood you to say that some houses had been pulled down and that that distributed more trade amongst the people, but you said that there was no increase of rent?—They do complain of rent being too high.

586. Do you know of foreign societies doing anything?—I don't know that they did; but they do help them. They do it upon a very fixed rule; they give 10s. More, generally, they won't give.

587. Do you find the distress among the class of small shopkeepers?—Yes; as a rule I could not help them very well, but I did find it.

588. Did you have any opportunity to inquire whether there had been any exceptional demand for parish relief?—I did not inquire.

589. (*Chairman*): With regard to the Westminster Union, this statement

was made to the Local Government Board by the Clerk to the Board of Guardians : 'I desire to state that there is no more than the normal amount of distress existing in the district,'* &c. (*reading*). Then from the Vestry of the parish of St. James's, Westminster, there is a return made, signed by Mr. Wilkins, the Vestry Clerk : 'In reply to your inquiries with reference to the special distress which is alleged to exist at the present time in the metropolis, I am to acquaint you that the Vestry have no reason to believe that, so far as this parish is concerned, there is any distress of an exceptional character, or that more persons are out of employment than is usually the case in the winter months,'† &c. (*reading*). That is February 24 ?—My district was in St. James's and Soho. There is an almoner for St. James's, who gave nothing, or next to nothing, saying that he found no need for it. He distributed £10, I think, whereas I distributed £120.

Rev. W. Curtis Hayward.

June 18, 1886.

590. (*Mr. Peters*): You spent the whole, then ?—No.

591. (*Rev. B. Lambert*): You found distress among the shopkeepers, but the parish do not seem to have done so ; they have had no application for reduction of rates. I have only one question more to ask, whether after the establishment of the fund you found a very considerable increase of cases ?—Well, the applications did increase, and would again, I have no doubt, if a fund was got up.

592. How many people were relieved ?—I should say about 25 per cent. were rejected, 75 per cent. were relieved.

593. You cannot tell how many applications altogether ?—No. You mean for the whole district ? I relieved about 130 cases, and I should say I relieved half of those relieved.

594. (*Mr. Hedley*) : Do you mean how many altogether in St. James's ?—I have got all the figures at the office.

595. (*Rev. B. Lambert*) : I want to know how many applications relieved. There were, you say, 75 per cent. relieved and 25 per cent rejected ; it would make 160 cases altogether ? - Not for the whole of St. James's.

596. (*Chairman*) : Well, you have it there—you relieved 130, which you say was about half of the whole ; which would therefore be about 260.

597. (*Rev. B. Lambert*) : I want the number relieved by the Committee. That would make it 300 ?—I don't think there were any more than that.

598. (*Chairman*) : Have we got it that there were only about 300 cases in the Soho district—that is, applications for relief ?—I don't know that.

599. (*Rev. Canon Legge*) : I think you attributed the distress to a want of work in the previous summer ?—Yes, for a considerable time.

600. Would it be on account of the rich classes spending less money last summer ?—Partly, but chiefly from general depression. I spent less.

601. You passed less money to the producers of goods ?—Yes.

602. But did you get a less quantity of goods ?—Yes ; where I had two hats I got one.

603. (*Canon Legge*) : You don't know if there was a labour yard ?—No, there was not. You could not have put these people into a labour yard.

604. (*Mr. Edgcombe*): Is this as it came before you (*indicating the application form*) ? It appears a great many were filled up already ?—Yes.

605. But I observe two forms—one is the Mansion House form, one not Mansion House at all. How did this one get filled up ?—If they could write they had to fill it.

606. Some charitable persons called your attention by letter to certain cases, I presume ?—Sometimes. If they did, I sent them one of these.

607. Did you in every case communicate with the employer ?—Yes, as a rule, though I cannot say in every case. I was so thoroughly convinced that the men were right in saying that they did not get as much work as usual, that I did not in all cases inquire.

608. You can hardly say as a rule you did inquire ?—Yes, as a rule I did ; it was the exception not to inquire.

* Return, Pauperism and Distress; printed March 8, 1886, p. 18.
† *Idem*, p. 49.

E

Rev. W. CURTIS
HAYWARD,
June 18, 1886.

609. Were these cases decided by the Committee?—No, by the almoner.
610. You say you did not go to the relieving officer; had you any guardian sitting upon the Committee?—No.
611. Or relieving officer, or Poor Law officer?—No.
612. (*Mr. Hedley*): Then, Mr. Hayward, you do not favour the establishment of a similar fund again?—No.
613. Have you any course you would suggest for the future in the event of distress arising?—I should say in the first place that I think it is a mistake, first, to say that there is no exceptional distress. You will not convince the charitable world that there is not; but I think that if the Society for the Relief of Distress or others would make an appeal for extra funds, and distribute them through their almoners, it would be done much more quietly.
614. You would strengthen the hands of the existing institutions?—Yes.
615. Would you adopt any other course?—I think that that would be sufficient; but they must increase the number of their almoners, and, of course, there would be the difficulty of getting efficient almoners. But I have been for several years among the poor, working more or less among them, and I know, I think, whether a man is trying to impose upon me or not.
616. (*Mr. Peters*): Have you not many men in Soho—hangers-on of theatres and cabstands, and so on—cadgers? You have a good many of that sort?—Yes, we have a good many.
617. Were the persons relieved by you out of the Mansion House Fund of a class you could not have expected to go for relief to the poorhouse? Were they of a superior class?—Yes.
618. What was the amount that passed through your hands?—About £400. We returned about £60.
619. Then you relieved the whole of the distress with £340?—Yes. I should not have wished to have had more.
620. What form of relief did you give—was it for food or what?—In very few cases did I consider it was given for food; but there were so many in imminent danger of being turned out of their houses.
621. Then it was to a large extent given to pay arrears of rent?—I did not infringe the rules, but sometimes I gave £1 for two weeks in advance, instead of 10s. for one week, where rent was in arrear and there was danger of being turned out.
622. (*Dr. Longstaff*): Do you prefer individual judgment to a Committee's decision on cases?—I do, as a whole.
623. Do you think, in panic cases of this kind, you can get a sufficient number of proper persons to distribute?—I fear there would be a difficulty in that.
624. Failing a supply of such almoners, would you have recourse to a Committee?—Yes.
625. In case of a Committee meeting again, can you suggest any improvement in the way of working?—No, I think not. We had a Committee afterwards, but we did not bring every case before it.
626. You consider on the whole your inquiry was reasonably adequate?—I think so.
627. (*Mr. Fremantle*): How did you deal with those who are out of work just now referred to as cadgers?—I generally said, 'You don't come under our rules; you have just as much as usual.' I certainly did not say this to the smaller shopkeepers.
628. And you found you had no difficulty in getting rid of the cases in that way?—There was some odium attached to it, but we did not relieve them.
629. (*Mr. Loch*): As an indication of distress you referred to the local Charity Organisation Committee as having sent you cases to be relieved by you as almoner. Their cases in 1884 and 1885 were not more numerous, I find on reference. Was there any other indication? Were the cases more numerous?—I don't think they were.
630. Then there was some other indication of distress than the number of cases?—Yes; it was not at all from the number of cases. In many cases when I went there I heard of distress; many said they never knew such distress in their lives.

Rev. W. CURTIS
HAYWARD.

June 18, 1893.

631. It was when you visited a case that had come before the Charity Organisation Society?—Yes, and the clergy.

632. (*Chairman*): They were more numerous?

633. (*Mr. Loch*): Then why was it that we did not get more applications?—Because there were many who object to go to the Poor Law and also to the Charity Organisation Society. They think they are under a ban, if they do, in the class of society in which they live.

634. Then what it comes to is this, that there is a Poor Law to which the people did not go; then there is a charitable administration set side by side with the Poor Law, and they did not go there. Was it because they were not suitable applicants?—I don't say they were not suitable, but they did not consider themselves suitable.

635. Then we are driven to the establishment of a third body—is that inevitable?—No, I think not.

636. What would you suggest in a future year? Would you put the two societies, the Metropolitan Visiting and Relief Association, and the Society for the Relief of Distress, on the spot to do the work?—Yes, and possibly the Charity Organisation Society.

637. What I understand is this: the Charity Organisation Society could not very well act, because by its method it would place applicants under a ban. Would this be due in part at least to the investigation?—Yes.

638. Then as a safeguard would there not have to be some investigation?—Yes.

639. What investigation would be sufficient, and yet come short of what we do?—Investigation such as I have spoken to you of. If you ask people whether you can go to the employers, they don't object. But if they go to the Charity Organisation Society you ask, What relations have you that can help you, and what employers, and so on, and it becomes rather onerous.

640. Suppose one of the people in St. James's had a relation who was a shopkeeper there, a well-to-do man, that would not come out in your investigation?—Well, but it would come out whether the person was in great distress or no.

641. Is it a cardinal point that relations should help?—I should not make it a point.

642. Would you think it at all an important point in a case, at another time than a time of distress?—I think not.

643. Take other questions. For instance, with regard to wages; I think that was one point you mentioned that might be omitted. Do you think if a man has been earning large wages that that ought to be considered?—Yes; but when he told me that he had been out of work, and other circumstances, I was convinced that his was a proper case. He was a sober man.

644. (*Chairman*): Was he a married man with a large family?—He had two children dependent upon him, and his wife was dying.

645. (*Mr. Loch*): Did he belong to a club?—I think he told me he was out of it. The man was peculiarly circumstanced: the whole house belonged to him, and he let it out to others, and the not being able to get his lodgers' rents had involved him in great difficulties. He did not like to give up the house.

646. (*Mr. Loch*): I was only using this as an instance to ascertain what points were dealt with; but the question of past wages is important?—Yes.

647. I understand that is a point you would leave out?—No.

648. Would you say, 'This man has been earning large wages; I cannot assist him'?—No; it does not follow from that he is not in great distress, if he is out of work.

649. In that case would you leave him to the Poor Law?—No. Then as a matter of fact, other details apart, the Poor Law would not be used in out-of-work cases in which the man has been earning large wages?—That simply means breaking up his home.

650. I only wanted an answer to the question. You would say, 'This man has had large wages, and therefore I would not assist him, but I would not send him to the Poor Law'?—I would not send a case to the Poor Law because he had had large wages.

651. Then, you would modify not only your investigation, but also your

REV. W. CURTIS HAYWARD.
June 18, 1886.

decision. Some differences you would introduce into the investigation by reducing the amount of inquiry; and you would also reduce the sharpness of your decisions? You would apply no test?—No.

652. Suppose you are dealing with a high-class artisan, you would not apply any sort of thrift test?—I did apply it. I went to the employer, and asked him how many weeks he got high wages, and if he got high wages for sixteen weeks out of the year I distributed that over the year.

653. You have had no instance of that?—Oh yes, I did that sometimes.

654. Did you pay back rent?—I never paid back rent. There was the case of a tailor who had been in an hospital; there was a family of nine children. I was told of the case at the Charity Organisation Society. It was a case that had not been filled up. The people were living in a Peabody Building, where they don't allow tenants to be in arrear. On my calling, the woman went into hysterics. She thought upon seeing me that I had come for the rent. When she recovered she said she thought it was the broker; she said, 'We owe a fortnight's rent, and they say if it is not paid to-day we must go.' I gave her 10s., and while I was there she sent down 9s. to pay for that week's rent.

655. (*Chairman*): Where was the husband when the woman was in hysterics?—He was there; he told me this.

656. (*Mr. Loch*): A pound then was used as a substitute for the charity of landlords. Might not they have been charitable instead and let the tenants off?—They would not have done it.

657. They would not have done it, because the landlord would not have been lenient?—No.

658. Then, in a house where there are a great many tenants, and the landlord acts on a strict rule, you would possibly have had to relieve a great many applicants, and the landlords would have had a large bonus for rent?

659. Then, as to this modified system of investigation, what staff would be necessary to carry it out, volunteer or other staff? Five people would not be able to do it for this district. Some one must make this investigation?—Oh yes. I never could undertake it myself again.

660. What is the population of that area?—I could not say.

661. (*Chairman*): Ten thousand?—I should think so.

662. You made use of a term, 'the charitable world;' what is the meaning of that term? Do you mean that there are a class of persons in London who are members of the charitable world, but who would entirely disregard distress among their relations and give their alms to strangers?

663. (*Mr. Edgcombe*): Am I to understand that you did consider thrift a necessary condition of your giving relief?—Reasonable thrift.

664. (*Mr. Freemantle*): Was there not another reason why the case should not go before the Charity Organisation Society, that able-bodied men were not eligible?—Yes.

MR. W. VALLANCE, examined.

Mr. W. VALLANCE.

665. (*Chairman*): Mr. Vallance, you are Clerk to the Whitechapel Board of Guardians?—Yes.

666. Is your evidence going to be more particularly with regard to the administration of the Poor Law, or had you anything to do with the Mansion House Fund?—No, I had not.

667. Were you invited to have anything to do with it?—I assisted a little the first day in the way of organisation, that is all.

668. Well now, do you live in Whitechapel?—I do not.

669. But you are there daily?—Yes.

670. Was there anything in the general aspect of the population and shops to lead you to believe, apart from your knowledge as an officer of the Poor Law, that there was exceptional distress?—Nothing was within my knowledge at all that indicated exceptional distress, but there was the usual winter distress.

671. After the establishment of the Mansion House Fund was there more

Mr. W. VALLANCE.
June 18, 1886.

evidence then—as far as the people's aspect was evidence—was there more evidence of exceptional distress?—There was no evidence within the scope of the Poor Law, but outside of it it was within my knowledge that large numbers of men were making their way towards London in the hope of securing a share of what was regarded as an inexhaustible fund.

672. About what time of year did you apprehend that people were coming into London?—Since the establishment of the fund became publicly known—February.

673. How did you know that?—From communications with the relieving officers, and on one occasion I was in the country, in Hertfordshire, and, inquiring there of the master of the workhouse, he told me that he was overwhelmed with tramps who were making their way to London. The evidence of the relieving officers was that the lodging-houses were overcrowded, and that whereas, not long before, some lodging-houses were scarcely paying at all, they then got more applications for admission than they could accommodate.

674. Then your opinion is that poverty was attracted to London?—Yes, certainly.

675. And that some were possibly cases invited into London by the hope of relief to be got?—Yes.

676. Well now, were there more applications? Was there an unusual number of applications for relief at your Board?—Compared with previous years, the pauperism was less. We had less real pauperism relieved in the Lady Day quarter than in any previous year.

677. That was paupers relieved?—The applications were normal, if not fewer.

678. You have given your opinion to the Local Government Board on February 7. You were asked to state whether there had not been an increase, a 'material increase, in the number of applications for relief" (reading). You believe that the distress was chronic or intermittent?—I do think so.

679. Did you find any difficulty in dealing with them?—None whatever. There was nothing exceptional about them.

680. Are you still of opinion that there was any amount of distress at that time; that it was of such a character that it could not be met by the agencies existing in the East of London?—I think that the distress could have been amply met by existing agencies without the aid of the Mansion House Fund.

681. (*Dr. Longstaff*): Are you speaking of Whitechapel only?—Of Whitechapel only.

682. (*Chairman*): I am a witness from the next parish. There is always more want in the winter than in summer?—Oh yes.

683. In the event of another such alarm could an arrangement be made for the way in which the work should be carried on next winter? You suggested to the Local Government Board a combination with the Charity Organisation Society?—There is a perfect understanding between the guardians and the Charity Organisation Society in Whitechapel. The guardians have never adopted a 'no out-door relief' policy; but have merely endeavoured to stem the tide of hereditary pauperism by guarding against permanency in Poor Law relief. The guardians, however, have not found it necessary to provide for even the temporary necessities of deserving cases, by reason of the representatives of the Charity Organisation Society on the board spontaneously undertaking to prevent the first step in pauperism. In 'no work' cases the guardians do not require the family to enter the workhouse, but, conditional upon the man doing so, voluntary charity undertakes to keep the home together; whilst, in the event of great pressure and cases arising in which there might be evidence of thrift, and in which it might not be desirable even to require the man to enter the workhouse, it would, in my opinion, be possible to come to an understanding with the District Board of Works for the application of a labour test in the form of additional cleansing of the streets, and this in the night-time.

684. Do you notice any number of small shops shut up in Whitechapel where goods are sold?—No, I have not personally observed it, but I am satisfied that

* Return, Pauperism and Distress (printed March 8, 1886), p. 11.

Mr. W. VALLANCE.
June 18, 1886.

the small shopkeepers have been among the chief sufferers during the past winter.

685. Did they weather it through?—That I am unable to say—whether the Mansion House Fund did help them or not.

686. Did you have any instance in which, upon an application for relief being refused, the applicant said, 'Oh, I can go to the Mansion House Committee'?—No.

687. You know, I think, of the adjoining parish of St. George in the East. We have it from St. George in the East that there has been increased application for medical relief,* &c. (reading). You believe that to be a correct statement of the district between you and the river?—Yes.

688. You don't wish, I think, to say much about the Mansion House Fund?—No, I know nothing personally.

689. What is the present condition of the population there now? Are they fairly employed?—Yes, equally as well employed as they usually are at this time of the year.

690. Is there evidence, generally speaking, of an improved condition among the population, comparing the year 1865 with the year 1885. Should you say that the comforts of the people have diminished in the East of London, or are their opportunities for getting what they want less than they were?—The condition of the poor morally and the conditions under which they exist, as compared with 1870, have materially improved.

691. Now, in what respect have they improved—has rent been raised upon them?—Yes.

692. Has better accommodation accompanied the rise of rent?—In some cases.

693. Are the sanitary conditions better?—Yes, clearly.

694. There has been less recourse to the doctor?—Yes.

695. I need hardly put the question that bread is very much cheaper, and food cheaper generally—and clothing?—Yes; bread is 30 per cent. cheaper than three years ago.

696. Have wages been reduced?—No, except the occupations in which women labour largely.

697. The sewers have done badly?—Yes.

698. These people have gone into other occupations, have they not?—I do not know whether sack-making has increased.

699. What has become of the population of 'stitch, stitch, stitch,' people, those miserable people who, as we know, were engaged in stitching before the machine came in?—They have largely entered into other departments of labour, where they are better paid.

700. Suppose a fund similar to the Mansion House Fund had been in existence, and that that had been distributed for temporary assistance of the sweaters, would it not have been extremely mischievous to them as a class?—Undoubtedly.

701. And would it not be so in other cases?—Yes.

702. And to have relieved that suffering by the direct application of money would have done harm?—If an example is needed, it is to be found in the circumstances of Whitechapel Union. Compare 1870 with 1886. In 1870 we had a stone yard, and outdoor relief, and so forth. The workhouse was only resorted to in extreme cases of absolute destitution of a home, and we had (take the sixth week of the Lady Day quarter—the first and second weeks in February) 1,419 indoor paupers and 5,339 outdoor, being a total of 6,758. In 1886 the numbers were reduced to 1,309 indoor paupers, notwithstanding that 126 of these were imbeciles, who are not included in the original number, and the outdoor were reduced to 70, of which number 54 were boarded-out children.

703. So that that leaves only 16 ordinary outdoor paupers?—Comparing these two conditions of things, we had at the relief office in 1870 a clamorous mob of the least deserving. It was known that outdoor relief was given in response to their parade of legal right, that the guardians were exercising a discretion, and it became a grievance if all did not receive it. The result was that we had demands for relief made in the Board-room in terms which showed that they regarded outdoor relief as their legal right, since it was not an uncommon

* Return, Pauperism and Distress (printed March 8, 1886), p. 28.

thing for them to threaten the guardians to go to their master (the magistrate) and compel them to relieve. But what is the result now ? A case came into the Board-room (for example) very recently: a very respectable widow with four children came and applied for relief, but when she applied it was seen at once that she was hopeful for the future, for she said : 'I thought if the gentlemen would take Johnny and Jimmy into the school for about three months I could get along.' But what are you going to do with the other two ? was asked. 'Well,' she said, 'my sister is going to take the one three years old, and the ladies have been very good and have taken the other, and I can get along if you will help me.' There was that poor woman, brave enough to enter into deliberation with the guardians as to her circumstances, and with their help she was able to go to service and earn £18 a year. There are other cases of a similar character. The poor do not come in now. The question is, ' If you do not come into the workhouse what can we do to help, as we don't want you to sink down into pauperism?' and the demeanour of the poor is altogether different.

704. Now you have given us some figures showing a very great reduction in the amount of relief given by the Poor Law ; has that been a continuous abatement ? Were 1882 and 1883 larger in numbers than 1883-84 ?—In 1882 the indoor was, 1,478 and the outdoor 105.

705. Now then, 1883 ?—1,482 indoor, 91 outdoor.

706. Now then, 1884 ?—1,418 indoor and 77 outdoor.

707. Then 1885 ?—1,370 indoor, 74 outdoor ; and in 1886, 1,309 indoor and 70 outdoor.

708. Then, as far as you can gauge the existence of distress from the Poor Law Returns, there is less cause for apprehension now than there ever has been ?—Yes.

709. You heard the expression ' charitable world '—do the charitable world find their homes in the East-end of London ?—I don't quite understand the question.

710. I suppose that it means the people who furnish the funds for charity.

711. (*Rev. Curtis Hayward*) : That was not my meaning at all ; I meant those who went about visiting.

712. (*Chairman*) : Then (*to Witness*) I will ask you another question. Are there many people in the East of London with sufficient means to contribute— not only sufficient sums—to contribute largely ?—Not many.

713. The incomes at the West-end are larger than at the East-end ?—Yes.

714. Do you consider that to be an advantage or a disadvantage to a district ? I will put a direct question. Suppose you could transfer Portman Square or Grosvenor Square to the middle of Whitechapel, would you rather be with it, than without it ?—Without it, if it implied merely additional almsgiving ; but with it for example and personal service.

715. You think the poor help the poor ?—Oh yes.

716. And that they are able to help the poor ?—They do help each other, and the demands upon relations are greater than they would be if there was a general system of indiscriminate charity.

717. I think you said that the tone of the people had been altered by a uniform administration ?—Yes ; the poor do understand a uniform administration, and the application of strict rules, especially when allied with efforts to lift them out of their pauperism.

718. You know a good deal about the administration of the Poor Law in other parts of London ?—Merely as to results.

719. Is it not true that the proportion of pauperism is less in the poor districts of London than in the rich districts ?—I believe it is. I tabulated the figures, but I have not got them with me.

720. Then you do not think 'the charitable world' would be an advantage ?— Not its money, but its service would.

721. You would hail with pleasure any person from the West-end coming to purchase a property at the East-end ?—Yes.

722. (*Rev. B. Lambert*) : With regard to what you said as to the additional cleansing of the streets, can you carry on that in dry weather ?—Oh yes ; there is an amount of cleanliness far beyond what the District Board would think

Mr. W. VALLANCE.

June 18, 1886.

Mr. W.
VALLANCE.

June 18, 1886.

essentially necessary. A street may be cleansed twice a week, but if it were cleansed daily it would be a great advantage.

723. You mean to say you could get such work as would not sometimes be mere fancy work?—I think it would be a useful work, which would not interfere with other people.

724. You think it really would be useful work?—Possibly it might be thought that it was work created for the purpose of giving it.

725. (*Dr. Longstaff*): Are you speaking of that in Whitechapel or in London generally?—Even in a well-to-do district there is a certain amount of cleansing that is done now; but if cleansing is not a daily cleansing, the introduction of daily cleansing would be a great advantage.

726. (*Rev. B. Lambert*): I am really seriously asking, because I tried to apply it in Greenwich in times of distress, and it was not possible in dry weather. Well now, another question. When you say that the condition of the working classes has improved, you mean as regards the Poor Law; you don't mean to say that the working classes generally at the East-end are improved, do you?—I don't know that they are earning more wages, but the conditions of their life have improved during the last sixteen years. There is the fact that the public-house trade has gone down very much. The poor are more sober than they were, and I think too that the poor are more thrifty than they were. Workers among the poor also say that rents are paid with greater regularity than formerly, and that they put by more in savings and penny banks.

727. (*Chairman*): Has not the rent of public-houses gone down?—Yes; that is necessarily an evidence of the trade having diminished.

728. (*Rev. B. Lambert*): I think it was you who made the statement, 'Comparing the present time with 1861' (*reading*); you gave evidence that there were more labourers competing in the labour market, with less work to be done?—I don't think that was my evidence at all.

729. Do you think there was any truth in that statement that there are more labourers in the East of London, and on the whole less labour distributed among them?—I don't think there can be any question about that.

730. That is so?—Yes.

731. When I was in Whitechapel there was a fairly constant supply of dock labour; and that would be casual labour?—That would be so probably.

732. Then the improvement in the labourers' condition that you spoke of; it was the moral rather than the material condition?—Yes.

733. (*Chairman*): There has been larger dock labour down the river?—Yes.

734. That has naturally reduced the number of vessels coming up to the London Docks?—Yes.

735. Have you ever heard that a distinct warning was given to the London dock labourers that they must expect the transfer of work, and they were invited to go further down the river, and they refused?—I don't know that of my own knowledge; but there has been a good deal of reluctance to follow the ships, because we ask the question, and it is shown that there is a reluctance to leave the neighbourhood.

736. (*Canon Legge*): Can you tell me what the area is of Whitechapel?—410 acres.

737. Has the population increased or diminished since 1870?—Slightly diminished.

738. I suppose there used to be loafers and cadgers in Whitechapel Union?—Yes; they have diminished materially.

739. Is that entirely because they have been improved morally, or that there is any truth in the suggestion that they have gone to other unions?—Some may have left the Whitechapel Union, but I must state my conviction that very few have gone by reason of the strict administration of relief, because very few return to Whitechapel by orders of removal.

740. Then you heard in Herts that tramps were making their way up to London, and told us that some lodging-houses were fuller?—When speaking of the lodging-houses I was speaking of Whitechapel lodging-houses.

741. There was a temporary increase in Whitechapel, then?—Yes.

742. And you think small shopkeepers are suffering as much as other classes:

is there any reason for that?—I referred to the moral condition rather than the pecuniary condition. I think the people are more sober, that they spend very much less in the public-houses, and consequently, what they do spend they would ordinarily spend with the shopkeepers.

743. That would tend to increase the trade of the small shopkeepers?—Yes; but during the winter, when the poor have not money, then of course the shopkeepers suffer.

744. Are any co-operative stores started there?—No, I think not.

745. You mentioned that women's labour is less well remunerated than formerly?—Yes.

746. Is that in consequence of relief being given to widows generally?—It is very difficult to attribute it to that. There is no doubt, speaking generally, that the grant of outdoor relief to widows must necessarily affect the rate of wages, because they are able to live for so much less. At the same time it is difficult to assume that the policy of administration would transfer a certain amount of labour from one class to another.

747. If the Whitechapel guardians gave freely to the widows it would lower the rate of wages?—Yes.

748. Have you any idea of the cost?—In the sixth week of the Lady Day quarter, 1870, the amount given in out-relief was £168. 17s. 4d.

749. I asked the question because you said that through the Charity Organisation Society there is an administration of private charity. Has that charity administered that amount of outdoor relief?—No; the Charity Organisation Society does not undertake the general relief of destitution, but merely to bring charitable help to bear upon the deserving poor whom it is desirable to save from the Poor Law, or for whom there is hope of doing a permanent good.

750. £168. 17s. 4d. was being distributed in relief by the guardians; do you suppose that at the present time nothing like that is being distributed now?—No, they are largely thrown upon their own resources and upon their friends.

751. There is no labour yard?—No.

752. Would a labour yard be a help?—There may be circumstances under which guardians would be justified in opening an outdoor labour yard, but I think the circumstances are little likely to arise if the administration is uniform. I lay stress upon it because we attribute to that our success. We have been uniform; there has been no division of the Board. Guardians have decided upon doing the right thing for the poor, and applying uniformly what they regard as sound principles in Poor Law administration.

753. Was it not decided some years ago that in the Whitechapel Union there should be no labour yard, but in Poplar there has been one almost exclusively for that?—The Poplar Union were some years ago authorised to make contracts with other unions for their able-bodied paupers.

754. (*Chairman*): Do you make use of the Poplar Union?—No; not at all.

755. (*Mr. Healey*): The Poplar Guardians now require the Poplar Union yard for themselves.

756. (*Rev. B. Lambert*) Were there any more paupers in the quarter immediately before? Did the Mansion House Fund relieve your applications at all?—No, they are tolerably even.

757. (*Chairman*): The figures you gave us were for the year, I think?—That was for the week, sir—the sixth week of the Lady Day quarter.

758. (*Rev. W. Curtis Hayward*): I think you said you have a good many dock labourers; has there not been exceptional distress among them?—No, not exceptional. There has been distress, the usual winter distress among those calling themselves dock labourers. If you get an exceptional spell of severe weather, there is more severe distress.

759. Has there been no depression in the shipping trade? I thought that here had been?—There has been depression in the shipping trade in some parts of England, I believe, but I don't know that there has been on the Thames.

760. (*Mr. Edgcombe*): No exceptional distress in Whitechapel?—No.

Mr. W. VALLANCE.

June 18, 1886.

761. If there should be, how would you deal with it?—I think] the ordinary agencies can deal with it.

762. Going to another question: the administration of the Poor Law is uniform; I suppose there are no Relief Committees of the Board?—We have no Relief Committees.

763. (*Mr. J. H. Allen*): You think that putting on men to sweep the streets at night will meet the difficulty?—Yes.

764. Why at night?—To remove the more deserving from the public gaze, and to leave them free to look out for themselves the following day. If they work through the night the more deserving would accept that form of relief.

765. Would there not be a difficulty in superintending the labour at night?—Yes, unless there is an understanding with the local authority. I don't apprehend any difficulty of that kind. I have the figures as to the work offered under the Mansion House Fund (*reading extracts*).

766. (*Mr. J. H. Allen*): Those people were put on by the Vestry?—No, the Vestry provided the supervision.

767. Who paid?—The Mansion House Fund. The one condition was that they should work and receive wages.

768. But in the event of the fund not being raised again, the Vestry would have to pay a man if they put him on at night?—No; I should be sorry to see the Vestry become a duplicate authority for the relief of distress. The exception of admitting the head of a family to the workhouse, and making the admission of the head of the family a condition of charitable relief to the family itself—admitting that, and admitting that there were deserving cases in which the head of the family should not be required to enter the workhouse, the charity agency would say, 'We will give a recommendation to the District Board,' and then under certain conditions he would receive his relief from the charity agency.

769. (*Mr. Hedley*): Is it not a fact that the dock labourers are never in permanent employ?—For the most part it is so.

770. (*Chairman*): You said those calling themselves dock labourers. I know, there are a certain staff of men who are known to be handy men, and there are a great number of men who apply from day to day?—Men who call themselves dock labourers, but who have belonged to every other trade.

771. (*Chairman*): Up to a clergyman?—Possibly, sir.

772. (*Mr. Hedley*): Might not these men always call themselves out-of-work labourers?—Yes.

773. Are you aware that there is more work done in the docks in the winter than in the summer, or in summer than in the winter?—I believe it is so to some extent.

774. (*Chairman*): It used to be affected by a wind; a west wind would put these men in great difficulties; but now most ships are assisted up the river, and I can say that the labour is more regular than it used to be.

775. (*Mr. Hedley*): Are the number of ships very much less in the winter than in the summer?—I think not; but, of course, adverse winds and severe weather have a marked effect.

776. (*Chairman*): There is an immense amount of wool taken to the London Docks. Do you not know that there has been a very, very large increase of building round the London Docks for the reception of that, and it involves a very large sum of money?—I know the wool warehouses have increased.

777. You would take that as evidence of a larger amount of labour required in the docks?

778. (*Rev. B. Lambert*): To a great extent labour is done by machinery. The hand labour has decreased.

779. (*Mr. Hedley*): Was it the fact that the demand for labour in the docks in March was less than it was in June?—We had no increase of applications from this class during the former month.

780. (*Mr. Peters*): Have you reason to believe that there has been increasing distress among the class above that?—I have not formed the opinion that there has been exceptional distress among any class of the poor. There are classes of poor who do suffer, and suffer acutely; but it cannot, I think, be said that in any special section the distress has been exceptional.

781. (*Rev. W. Curtis Hayward*): Is trade the same as it was ten years ago?—No.

782. (*Mr. Fremantle*): Is there a similar moral improvement in the ratepayers? Is the improved system of Poor Law administration apparent in the class above the pauper class?—The Poor Law guardians would not have been able to carry on their work successfully without the sympathy of those outside. When it was found that the ultimate object of the guardians was to draw a distinction between pauper relief and charitable assistance definiteness of aim was given to both Poor Law administrators and voluntary workers, whilst co-operation between the two agencies was in no small measure promoted. The diminution which has taken place in Whitechapel pauperism is largely attributable to the earnest efforts of voluntary workers to redeem the poor from pauperism and dependence.

783. This improved care for the poor, this greater sense of obligation to care for the poor belonging to them, does that result from the action of people in Whitechapel or people from outside?—Much, I think, from the outside—ladies from the West-end of London. But there is some increase of sympathy inside.

784. Do you think it is any way possible that the opening of the Mansion House Fund could have diminished your applications at Whitechapel?—As a fact the applications did not increase. The applications by reason of the uniformity of administration were tolerably regular.

785. With respect to medical orders, you told us the total number of people in receipt of outdoor relief in 1870, does that include medical aid?—None of those figures included medical relief only.

786. Then the practice of giving orders for meat and grocery is seldom resorted to at Whitechapel?—Very seldom.

787. (*Chairman*): Have you a number of medical cases in that report?—No; not cases of medical relief only.

788. (*Mr. Fremantle*): Can you tell us the number of medical cases?—The number of medical orders given in 1885 was 3,284; in the previous year 3,109.

789. Do you think on the whole that the sanitary surroundings of the population have improved?—Yes, undoubtedly.

790. Do you know whether friendly societies have spread in Whitechapel or not?—I am afraid they are not spreading to any appreciable extent. Where medical orders are granted the condition is usually attached that the man shall make an effort to get into a sick club.

791. Have you ever recovered the money given for medical relief on loan?—Not by legal proceedings.

792. (*Mr. Loch*): You have heard what Mr. Curtis Hayward said of Soho, and you have described the plan of co-operation with charity that you had found to answer in Whitechapel; was anything related about Soho that made you think that your plan would not answer there?—Not at all.

793. Have you found that the Charity Organisation Society were too rigorous in their inquiry?—We have never had to complain of it.

794. Do you think that the charitable relief which was distributed last winter among the poor would create that feeling of dependence and expectation to receive relief which was formerly stimulated by ill-administered Poor Law relief—charitable societies would bring about the same evils as the ill-administered Poor Law?—I do.

795. So that you think the tendency of these funds would be to repeat the old evils in a new fashion?—I do.

796. Could we avoid a popular scare by having, so to speak, a weather gauge?—It might be possible.

797. You think the panic arises from an inexact knowledge of facts?—Yes, in some measure, but with an exact knowledge of facts you cannot always restrain impulsive benevolence.

798. Would you in a time of distress substitute for the labour yard the parish charity labour which you spoke of?—Yes, I think that the function of the Poor Law should be clearly defined—that the Poor Law is designed to relieve destitution, and that that relief is given in obedience to a claim which the

Mr. W. VALLANCE.

June 18, 1886.

Mr. W.
VALLANCE.
June 18, 1886.

poor are legally entitled to urge, and, that so, the question of the individual is not primary in the matter at all ; but the question is what is good for the community. What do the interests of the community require in this case ? To put bread into a man's mouth to-day, knowing that he will be hungry again to-morrow ? What is done should be done in the interests of the community and not the man. We should try to lift the poor out of their condition ; to aid them permanently and effectually, and remove the cause of distress rather than relieve the distress itself.

799. Do you think that there is any difficulty or very great difficulty in bringing about the co-operation of the guardians and the District Board ?—The suggestion was made in the case of the Mansion House Committee, and with the exception of day instead of night work it was carried out.

800. (*Chairman*) : It gives trouble, does it not ?—Oh yes.

801. (*Mr. Loch*) : As a matter of fact—as to the relief of applicants for relief - do you think that the poor in Whitechapel are better relieved now than they were ?—I have no doubt of it ; the wants of the deserving poor are better met now than formerly.

802. You would not approve of the relaxation of your principles ?—I would not.

803. (*Chairman*) : And you have never been called upon to relax them ?— No.

804. (*Mr. Loch*) : You think that the charitable aid that will come to the relief of the guardians will meet the whole difference ?—I do.

805. If charitable effort were brought in you would apply thrift tests, and so on, and you don't think there is anything like that that might not be applied to other districts ?—I do not.

806. Take Mr. Curtis Hayward's evidence as to Soho, do you think that system of applying the thrift test could be carried out more regularly than it there was ?

807. (*Mr. Hayward*) : How would you put a tailor or a silversmith to sweep the streets ?

808. (*Mr. Loch*) : In those cases of artizans could you apply the charity labour to them ?—You could not apply the charity labour to every class, but to the large bulk you could. Where a man's hand was delicate there is no reason why an exceptional case should not be made of it ; but there is no hardship in taking the broom.

809. Though you had workmen of a better class, there would be no difficulty in giving them work that they could do ?—In the case of the Mansion House Fund there were exceptional cases, and we were asked to assist, and we assisted to the extent of giving the Committee a contract for cleaning windows which we had before given to a West-end association, and we paid the Committee for it. In other cases we set them to do work which would not ordinarily be done—the cleaning-out and re-arranging certain stores, whitewashing, and repairing, and so forth.

810. (*Chairman*) : Then you transferred the distress to the West-end by employing them instead of the West-end Association.

811. (*Mr. Peters*) : You think it is desirable to apply the labour test in the case of non-provident men ?—Yes, it is specially a workhouse test.

812. (*Mr. Hedley*) : Did you say you strove to make men join benefit clubs ? Did you recommend any as thoroughly sound ?—No.

813. Are you aware of any clubs that are open for dock labourers to join anywhere in the East-end, that you believe solvent and sound, other than the Hearts of Oak and the large ones ?—No, I am afraid I cannot.

814. (*Chairman*) : Are there any purely medical clubs ?—Yes, at the dispensaries.

(*The Committee then adjourned.*)

FRIDAY, 25TH JUNE, 1886.

Present—SIR J. TILLEY, in the Chair.

Mr. F. J. S. EDGCOMBE,
Rev. W. CURTIS HAYWARD,
Mr. J. H. ALLEN,
Mr. A. G. CROWDER,
Mr. E. PETERS,
Dr. G. B. LONGSTAFF, and

Mr. C. S. LOCH, *Secretary*.

MR. T. GAGE GARDINER, examined.

815. (*Chairman*): What particular district do you represent?—St. Mary's, Newington.

816. Are there any particular points on which you wish to give evidence?—No, I think not; but, as to the working of the Mansion House Fund in Newington, I have come to a general conclusion.

817. Were you one of the almoners of the Union?—Yes; for the whole of that part of the Union.

818. Did you know anything of any particular distress in that district last winter?—I think from the work of the Charity Organisation Society that times were a little harder than usual, but I was of opinion that it was undesirable to create a fund, which I thought would do more harm than good.

819. You rather took it up in the hope of minimising the evil?—Exactly.

820. What amount of money was intrusted to you in the first instance?—The first cheque we had was £150; the entire sum was £2,100.

821. And, in distributing that, did you adhere to the Mansion House rules that were laid down by the Committee, indicating the sort of persons who were to be relieved, and the sort who were not?—Yes; approximately. Before the Mansion House Fund sent down rules we had formed our own. We relieved a great many chronic cases, in spite of the rules; and the Committee systematically supplemented parish relief, so far as regards the labour-yard. They regarded it as a test of the man's willingness to work, and as to his respectability.

822. In other words, you relieved people who could have been relieved by the Poor Law—that were being relieved?—Yes; and we carried it to some distance, because we wished to make it a test. After they had given relief for three or four weeks, some of the members proposed to make it a test that a man, before receiving more, must be able to show that he had done two days' work in the labour-yard; but that was overruled.

823. But I suppose you did not communicate much with the relieving officers before you began to distribute the fund?—The first two or three days we found it practically impossible to do so, because Mr. Walrond came down and insisted that, if we carried out our rules, there would be too great delay. Public opinion would not stand so much care being taken, and therefore we deviated to some extent from our scheme; and we literally at first had not sufficient staff to make up our lists and send them to the relieving officers, but after the first three or four days we sent the list to them daily, and they marked it off.

824. Then, after a short time, the fund was better distributed?—It gradually improved, till at the last it was fairly well administered, because the Committee by that time had acquired some experience of that kind of work.

825. Upon the whole, were there any cases that you relieved which could have been equally well relieved by the Poor Law?—Yes; one can commonly tell by the applicant's appearance whether he is a parish case or not; and the great bulk of the cases that came at first were parish cases; while the artisan would not come near us. But as time went on, and as the application of the rules became more rigorous and more careful, a better class of men did come, until at last the good cases were, I should say, in a decided majority over the Poor Law cases.

Mr. T. GAGE GARDINER.

June 25, 1886.

826. After you received the Mansion House rules you adhered to them?—Yes; the Chairman insisted on rigorously holding us to those rules.

827. How did applications come before you? Were they given by person or by letter?—The Committee determined to set up a big board over the office, which was in the main street of the neighbourhood, and that attracted people. We insisted that the head of the family should come.

828. Had you only one office?—Yes.

829. What is the population?—107,000.

830. How many applicants came?—2,026, exclusive of some common lodging-house cases, of which we took no heed whatever.

831. Each applicant was seen by some representative of the Committee, and his application taken down?—At first we attempted an application form of the Charity Organisation kind.

832. Did you succeed in getting the information by taking it down as the Charity Organisation Society would take it down?—No; because the members of the Committee did not know how to do it, and this form we had to reject.

833. And suppose they had been willing, could they have taken all the applications at one office?—No; we should have had to take another office. I was anxious to do it, but the Committee did not agree with me.

834. What amount of inquiry did you make on each occasion?—We had a staff of eleven inquiry agents, five clerks, and five messengers. The inquiry came to this: the house was visited, inquiry was made of the relieving officer, and a reference was seen; and upon that relief was given upon for one occasion.

835. Was the employer seen?—Generally not; before relief was given again, however, if we had any doubt about the person, we communicated with the employer by letter.

836. Were those letters responded to usually?—Yes; but I should say that the inquiry of the employer was not made so frequently as it ought to have been made.

837. Before what tribunal did the cases go?—Before a Committee consisting of two or three people.

838. And they decided to relieve and how much to relieve?—The General Committee adopted a scale, which was roughly adhered to, and the scale was taken from the exceptional distress paper published by the Council of the Charity Organisation Society.*

839. The Committee had upon it Poor Law Guardians?—Yes; one of the Guardians was the most vigorous member—Mr. Dover.

840. You were not able at first to communicate with the relieving officers?—No; but during the remainder of the five weeks—after the first few days, I think. There is a labour-yard open every winter, which is still open. The Guardians have tried to close it, but they say they cannot.

841. Have you any suggestions to make as to what you would do?—If I could prevent the formation of a fund, I would do so.

842. How would you meet the distress—what would you do?—In the main I should rely upon the Poor Law. For the rest the hands of the charitable agencies now at work in London would naturally be strengthened.

843. Suppose a great distress occurred like the Manchester distress?—I am not prepared to answer that question.

844. Perhaps your answer would come to this; that in case of exceptional distress the provision should be different from that for ordinary severe distress?—For the last I would make no provision whatever. So far as I can see at present, the case of flood and fire is the only case of exceptional distress which would be considered by me.

845. (*Mr. J. H. Allen*): Your Committee was not the Charity Organisation Committee?—No.

846. Who formed it?—It was formed by the guardians and all the clergymen holding benefices in the two parishes of St. Saviour's Union, with the Nonconformist clergy in addition.

847. How were they appointed? Did they appoint themselves?—In the

* 'Suggestions for dealing with Exceptional Distress.' December 1884.

first instance a meeting was called at the Mansion House on February 15. A Committee was then appointed for the whole of St. Saviour's Union; the St. Saviour's Union Committee, of which I was one, subsequently held a meeting, and resolved themselves into two Committees. We who formed the Committee for St. Mary's, Newington, nominated a large number of persons whose names occurred to us.

Mr. T. GAGE GARDINER.

June 25, 1886.

848. Did you think it a satisfactory way of distributing relief?—No, most unsatisfactory.

849. You prefer it in fewer hands?—Very much.

850. Would it be possible to have a charity labour-test in your union?—On this recent occasion I was most anxious to try something of the kind, but could not obtain the means. There were very few spaces (if any) which could have been cleared by Lord Brabazon's association.

851. Suppose the vestry had allowed you to sweep the streets at night, would you have tried that?—That, personally, I should have liked to try; but it was not suggested that it be done at night.

852. Would not that interfere with the contractor?—Yes; and I think there would also be this other objection to doing it in the daytime—your really respectable artisan would object to be seen by his friends sweeping the streets.

853. There is no possibility of getting a charity labour-test in your union?—I was not able to get one.

854. Is the labour-yard open now, do you say?—Yes; the Guardians closed it twice (I believe) and re-opened it.

855. (Mr. A. G. Crowder): Is it your opinion, with regard to the labour-yard, that the public would not be satisfied with the relief being administered entirely in that way if the labour-yard were large enough?—I am afraid it is too reasonable, and not sufficiently sentimental.

856. Did any other form of test except a labour-test of destitution occur to you?—No.

857. (Dr. Langstaff): You think, Mr. Gardiner, the Committee went against the rules of the Mansion House Fund in the way in which they made use of the labour-yard, and the way in which they relieved chronic cases?—Yes.

858. And were you in harmony with the Committee, or opposed to them?—I was distinctly opposed to them in regard to the relief of chronic cases. The number of applications made to us was 2,026. Of these they attempted to relieve 1,574, but of that 1,574 to 295 they gave single sums of 2s. 6d. or 5s., and gave them no more; so that it would be fair to say that out of 2,026 they relieved about half. That, to my mind, was too large a proportion, and included a great many chronic cases. They would occasionally relieve the family of a man who was a known drinker, and when remonstrated with, said they must think of the wife and family.

859. Then I take it, Mr. Gage Gardiner, you were part of a minority on your Committee, and that your influence with the Committee slowly increased?—At first they looked upon my views as a hobby, or a fad.

860. And they gradually learned that there was something in your fads?—Yes.

861. They found themselves deceived?—Yes; when some of these gentlemen tackled an applicant they did not know what questions to ask him. On the first day a man came in who was a thorough soaker, and had sixteen shillings given him there and then. I protested. A member of Committee said yes, no doubt he drank, but the weather was cold, and he had a large family, and we must relieve the distress.

862. That was given in money?—Yes; but afterwards the relief was often given in kind.

863. Your principle was to give in money?—Partly in money and partly in kind.

864. Do you think there was any advantage in giving in kind?—I think the advantage was very slight; the tickets were sold.

865. You know that—for drink?—I don't know that they were sold for drink, but they were sold.

Mr. T. GAGE
GARDINER.
June 25, 1886.

866. Have you any reason to believe that any portion of the sum went to the benefit of the public-houses?—I cannot prove it; but I have seen men come back to the office very much the worse for drink after having received it.

867. Is it your opinion that the existing agencies could have been expanded for the occasion to meet the extra work, and could have done the work better than these Committees did—scratch Committees?—I certainly think so.

868. Could you have got assistance from the Newington Committee of the Charity Organisation Society?—I think their hands could have been strengthened. The difference, to my mind, is this. Owing to the action of the Mansion House Committee a large number of persons, entirely unaccustomed to dealing with distress, were called together and forced to administer a large sum of money on the large scheme. If the other plan had been adopted—to use existing associations—you would have had people of some experience.

869. Of the rules that you adopted, are there any which experience has taught you were of importance, and some which might have been omitted?—I think it was of importance that the head of the family should be required to attend at the office. I do not think that any of the rules that we made should have been omitted.

870. You think it necessary to work upon principle in each case?—Yes; and that the Committee should bind themselves to stand by their principles. I had great difficulty in getting the Committee to do that. They guarded themselves; that is, they refused to call their rules rules, but they called them general principles of relief.

871. Have you any evidence yourself of there being dearth of work in Newington, now?—I cannot say that I know that the dearth of work is greater this year than last year, but district visitors and clergymen are constantly telling me that there are more people out of work than usual.

872. Your experience at the Charity Organisation Society does not give you evidence one way or the other?—No; because it is generally known that we do not relieve people whose distress is caused by being out of work.

873. (*Mr. Loch*): Do I understand that these are the rules adopted by the Committee, and not the Mansion House rules?—No; the principle is the same, because the rules which we drew up came for the most part from the Council of the Charity Organisation Society, and the rules of the Mansion House had practically the same source.

874. Taking some of these heads, 'No question of payment of rent to be entertained'—can that be enforced?—No; we subsequently, systematically, would pay the current rent. For some time the Committee would not, but it was found that a part of the relief almost always went in rent. They refused to believe that that was the case, but I was often present when the applicant came a second time, and I asked him how he had spent his money, and the Committee found that some did go in rent, and the landlords therefore benefited.

875. (*Dr. Longstaff*): Would you still maintain the rule against rent?—I would pay current rent, but not back rent.

876. As a matter of fact, apart from the payment of current rent, when you gave more than enough to meet current rent, did the balance go to the landlord?—Very seldom: I should say generally not. The landlord was satisfied when he got the week's rent.

877. Taking the next—'That it is desirable to reinstate men fallen out of clubs and benefit societies'—I suppose the larger number were not benefit society cases?—The majority were not benefit society cases. As a matter of fact, out of £1,850 received we spent £140 on clubs.

878. At what period of time did that occur?—That was in the last fortnight or three weeks.

879. As the work got better done this form of relief was given?—Yes; it was partly for this reason. I was very much distressed to see the way in which the money was being squandered, and I thought that what was put into clubs was wisely used: at my instance a large number of men were placed in clubs who had never been there before. We paid the entrance fee and first quarter's subscription.

880. (*Mr. J. H. Allen*): Could people keep up their subscriptions?—Not always. But it was a safe place for the money. It could do no harm; it benefited the clubs, and, in that way, the working classes.

881. Did you spend any money on emigration?—Only one small sum, though I proposed it many times. But we spent money on migration.

882. (*Chairman*): Have you any evidence that rents were raised in consequence of the Mansion House Fund?—I have no evidence.

883. (*Mr. Loch*): Do you think that the test of belonging to a club is of any value in taking down the case?—Distinctly.

884. Judging from your experience, did you find that that could be utilised as a first sifting of cases?—I was always in favour of giving a larger amount of relief to a man who was in a club than to a man who was not, even if we had not made any inquiries before.

885. If it became generally known in a time of pressure that men belonging to clubs would have favourable consideration given to their cases, would it be a good method of parting those who should be assisted from those who should not?—Certainly: I went so far, towards the end of the fund, as to propose to the Committee that we should not relieve anybody who had not been within the last two years a member of a benefit society. The proposal was rejected on the ground that it was too hard and fast a line.

886. (*Mr. Peters*): Did not the Mansion House Fund deal with that?

887. (*Rev. Curtis Haywa'd*): Would you not in that way exclude some of the most undoubted, if not the most deserving cases? Would it not have been found that they could not keep up the club? These are the people who most want you?—I do not think so. The limit was wide. Anyone who had belonged to a club within two years was to be eligible.

888. Do you not think this distress was coming on for more than two years?—I hardly like to express an opinion. But I think the decent, provident man would not have fallen out of his club two years ago. I do know this. I know a man who was placed in a club two years ago; that man has a wife and four young children, and though he is only having £1 a week, he has kept up that club. It must be remembered that from the Benevolent Fund of the club members' subscriptions are sometimes paid.

889. (*Mr. Loch*): I understand that a very large number of people who applied were those who ought to have been left to the Poor Law?—Yes.

890. Then, in the first place, there were a certain proportion of benefit society's men. Between these and those that ought to have been left to the Poor Law—there was a section to which thrift-tests of various kinds might have been applied—*e.g.*, as to having a large number of things in pawn, owing to the pressure of distress?—We always regarded that as evidence of respectability.

891. And you had not any difficulty in applying that test in the main—the difficulty in the way of investigation?—No; properly asked, people had no objection to such inquiry.

892. Is there any other way in which, speaking roughly, you could discriminate between the suitable and unsuitable cases—would the neighbourhood—the class of cottage or house he occupied, be a test of value?—It is to people thoroughly well acquainted with the district. What I found was that those who worked the Mansion House Fund were unacquainted with the various streets in their parish. One man would know one, and another another, and if the whole Committee had been present every day they would have been of great value; but the number of gentlemen who fairly regularly attended was only four or five out of forty-five members.

893. With regard to the test of the labour-yard, were the payments to the workers and their families sufficient to meet any prejudice there might be in the minds of the public as to the workers starving, even though they were receiving relief?—Our guardians do not give money to those who are working in the labour-yard. They relieve in kind.

894. Would there be a feeling of security that cases referred to the labour-yard could be left to the Poor Law authorities, so that there would be a clear division between charity and the Poor Law in that matter?—I don't think the public would be content with that course.

Mr. T. GAGE GARDINER.

June 25, 1886.

Mr. T. GAGE
GARDINER.

June 23, 1886.

895. But even if the amount given, whether in money or kind, was a considerable amount, amounting to 2s. 6d. or 2s. a day, which was what was paid by the Wandsworth guardians in relief work?—I should say you would not get the St. Saviour's Union guardians to give such relief.

896. So that the test of the Poor Law labour fails because of the amount paid in relief?—Yes; and because of popular prejudice. I don't know how far it would go in times of pressure.

897. One experiment which was tried in the year 1836 was that the people who were in distress were invited to come to the workhouse and board there for the day, receiving their meals and working there. This acted as a strong deterrent, and not a single case of starvation occurred. Would such a thing be practicable in a London union?—I am not prepared to answer the question.

898. If there was that amount of exceptional distress which would not justify a large fund, but might create a real pressure upon Charities, would you suggest that money should be collected in a private manner? We do not want to create applicants, but to relieve distress.—It would be better if the money could be collected privately than by advertisement.

899. How would you propose to extend the Charity Organisation Society Committee, if you had had it in your own hands this year?—I should have tried to get some of the old workers to return for the time; and I should have asked some of the more experienced district visitors in the various parishes for their special help.

900. In that way you would have got together a band of ten or twenty workers?—I should think I might have got together fifteen to twenty workers.

901. Working on that plan, you might have always kept before you some of the final results, and relieved such as were provident, and barred the defaulters altogether, or would you have had to set that aside?—I think it would have had to be set aside. I don't think the Charity Organisation Society Committees would adhere to their principles if large sums were coming in again.

902. Really, then, it is a fact that a large sum of money is undesirable?—Yes; and the unreasoning kindness with which it is administered.

903. (*Chairman*): In other words, the fund demoralises those who give, as well as those who receive.

904. (*Mr. Loch*): The fact is that statements are made in this or that paper, and there is a sort of hot feeling in the public mind that something must be done. Do you think it would be possible for a supply of information to be obtained from employers and employés, too, which could be put before the public systematically, so that we might have a weather gauge, as it were, if there really was distress?—I have considered that question, but cannot answer it.

905. Would the employers in Newington have helped you if we had, earlier in the winter, tried to obtain information?—I could have got information from, I believe, some of the largest employers.

906. That would have been of real value as a test, would it not?—Yes, I think it would. I cannot see why the pauperism returns are not a good indication. The guardians of St. Saviour's Union published a comparative return, up to a certain date in February, for four years. That return showed that the number of paupers in 1886 was smaller than it had been in any of the three years preceding; and it appears to me that there you ought to find a good test. It is commonly said, and is perfectly true, that the better class artisan will suffer the direst possible poverty before applying to the guardians, but you must remember that he deals with people in the social scale rather below him, and they again deal similarly in their turn, so that if there is real distress among the class of people to whom alone we think charitable contributions should go, if to anybody, that must be shown by the Poor Law return.

907. If you were going to get information, would you go to a large employer or a small employer?—I should go to both.

908. Do not the large men continue their business while the smaller men stop? Cubitt does not fail, but the small builders failed.—Just so; but Cubitt diminishes the number of his hands. Hands whom he had employed for years had been temporarily struck off this year for the first time, as I was told.

909. (*Rev. Curtis Hayward*): And yet you say there was not exceptional distress ?—It depends on what you call exceptional distress.

910. It was not the weather that threw them out, was it ?—It was in the time of cold weather that I came across two or three of these workpeople.

911. But there is a general depression in trade, is there not ?—Most certainly.

912. (*Mr. Loch*): Granting that the Poor Law returns might be taken as a test of the amount of distress, was it not the case that in the past winter there was a good deal of distress among better-class artisans, that upper end of the scale ?—Yes ; but generally the better class of artisans was not reached by the Mansion House Fund, as it was administered in St. Mary's, Newington.

913. I noted that. And, first of all, could we not have learned from the friendly societies and building societies as to that upper class of distress ?—Yes ; in fact an attempt was made with some of these societies.

914. Too late ? Not in November or December ?—No.

915. If we had gone to them we must have learned who was in distress, and could we not have relieved them better ?—I think their information would have been a valuable indication as to the want among the better class of working men.

916. Did you have any working men on your Committee, or in co-operation with you ?—We had one who never came to the Committee because before he joined the Committee had resolved to do their work in the day-time, and not at night.

917. (*Dr. Longstaff*): Mr. Curtis Hayward has referred to depression in trade, and you have also. Is it not possible that there might be considerable depression of trade, and very few artisans be effected ?—I think it possible, but hardly likely.

918. Is it not a fact that large houses now are doing work at a very small rate of profit ?—I don't know whether employers or employed are suffering most. I have no doubt that people are supplied, and profits are low, and that wages have come down ; but also inferior hands have been discharged. I don't know what it may be in the north, but I know this, that a great many men are temporarily dismissed on account of slackness of work. I know a man well who is now out of work, and who had for years been continuously employed. He had been employed at the docks on a superior class of work. Together with a mate he was discharged in January, the men being told that their services would not be wanted again till July. Immediately afterwards the employer subscribed fifty guineas to the fund for the unemployed.

919. (*Mr. J. H. Allen*): Does not the pressure show the need of emigration to assist the good class of men out of work ?—That question I am not ready to answer ; but it does show, I should say, the necessity of teaching the working people some means of limiting the number of their families.

920. If you cannot do that, you must help them to emigrate ?—At any rate, the population question deserves as much attention as the emigration question.

921. (*Rev. Curtis Hayward*): As to test of property, you say you looked to the pawn tickets—did you test it by the rate book at all, to see whether they had paid rates when they were in work ?—One instruction to the agent was to make a report as to the date at which rent had ceased to be paid.

922. (*Mr. Loch*): Your general conclusion is that in dealing with exceptional distress you want well-directed charitable work ? Taking a district like your own, Newington and St. Saviour's, do you find the people who are making money in the district are residing in the district ?—No ; generally not. In St. Mary's, Newington, there are very few large employers. Mr. Tarn, of Lancaster Gate, is the largest employer of labour in Newington.

923. Would it be possible to get that skilful charity on the spot if those who employed the labour of the district were to care for the district themselves, and put their leisure, so to speak, into it ?—That would make a very large difference.

924. Practically, so far as that power is available, it is not exerted, by the rich and well-to-do who make their money in the district ?—No.

925. Therefore the people who are responsible are not fulfilling their

Mr. T. Gage Gardiner.
June 25, 1886.

responsibility for the district?—If they are responsible, they are not fulfilling it.

926. So far as the Mansion House Fund is concerned, it acts as a substitute for the real actual responsibility of these people?—I cannot say it acts as a substitute.

927. But there is nothing else to take its place.—And therefore I say that until these people, and people generally, are disposed to give up a great deal more of their time than at present, to helping in some form or other those whose circumstances are less fortunate than their own, such a fund as this should not be created.

928. Therefore the mismanagement of an exceptional distress fund would point to a radical defect in Newington?—I should say it pointed to the want of civilisation in London generally.

929. Did the Poor Law officers look through their books, or simply say, 'I don't know such a case'?—If the case was receiving relief, they made a note in the list that was sent to them; if not, they made no note, unless it was an exceptionally bad case, and then they warned the Committee.

930. Then the reference did not answer all the purposes it might have done?—At first relieving officers were most obliging in making suggestions as to the cases, but on one occasion one of the relieving officers recommended a case which was shown to be a bad case, and as a number of guardians were members of the Committee, the relieving officer heard of it again; and the other relieving officers took warning by that, and afterwards confined themselves to definite information.

931. Do you think it a good plan to distribute forms to be filled up by applicant themselves? Would you adopt that plan again?—To tell you the truth, I never saw that the form was of any value whatever.

932. If you worked the fund as you think it desirable, would the staff have to be increased?—I don't wish it to be understood that I favour having a fund at all, except in cases of distress arising from what is sometimes called the act of God—that is to say, fire or flood.

933. But dealing with it, as you would deal with it, this year you would not have to incur a very large extra expense of machinery? Suppose it had been in your hands, would you have had to employ a very expensive machinery?—It is very hard to say what number of applications would have been made if the fund had not been largely advertised.

934. Two or three extra agents would carry it a good way, would they not?—Yes.

Mr. W. H. O. JACK, examined.

Mr. W. H. O. Jack.

935. (*Chairman*): You are specially connected with the Charity Organisation Society?—I am agent for the Lewisham Committee.

936. Then in that capacity you have special knowledge of questions affecting the Poor Law?—I have only been two years in that position, and I cannot say that I have any special knowledge.

937. You only acted for the Charity Organisation Society. Did you help to distribute the Mansion House Fund?—At the time of the starting of the Mansion House Fund, Mr. Bramly, the Hon. Sec., joined the Mansion House Committee, and I was deputed by the Charity Organisation Committee to assist the Mansion House Committee in inquiry and office work.

938. Did you find they were distributing the fund in a manner contrary to the rules laid down by the Mansion House Committee in regard to chronic cases?—No, I think not.

939. You have no knowledge?—I can say that they did not deal with chronic cases. They were referred to the Poor Law.

940. So far as you helped, were you assisted by the relieving officers?—Yes, when our inquiries required us to consult them; but they were inclined to be lenient to people always on the rates, and who, whether there was a Mansion House Fund or not, would still be in want.

941. Did you find that the relief was being badly distributed?—At first it was

Mr. W. H. O. JACK.

June 25, 1886.

badly distributed, because they commenced before the Committee was regularly formed ; but after the Committee had settled down in working order it was well and carefully distributed.

942. When it had got into this better state what kind of people did you assist ?—The class of people which came to us were labourers, and artisans, and mechanics—a very large proportion of them were labourers.

943. Could not those labourers have been relieved by the Poor Law ? —They could have been, but it would, I think, have been better to arrange some relief works.

944. You are specially in favour of relief works ?—I think it is a better plan. By a labour test you can weed out the loafers.

945. In a place like Lewisham could you have relief works ?—Yes, roadmaking. There are many in Lewisham that are not yet made up.

946. Work which is now done by the vestries ?—Yes.

947. They would have been assisting the vestries ?—Yes, and relieving the rates by taking these people away who were otherwise receiving outdoor or indoor relief, or in the labour yard.

948. I don't know how that would have relieved the rates.—There is a large number of roads which are not made up. They must be made up at some date or other, at the expense of the owners of the houses in those roads. That work might be given to a large number of men out of employment during the winter or a time of depression.

949. (*Dr. Longstaff*): If the people living on either side of the road had been compelled to contribute ?—The owner of the property is responsible for the cost of making up the roads.

950. But as a rule the making up a road is postponed till a certain proportion of the inhabitants ask to have it made up—then the order of apportionment is made.—Is it not sometimes the case that a portion of the money is paid, yet the vestry waits until all the owners have contributed ?—Suppose that £1,000 is necessary to make up of a road, and £800 paid, it would not be at all out of the way for the Vestry to provide the £200.

951. What I understand is this : that you would be in favour of accelerating the process of making up the roads without relieving people living in the roads from their liability, though the vestry would meanwhile supply the deficiency for doing it ?—Yes, and (if legal) charge an interest on that deficiency; and if the owner refuses to pay, collect the rent until it is paid.

952. Would you not have been benefiting speculative builders or proprietors ? You would have improved the property ?—I am speaking of roads already built upon.

953. (*Chairman*) : Upon the whole, so far as you are able to judge, was good done by the Mansion House Fund in the neighbourhood of Lewisham ?—I think so, but a great deal of the money no doubt went to people who did not deserve it, which, with necessary precautions, would not happen again.

954. Then you think that machinery might be established to prevent it ?—I think the existing machinery could be utilised and improved.

955. Does your Lewisham district correspond with that map ?—The Mansion House Fund deals only with Lewisham civil parish. Eltham and Sydenham had, I think, local Committees.

956. Do you know the population ?—I can get it.*

957. I think you said you acted as inquiry officer ?—I did.

958. Were you the only one ?—No ; the Hon. Sec. of the Charity Organisation Committee and the two Hon. Secs. and some of the Committee of the Mansion House Fund, assisted.

959. Do you know how many applications were made ?—It is given in the report of the Lewisham Committee—474.

960. Were these applications made personally ?—In the first place, the Central Committee at Greenwich forwarded to the Lewisham Committee a quantity of application forms, which were distributed to district visitors,

* The Lewisham Union, including Eltham and Sydenham, had in 1881 a population 73,314.

Mr. W. H. O. JACK.
June 25, 1886.

clergy, &c., and after they were filled up they were placed in a box at the entrance. They were taken from the box three or four times a day, and sorted and inquired into.

961. When you started to make these inquiries were these forms filled up by the district visitors?—If they came filled up by a district visitor they were returned, and had to be filled up by the applicants.

962. You are familiar with the practice of the Charity Organisation Society?—Yes, for two years.

963. Were the inquiries you made for the Mansion House Committee similar to ours?—The application forms were given to the inquiry agent to obtain any information he could; the Charity Organisation Society's books were looked into to find anything concerning applicants. During the two years I have been at Lewisham I have known a number of people as public-house loafers. Many of these applied, and were at once written off.

964. If they were strangers, did you make the same inquiries as you would have made for the Charity Organisation Society?—There was not time, but their case was carefully looked into.

965. Your report was expected to be ready in a few hours?—Yes; probably by six or seven in the evening.

966. You had no chance of inquiring of employers? Did they give money on account and pursue inquiries afterwards?—In some cases, I think, it was done; but, generally, when the case was pressing, it was placed in the inquiry officer's hands, and was immediately seen to.

967. In many cases the inquiry officer resided far off?—They resided in Lewisham, Blackheath, or Lee.

968. Did a single member decide the cases, or a Committee?—No, I never saw less than four decide a case.

969. (*Mr. J. H. Allen*): In the event of exceptional distress happening next winter, should you recommend another Mansion House Fund or not?—The Mansion House Fund might do a deal of good if properly managed, but this one was a general scramble. The applicants seemed to think, the money having been subscribed, it was to be given them whether deserving or not. Some of the applicants who saw the Committee demanded—they did not ask.

970. Was there any labour test in your neighbourhood, and, if so, what?—The Committee made an arrangement with Mr. Carline, the local surveyor, to make and level a road. It was a road which would, perhaps, never have been done otherwise. At first we referred applicants to the surveyor, telling them that he would find them work; this worked badly, as they did not apply, but came back and said he had refused them. We adopted the practice of writing to the applicants, and when they attended, offering them work. I wrote to forty the first day; out of that number we obtained eleven, and these eleven were not of the right class. We finally wrote to 145 men and obtained 50.

971. What class of men?—They were labourers.

972. Not chronic cases?—Yes, I think many were.

973. Men who were always out of work in the winter?—Yes, most of them.

974. Men who were employed in the gardens—the market gardens?—Yes, and other work—*i.e.*, labourers.

975. And the market gardeners are always out of work in severe weather?—Quite so.

976. Are you in favour of the labour test?—I think it is the only means of testing whether a man means to work if he can obtain it, or prefers to accept charity.

977. Some kind of labour test you are convinced is necessary?—I am, if the rate of wages was increased.

978. What did you give?—Fourpence per hour for seven and a half hours.

979. Don't you think that sufficient?—No, sir. My experience is, it stamps the work as being too much of charity, and the men will only put the amount of labour to it you can get for charity work. I think if they were paid 4½d. and the best 5d. per hour, you would have less grumbling and better work.

980. Fourpence per hour for seven and a half hours ?—Yes ; that is 2s. 6d. per day of seven and a half hours.

981. You don't think that with the lower rate of pay you will ever get real work ?—I am convinced that you will not, unless you stand watching them.

982. You think a halfpenny an hour will make the difference ?—Yes, the lower rate stamps it as charity work. It is surprising what a man will do for the other ½d. or 1d. per hour.

983. Then you actually did employ fifty men in this way ?—Yes.

984. Did the majority of them skulk ?—Yes, and also through lax supervision they got drunk on the work.

985. And they were men of the lower class, most of them ?—They were of the labouring class. Some of the artisans and labourers preferred to go about with a box, drum, and banner, and get 5s. a day. These were that class of men who talk politics in a public-house the best part of the day, and prefer anything to work.

986. The artisans you came across were the dregs of the class ?—I do not think the Mansion House Fund generally reached the best of the artisans and labourers. These are generally too independent to ask charity.

987. (Dr. *Longstaff*) : Do you think there was exceptional distress among the exceptionally good artisans ?—No ; not more than, from depression in the building trade, there has been for some years.

988. (*Mr. Peters*) : If there had not been any Mansion House Fund, do you consider that there would have been very great hardship ?—No, I don't think there would have been in Lewisham, because Lewisham has so many churches and well-organised District Visiting Societies, who give relief outside. There are also a great many charitable people, whom I have heard called ' free lances,' who give relief on their own account.

989. Then practically you would say there was no occasion for the Mansion House Fund in your district ?—I think not.

990. How many applications had you ?—You have it in the report.

(*The Secretary read the figures from the report.*)*

991. Do you consider, as a rule, that the cases which are here described as deserving cases were deserving cases really ?—I should not like to give an opinion, unless a better or longer inquiry could have been made.

992. (*Mr. Loch*) : As a fact, it is quite clear that these men who were set to work, under the arrangement made by you, were men of the chronic class—out of work every winter ?—Yes, many of them ; others were of the loafing class, a few respectable—they were a mixed lot.

993. There would be no hardship whatever in many of these men receiving their relief in the stoneyards ?—In some cases not.

994. Therefore, so far, the charity labour would be simply substituted for the stoneyard ; it might just as well have been the stoneyard under the Poor Law authorities ?—Yes ; we endeavoured to obtain the best of them. I am not in favour in all cases of the stoneyard test ; it is too demoralising for a respectable man.

995. Though you endeavoured to obtain the best men, they were of this chronic class ?—Yes, with some exceptions.

996. But who provided the money for this charity labour ?—£50 was given by the Lewisham Mansion House Committee.

997. Was that money given in connection with Lord Brabazon's Association ?—No.

998. Had you any connection with that Association ?—Yes. I have the management of the work at St. Mary's churchyard. £400 has been given from Lord Brabazon's Association to lay this out.

999. Are the same men working there ?—A few. There is considerable difficulty in getting labourers to work there.

---

* ' The number of applications received was 474. These were all carefully investigated by the voluntary almoners, assisted by the Committee's officers, who visited the homes of the applicants, and 321 were reported as deserving of relief.'

Mr. W. H. O. JACK.
June 25, 1886.

1000. Why?—Because the building trade is looking up.

1001. So that the charity work is being carried out in a competitive manner with the building trade, which is getting into full swing?—Improving, but not in full swing. Not competitive; we don't compel labourers to come there.

1002. If he prefers the charity work, as he can have it to do, he is so far prevented from working at contract prices under a builder's foreman? No one prevented him, he had his choice—charity work and 4d. per hour, or contract work at 6d. per hour.

1003. So that the Boulevard Association work is being done by this set of men, more or less?—Yes. A class of men, many of them, I would not give 2d. per hour to, if I were a builder.

1004. And it is not meeting any particular demand weekly?—It has already found work this week for 24 men.

1005. But that is not in response to a distinct demand?—No. Most of them are men who would rub along somehow.

1006. Would those 24 men be good for emigration? I have pushed emigration very strongly. I have had many promises, but I find generally excuses are made at the last moment—that the wives will not emigrate.

1007. But these men who will not emigrate are out of work every winter What wages do they get in the summer?—If they get work, 5½d. to 6d. per hour.

1008. Speaking roughly, for a week, would he be able to earn his 25s. a week?—No, I don't think he would, because he would work a short day on Saturday, and would stop for rain, loss of time, &c.

1009. And being unable to do that (and as a married man), is out of work every winter?—Generally so.

1010. And yet he won't emigrate, though physically able to do it?—No, he will not.

1011. If he felt that this money was not forthcoming, do you think he would be induced to emigrate?—Or else to shift from the neighbourhood.

1012. (*Dr. Longstaff*): Then you think they look out for this? I have had men who said, 'Mr. Jack, if there's another Mansion House Fund next winter I hope you'll remember me.'

1013. (*Mr. Loch*): But charity work is keeping on the spot men who would make good emigrants and might be induced to emigrate? If he were driven to extremities he might emigrate?—Unless he could go to the labour-yard.

1014. Are they as happy in the labour-yard as in the charity work?—Yes, I think so. However lazy a man may be, I think he would rather have strict supervision. If not, he turns it up, and prefers to loaf about the streets. I think they are more contented in the labour-yard, where they are strictly supervised.

1015. The labour-yard, so far, would be equivalent to extreme pressure?—I think so.

1016. And if the labour-yard was not open ordinarily there would be an inducement to them to move or emigrate?—Yes, the bad ones. I know many a decent labourer who went in last winter who would not have done so unless he had been driven to it.

1017. Supposing the labour-yard is shut and the charitable work only available for such men as you have just mentioned, do you think that would answer?—I think the charity work would answer if done by measurement.

1018. You want contract, do you?—No, sir.

1019. Treat them as if they were under a contractor?—Yes. Because it may be charity or relief works is no reason a man should skulk.

1020. Would you take more gangers?—No, one ganger would be quite sufficient if he were up to the mark.

1021. How was he chosen?—He was appointed by Mr. Carline, the district surveyor.

1022. Lord Brabazon's work is 2s. 6d. a day?—No, it is only five hours a day—1s. 8d.

1023. Did they give breakfasts?—That was done in some places; we had no conveniences for such an arrangement.

1024. If the man has to be paid at all, do you think it better to pay him partly in breakfast and partly in money?—I think it better to pay him in money.

1025. (*Chairman*): From one of Mr. Loch's questions it would lead you to suppose that idle people would make good emigrants?—Yes; if they were taken abroad, and left to shift for themselves, they might do it.

1026. With regard to a suburban district like yours, is there any suggestion you have to make for exceptional distress?—Supposing another Mansion House Fund were formed, the first thing to be given is a labour test. No money should be given to able-bodied men unless it was earned. But the work should be done by measurement, and so much should be expected from each man, allowance being made for old men.

1027. (*Mr. Allen*): You must have strict investigation of the cases?—Yes, and while making strict inquiries applicants who were able to work should be referred to the relief works.

1028. (*Mr. Loch*): That would be with special reference to the wants of your own district?—I think so. In Lewisham there is a very large proportion of labourers. They were the largest proportion who applied to the Mansion House Committee for relief.

1029. Just now there is a demand for a certain number of labourers for Queensland for service; I think £20 is the money. After that they can earn very much higher wages. Do you think you could get six or eight men who would take that?—No, not one. I have taken great trouble about emigration, and find they back out at the eleventh hour.

1030. That is to say, we are keeping on the spot a number of people who will not work properly?—If the work was done by measurement it would be too hard for them; they would either migrate or emigrate.

1031. Therefore you would be very strict with them?—I would make no exception with able-bodied men.

1032. But taking the character of the Lewisham public into question, I suppose they would highly disapprove of such a plan?—Yes; we offered 145 work, but only 50 accepted it.

1033. The rest got relief somewhere?—Yes, but not from the Mansion House Fund.

1034. And they did not go to the Poor Law?—No.

1035. So that the whole difficulty is the feeling of the public as to their responsibility. You cannot apply any system in the present circumstances to meet the case. I think you would find that the public would hold your hand; they prefer to keep them. Those 90 who refused were able to live somehow on the public, and that would be likely to occur in any future year?
Yes. At St. Mary's Church on the last Bank Holiday I resolved to work all day, to know which of the men would come up. Three men did not come, but were loafing outside of a public-house three parts drunk the whole of the day.

(*The Committee then adjourned.*)

Mr. W. H. O. JACK.

June 25, 1886.

FRIDAY, JULY 2ND, 1886.

Present—MR. A. PELL, in the Chair.

Rev. W. C. HAYWARD, Mr. A. G. CROWDER,
Mr. J. H. ALLEN, Rev. BROOKE LAMBERT,
Hon. and Rev. Canon LEGGE. Hon. and Rev. A. C STANLEY.

Mr. R. HEDLEY, attending on behalf of the Local Government Board.

Mr. C. S. LOCH, *Secretary*.

THE HON. AND REV. CANON LEGGE, examined.

The Hon. and Rev. Canon LEGGE.
July 2, 1886.

1036. (*Chairman*): You are Vicar of Lewisham?—Yes, for seven years. I have been resident in Lewisham for 19 years.

1037. In addition to that, you are Chairman of the Lewisham Board of Guardians?—Yes.

1038. How long have you been guardian on that Board?—Sixteen years.

1039. And Chairman for how long?—This is the third year.

1040. Just incidentally, are your guardians appointed for a period of three years?—No, for one year.

1041. Have you acted in any way on behalf of the Mansion House Fund? Very little. I was a member of the Local Committee.

1042. At what date did you become a member?—Some time in February. As soon as it was formed.

1043. Did you continue a member till a month ago?—Till it ceased to exist.

1044. Now are you pretty regular in your attendance at the Board?—Yes.

1045. How often do you meet?—Once a fortnight, but committees in the alternate weeks.

1046. You have Relief Committees, then?—Yes.

1047. Your relief is not administered by the Board, but is distributed through the action of Committees. How many?—Three Committees.

1048. And these Committees have a certain area, I suppose?—Yes, which correspond with the areas of the Relieving Officers.

1049. Do you know at all what proportion of indoor to outdoor paupers you have?—The outdoor paupers vary so very much.

1050. Take the first day of the year—have you more outdoor paupers on your list than you have in the house?—I am afraid I cannot tell you.*

* Canon Legge writes:—The following statistics will furnish answers to some of the questions asked in evidence; and may form a convenient schedule to my evidence.

The Lewisham Union Workhouse is certified for 506 inmates all told.

The *Able-bodied Men's Wards* accommodate 120.

These wards were *full* from December 12, 1885, to March 6, 1886.

The *Number of Persons in Receipt of Outdoor Relief* were as follows:—

	1st July, 1885	1st Jan., 1886.	1st July, 1886.
In receipt of General Relief	929	2,045	1,094
„ Medical Relief only	67	54	21
Totals	996	2,099	1,115

The number of men (separate cases, mostly heads of families) relieved in the *Labour-yard* during the six months ending March 25, 1885, and 1886, respectively, were:—

		£ s. d.		£ s. d.	
1884–85 ... 271	at a cost of	710 12 9¾	or	2 12 5¼	per head.
1885–86 ... 416	„	1,469 15 6¼	„	3 10 7¼	„
Increase 1885–86 ... 145	„	759 2 9	„	0 18 2¼	„

1051. (*Mr. Hedley*) : Many more outdoor paupers than indoor.

1052. (*Chairman*): Perhaps you would not mind—taking the first of January—hunting it up. The numbers on the poor list and the number of indoor, including the medical cases out of the house.—The proportion would vary very much in summer and winter. It may be an advantage to answer for both.

1053. In winter you think it would be very much larger? Could you give us the same figures for the first of July 1885?—Yes.

1054. You are aware, I believe, that the Mansion House Fund came into operation about the 11th February?—About that time.

1055. Now, had there been any increase of distress apparent to you as Chairman of the Board, previous to February, beyond what you would have expected to have been brought under your notice at that time of the year?—Yes, there had.

1056. Very much more?—Very considerably more.

1057. Something like 20 per cent. more?—I should think so. I have got here the actual number of cases relieved during six months ending March 1st, 1885, and during the six months ending March 1st, 1886. In the six months ending March 1st, 1885, the number of cases relieved was 3,360 outdoor relief.

1058. That was in 1885?—Yes. For the six months ending March 1st, 1886, the number was 4,868.

1059. Now the indoor?—The indoor I cannot give you. Very slightly increased, I think.

1060. The indoor was very slightly increased. Was the house crowded? Were you unable to receive more?—We were, in many of the wards; but several wards are for special cases—children and so forth.

1061. The ordinary wards were full?—Yes.

1062. Can you say that you had any more able-bodied adults in the workhouse at this time than usual?—Yes, we had.

1063. Did you make freer use of the workhouse test during the winter, or act upon the same lines as usual?—We made a freer use of it.

1064. Did you use it more freely than at any other times? You had more applications for relief occurred in 1886 than in previous years?—Yes.

1065. You had, according to your figures, had you not, 1,500 more cases?—Yes.

1066. How was it that you admitted 1,500 more cases to the receipt of outdoor relief without any corresponding rise in the indoor?—1,500 includes every child.

1067. (*Mr. Hedley*) : They were not cases then—they were individuals?—A man and woman and seven children is one case.

1068. (*Chairman*): Then, when in answer to previous questions you have mentioned cases, you referred to individuals?—Yes.

1069. How was it you admitted 1,500 more people to outdoor relief without

The Hon. and Rev. Canon LEGGE.

July 2, 1886.

The scale of remuneration was unchanged, and the increased cost per head is accounted for by (*a*) The larger number on an average in the families.

(*b*) The provision of boots for the children in a large number of cases during the later months of the long winter.

The number of families assisted to *emigrate* by the Guardians was during the same six months:—

			£	s.	d.
1884-85	...	... 4 families, at a cost of	89	16	0
1885-86	...	... 7 ,, ,, ,, ,,	142	0	0

The number of *Casuals* relieved during the same period was:—

| 1884-85 | ... | 1,894 casuals, at a cost of | 95 | 0 | 6 |
| 1885-86 | ... | 1,803 ,, ,, ,, ,, | 87 | 11 | 0 |

The expenditure on Outdoor Relief in the Union during the same six months was £920. 9s. 6d. more in 1885-86 than in 1884-85; of which, £759. 2s. 9d. was expended on Labour-yard cases.

The Hon. and Rev. Canon LEGGE.

July 2, 1886.

any corresponding indoor relief?—Because we could not have taken anything like the proportion of increase into the house, from want of accommodation.

1070. Did you make offers of the house till the house was quite full?—I don't suppose we offered the house in every instance. I don't suppose a fortnight elapsed without an offer of the house being made.

1071. But still again, I want this answer—Did you make the offer of the house till the house was so full that you could not use the workhouse test any longer?—I should think we did, because we did till the house as far as able-bodied men were concerned.

1072. Had you beds made up in the Board room?—No.

1073. In 1881?—In 1881 the house was only half the size.

1074. Would you, Canon Legge, be able to let us know whether the house was at any time so full that you were prevented making use of the workhouse test?—Yes, I will.

1075. Will you tell us whether it was full up to the certificate of the Local Government Board—that you will let us know?—Yes.

1076. Did you put on any extra inquiry officers when you had this large number of fresh applicants? We had quite recently appointed three assistant-relieving officers.

1077. Were the officers old hands?—Yes.

1078. Are you on one of the Relief Committees?—Yes.

1079. Now, we will take your own Relief Committee—did you see all these persons? Did they all—that is, the parents or representatives—come before the Board?—So far as my Committee was concerned, they all did. The relief was given for certain periods.

1080. For how long a period do you give it, not during sickness, do you?—Do you mean sickness of the man.

1081. Do you ever grant relief for the term of sickness?—No.

1082. It was always for a specified time?—Yes.

1083. With regard to these exceptional cases, what period did you have?—Six weeks.

1084. Was that your general order?—General in the first instance.

1085. You did not vary your rule in the winter of 1886?—No, but if at the end of six weeks a man applied again, we considered whether we should allow him to continue to work in the labour yard or tell him to come into the house. We would often grant him permission to go again into the labour yard for a short period.

1086. When you offered the house, was it accepted?—In very few cases—in some.

1087. Was not that rather a proof that they could have done without the outdoor relief? What relief did you give generally in these outdoor cases?—In money and kind, according to our scale.

1088. You have the scale?—Yes.

1089. In any case did you give outdoor relief to able-bodied men?—Not, except in the labour yard, in any case.

1090. At what time did he come?—At nine o'clock.

1091. And remained till ——?—Four in the afternoon.

1092. And that in fact was the test?—Yes.

1093.—Was the relief you then gave him supposed to be enough to support those dependent on him?—It was supposed to be adequate for the number in family to supply them with the necessaries of life, but not to pay rent.

1094. What was the character of the people? What class did they belong to?—The majority belonged to the class employed in the building trade and the brickfields. But there was a considerable percentage of persons of a somewhat better class—the artisan class.

1095. Now, with regard to the building class, before you admitted them to relief, were inquiries made as to what they had been doing in the previous two years, and previous life?—Yes, in every case I think we had an investigation.

1096. Did they satisfy you that the trade had been so bad they could not help their position?—Yes, there was no doubt I think about that, and the larger portion of the distress we thought arose from the length of the winter.

1097. But the long winter, as we will call it—would you not agree with me, did not begin until March, whereas relief began in February? It was an open winter up to February?—If I remember right we had a good deal of frost earlier than that though it was not continuous, it was sufficient to interfere very considerably with building.

1098. I'll put the question in another way, when did these people begin to apply to you?—As early as November.

1099. That will do. Then the winter had nothing to do with it. They had been doing badly in the summer?—Yes.

1100. Then all through the winter the cases I suppose rather increased than not?—All through the winter. As the winter continued some applied who had never been in that position before.

1101. Now just leave the Poor Law for a moment. Did you find that much distress was brought under your notice as a clergyman over and above these applications?—Not very much.

1102. Do you think that the exceptional distress was confined to the artisan class of your district?—Yes, I think so.

1103. Did much money come from the Mansion House Fund? Did you know much about the Mansion House Fund?—Yes.

1104. Did that tend to reduce the pauper list, or did it reduce the pauper class?—No, but I think it helped to prevent an increase. We were able to refer some—who applied for the first time—to the Mansion House Relief Committee, so as to prevent them from becoming paupers.

1105. Was there any correspondence kept up between the officers of the Poor Law and the gentlemen who represented the Mansion House Fund?—Yes, in Lewisham we were in constant communication, and there were two or three guardians who were members of the Mansion House Committee.

1106. Do you think on the whole that the Mansion House Relief Fund was a benefit to the population in your district?—I don't think it was required. I think it was on the whole wisely administered, because we had the advantage of having the experience of the Charity Organisation Society's Committee.

1107. You don't think the Mansion House Fund was required, but you do think it was rightly administered?—Yes.

1108. Would you do anything yourself to promote the establishment of another?—No, certainly not.

1109. Even though you are aware that though we have got free of midsummer day there is lack of work among your population?—No, I should rely upon the neighbourhood to help.

1110. And would you resent help coming from the outside? Would you be disinclined to have it?—Yes.

1111. And you think your parishioners would in that case be more prepared to accept the duties that belong to neighbourhood?—I think they would.

1112. Do you think that where this principle is rightly observed, sensational work like the Mansion House Fund would supersede it?—I think that is likely to be the result.

1113. I suppose you have a good many rich people?—Yes, in the Union—in the neighbourhood.

1114. It is not a very poor district?—It is a poor district. In a very poor district the principle might be maintained by affiliation to a wealthier district; a system already in operation in some cases.

1115. (*Rev. B. Lambert*): I think we understood that your accommodation as regards the Local Government Board certificate was not exceeded; you kept up to the certificate and no more?—Our certificate, I think, shows a considerable amount of accommodation not used, but it is accommodation for special cases, and not available for able-bodied men.

1116. You said that you had many bricklayers, was the outdoor applicant generally of a superior class?—No.

1117. But superior to what have come in other years?—Well, the number was very large, and I should not think the majority were of a superior class; but many were.

1118. I ask, because some one looking at your labour-yard told me that the

The Hon. and Rev. Canon LEIGH.

July 2, 1896.

class was very much superior. Now did the Mansion House Fund reduce your labour yard?—No, but I think it prevented it increasing.

1119. Now then, did you make any use of the Local Government Board suggestions of March 1886, allowing the guardians to supply labour in other matters than the labour yard?—We kept ourselves in communication with the District Board of Works, and the Board did employ a certain number from the labour yard on works which would not have otherwise been undertaken.

1120. I must ask how far that letter is still in operation?

1121. (*Mr. Hedley*): It was only a letter of suggestions, but it would still stand good in another winter.

1122. I understand that at Lewisham all you did was to lay out some new roads. Do you think that in a future year the suggestions in the letter would practically enable us to get rid of the labour-yard test?—I would not say that it would enable us to get rid of it altogether. I would mention that the Local Mansion House Relief Committee applied a certain portion of their funds to the payment of labour.

1123. (*Chairman*): A sort of encouragement?—Yes.

1124. (*Mr. B. Lambert*): Would you kindly tell me in what directions you think you could place labour?—Well, I heard Mr. Vallance's proposition in regard to the streets.

1125. Do you think those could be done?—I think there are objections.

1126. Is there anything else you think of?—It must depend on the locality. In our case you mention roads. There was some work done by the Board of Works in making up roads, the cost of which must be repaid by the owners of the houses. The grant from the Mansion House Fund was used for improving a road by levelling a piece of rising ground in it—a work that never would have been done otherwise. That was paid for at a lower rate of wages.

1127. And you think the work could be done in future?—I think so, in our Union.

1128. And no other plan has suggested itself to you?—Since the Mansion House Relief Fund has been closed, we have undertaken to lay out our churchyard as a garden in connection with Lord Brabazon's Association.

1129. (*Chairman*): Just to follow it up, was any of the work that was done of an unremunerative nature? Some was remunerative labour as in the case of occupation roads. But was part spent on unremunerative work?—The whole of the grant from the Mansion House Fund was spent on unremunerative work.

1130. (*Mr. B. Lambert*): In regard to the other matter that you mentioned— you said that you thought the ordinary charity of the neighbourhood could meet this time of distress; now may I ask how you would suggest to meet the case of a man out of work, whom you did not intend to take into the Union? What would you do with him?—I don't know what cases there would be like that. If a man was out of work, there is nothing for him but relief from the parish.

1131. You do intend to make them appeal to the parish?—Yes.

1132. (*Chairman*): That is if he has no relations who would help him to tide over the difficulty?—Yes.

1133. (*Chairman*): I have just one question before we leave this. Has the amount of building in your neighbourhood sensibly decreased?—It has; and more especially in proportion to the population, and the explanation is this, that of the small class of cottages which formerly employed local labour a great, many of them are unlet; and where larger works have been undertaken, the contractor has brought his own men, thus increasing the population and not giving employment to the builders in the locality.

1134. (*Mr. Loch*): Is the bulk of this distress chronic, do you think?—By chronic, you mean always coming after the summer?

1135. Yes, and lasting for the winter year after year, for the last four years say?—I think the bulk of it is.

1136. Then practically if it is not to be relieved by our charitable relief funds —which I understand in regard to a large proportion of it would be your opinion—would those people apply naturally to the Poor Law?—A considerable number would.

1137. If they were left to themselves?—Yes.

1138. Are they left to themselves? As a matter of fact is there not a lot of small charitable relief from one source or another drifting their way?—A great deal too much.

1139. And that prevents their coming to a decision as to moving or coming to the Poor Law?—Yes.

1140. And therefore we are keeping an amount of chronic distress which we are giving sops to occasionally?—Yes.

1141. And the Charity Relief Fund is accentuating the evil?—Yes.

1142. And it destroys thrift, does it not?—I think we are improving as to thrift. We have a self-supporting dispensary, and the number of members increases regularly.

1143. Did you find that the members of the dispensary were people who applied for relief last winter?—I think not.

1144. Therefore, it follows that the chronic distress can only be relieved by the thrift of these people?—Through the Poor Law, do you mean?

1145. No, chronic distress could only be met by the thriftiness of these people.—Quite so. There are two classes of workmen, one regular and thrifty, and the other irregular, which last class falls back persistently on indiscriminate charity.

1146. Then if this charity were away, they would be tempted to be thrifty, or move; and the key to the difficulty lies there—in their increased thrift or getting regular work, and not on relief at all?—Yes, but a large amount of work cannot be regular—the jobbing gardeners' work and builders' work.

1147. (*Chairman*): Are you acquainted with the wages in your neighbourhood?—Yes.

1148. And these people take exceptionally high wages because their work is so casual and irregular?—Four or five shillings a day, not more.

1149. (*Mr. Loch*): In view of the necessary irregularity of certain work, do you think that that could be met by these people having alternative trades to work in the intervals?—I never thought that out.

1150. But, practically, unless some solution of that sort is arrived at we must be perpetually in this dilemma?—Yes.

1151. Have you, in connection with the schools of the district, any settled plan of teaching another trade—that men, such as gardeners, should be taught wood carving and toy making?—No.

1152. Do you think, with a certain number of charitable people in your neighbourhood, that their attention and energies could be given in this direction? The dilemma is just this. The state of trade brings intermittent labour and consequent distress unless there is thrift to make up for it, and during the slack period the workman must go to the poor-house and charity. The only thing then is to give them work which will supplement their regular work. What I want to ask, is whether attention is being paid to any such solution of this problem?—There are very few who have the leisure and the means to promote a scheme of that kind.

1153. But there would be the ordinary schools to promote a movement of that kind?—Yes, but the whole time is taken up preparing for examinations.

1154. But then there are night schools?—Yes.

1155. But they don't teach industrial work there?—No, not that I am aware of.

1156. So that, if in foreign countries they do this, the best means of getting industrial training are not made use of by us?—No.

1157. Did the local people subscribe to the Mansion House Fund?—I did not advise them to.

1158. What I wanted to know——

1159. (*Chairman*): Canon Legge says that the Lewisham district was obliged to have a Mansion House Fund of its own.

1160. (*Mr. Loch*): But, as a matter of fact, do you suppose that the condition of things is this: that a large number of people in London gave money to the Mansion House Fund, the proceeds of which were distributed in districts comparatively rich? In Lewisham was the fund raised by the Mansion House

The Hon. and Rev. Canon LEGGE.
July 2, 1886.

utilised in comparatively rich districts in Lewisham?—It was used in a district in which there are a sufficient number of well-to-do people to provide against any emergency.

1161. And were those people subscribers to the Mansion House Fund?—That I cannot say.

1162. But it is quite possible. I suppose that money collected from the rich people of the metropolis was being used for a comparatively rich part of your district?—Very little, I should say.

1163. That is, it so happened that one large donation covered the wants of the district?—Our proportion of the fund was not a very large one—we did not have a third of the whole amount assigned to the Greenwich district of which we formed a part.

1164. Then, practically, the wants of the district were relieved by a portion of one large donation, and the call on the other people was not so great as it might have been had the work been done locally?—Yes.

1165. And there was a frightful amount of begging going on at the same time?—Yes.

1166. (*Chairman*): You have been asked about supplemental industry, whether these casual people, jobbing gardeners, should not be trained to fill up the intervals of time when they are not employed in the gardens. You said, I think, that no attempt had been made?—We had an industrial exhibition which was intended to promote that kind of employment.

1167. But why should a man take up a position of that kind?—We gave no outdoor relief to able-bodied men without work in the labour yard. We used that freely.

1168. Is there a medical examination of the persons going to the labour yard, if they say they are unable to do the work in the labour yard?—There is a variety of work, including wood chopping, but if any men say they are unable to do any work, they have to submit to a medical examination.

1169. Had you ever to take a man before the medical officer?—When at work? I don't remember a case.

[*The Committee then adjourned.*]

FRIDAY, JULY 9TH, 1886.

Present—Mr. F. J. S. EDGECOMBE, in the Chair.

Mr. J. H. ALLEN,   Hon. and Rev. A. C. STANLEY,
Mr. C. S. LOCH, *Secretary.*

Mr. T. MACKAY, examined.

Mr. T. MACKAY.
July 9, 1886.

1170. (*Chairman*): You were an Hon. Secretary of the Mansion House Fund Committee in St. George's-in-the-East?—Yes.

1171. How much money was placed at your disposal?—About £300 personally; the whole Committee for St. George's Parish had about £2,000.

1172. All these figures are contained in the printed Report?—Yes.

1173. What instructions did you receive from the Mansion House Committee?—None, till a fortnight after we had started, and by that time we had drawn up rules of our own.

1174. Did you act upon the Mansion House rules?—We continued to act on our own rules; the Mansion House rules were rather wider than ours. I may say there was one thing we did not do. The Mansion House Committee told us not to pay back rent. We had commenced paying back rent, because we found that the arrears of rent were the chief cause of the distress people were in, and we continued to pay it.

1175. Your rules and the Mansion House rules were substantially the same rules?—Yes; not much difference.

Mr. T. MACKAY.
July 9, 1888.

1176. You laid more weight upon some points than they did? Yes; there was one point—about the workhouse test—we did not attempt it, although it appears in our rules.

1177. You have no means of applying any Poor Law labour test except the workhouse in your district?—No; we had no labour yard. We had a small sewing class towards the end.

1178. How far did you comply with the rules?—We did comply with them as far as possible.

1179. Then there were little or no cases of chronic distress? We were supposed to have nothing to do with chronic distress; it was out-of-work cases we felt ourselves authorised to relieve—only out-of-work cases.

1180. Were these cases of habitually out of work?—In that neighbourhood, if you asked a dock labourer whether he was out of work, he would say 'yes' if he had not got work on that day. They have no regular employment; they may be at work three days in the week, and on the other three they would say they are out of work. The dock companies do not know the number required each day.

1181. How did you arrive at the applications? Were they made by letter, or were they made personally at one or more offices?—The first day or two they came by letter. They were forwarded from the Mansion House Committee. Mr. Turner, the chairman, received them, and sent them to the almoners for the various districts. After that we had a public office, and we had such a crowd of applicants that we were obliged to have, I think, four policemen to keep order.

1182. After the first days you received personal application? Did you continue that?—Yes, but when we thought we were getting towards the end of our money we shut up the office.

1183. Were a great many of the applications you received made personally at your offices?—Yes; 80 per cent., I should say.

1184. Could you take down the particulars with the staff at your disposal?—The applicants calling at the office, if they could write, were given a paper to fill up, stating name, number in family, cause of distress, &c.; if they could not write, a clerk took down the application. These papers were sent to me. At first I tried to attend to them all myself. I got the Charity Organisation Society to make some inquiry, but the applications were so numerous that we were 'swamped.' After that, Mr. Turner, the rector, lent me a room, and helped me to organise a Committee. This Committee consisted of one of his curates, the nurse, a mission woman, one of the priests from the Roman Catholic Church, who occasionally attended, two or three gentlemen connected with some of the Nonconformists' churches in the neighbourhood, the City missionaries, the relieving officers and the sanitary officer of the parish. The applications were read over to this Committee—generally someone knew the various applicants; if not, a member of the Committee visited the home and reported. This was done in the morning. I spent the afternoon or evening in going over these reports, and the ultimate decision was left with me. It is practically impossible in this neighbourhood to find out if a man is out of employment or not. We had to give it up as a bad job. If a man had a decent home, and belonged to a club and seemed a provident fellow, substantial assistance was willingly given.

1185. When you got the report, was the case left with you?—Yes.

1186. Such inquiries as you were able to make went mainly to a question of general character?—Mainly, but I do not think they were worth much. There was no employer to consult. The neighbours were most of them applicants themselves. The parish clergyman, in his civil capacity, knows most about the people. Everyone in his parish, whether of his congregation or not, goes to the vestry for advice and assistance when in want. The Roman Catholics and Nonconformists know their own congregations, but our applicants were not, as a rule, of the church-going class, and, except as stated, nothing very definite could be got from the clergy. The relieving officers and sanitary officers naturally know the districts well, and assisted us a good deal. But, on the whole, the investigation, I felt, was rather a farce.

1187. A considerable number of people, then, were relieved who ought not

G

Mr. T. MACKAY.
July 9, 1886.

to have been relieved?—I know one or two were. I saw one woman very drunk the day after she got relief. We got hundreds of applications every day, and it was very difficult. We were told that we were to spend the money, and were urged to hurry.

1188. Had you any communication with the Poor Law people?—The two relieving officers used to look in at the meetings of the Committee I have described. There is no outdoor relief given in St. George's, and, therefore, no chance of overlapping with Poor Law relief.

1189. There are few large employers of labour in that part of the world?—There are some, but, I think, none of their men applied.

1190. Were any of those serving on the Committee?—Yes. Mr. Sly, who is a large sack manufacturer, and Mr. Petherbridge. Mr. Sly employs a number of women, and at slack times they are not constantly employed, and some of them would no doubt apply.

1191. (*Mr. Allen*): Was there any great exceptional distress last winter?—It is a difficult question. I was anxious to find out, and when they were getting this thing up, I went myself to the pawnbrokers and asked them. They said they did not think there was. They were not doing so much business. One man took me round and showed me his books. There was a falling-off in the business that he had done. Mr. Turner suggested that this was evidence of exceptional distress, and that the people had pawned most of their things. The pawnbroker said he thought not, that for some years trade had fallen off. He thought the people were more thrifty. They kept a little money in hand, and did not bank with their pawnbroker as they used to do.

1192. The pawnbrokers, perhaps, could not say whether that was so or not?—The two pawnbrokers agreed that pledges were being redeemed quite up to the average. I also asked one of the grocers. He was of opinion that there was a good deal of distress. The question I generally asked applicants was: 'Have you got anything in pledge?' and they told me. I said I supposed they had to do that every winter. They said, 'Yes, they did; but this winter more than usual'; and I think that was the case. These dock labourers—there are very few artisans—get fair wages in the summer, and buy furniture and Sunday suits of clothes, and in the winter they put them into pawn, and get them out in the spring. They do this every year.

1193. Do you think, from what you have heard and seen, that there is likely to be an outcry again this winter?—There is no reason why there should not be. I don't think that there is any exceptional depression in the shipping trade (that trade has been bad for some years), but a good deal of the trade is leaving St. George's and going lower down the river. It is not a rising neighbourhood.

1194. You say that greater care should be taken to ascertain if exceptional distress exists—you would get information from the Poor Law authorities and clergy. What greater care would you take than that?—There are various charitable societies who know something. Inquiry should be made by districts. As far as I know, no one in East London was consulted about this.

1195. And supposing that distress was proved to be prevalent, would you advocate another Lord Mayor's Fund again?—I confess my own experience was that it was not satisfactory. We may have managed it badly, but I don't think we could have done it differently.

1196. Would you advocate a labour test in all cases before assistance was given?—I would unless a man showed that he was a provident man and had belonged to some friendly club. I don't see how else you can check it. If you go out into the streets and say your pockets are full of sovereigns to be given away, you will have to have four policemen at the door.

1197. Do you know what Mr. Vallance's plan was—sweeping the streets at night?—Yes; but there was the difficulty about that that they have a contract in St. George's. It would have been putting money into the contractor's pockets.

1198. He thought the streets might have been swept twice where they are now swept once?—That is so. My opinion is not worth much on that.

1199. If you have not a labour yard, what form would your labour test take?—We should have to arrange it with the parish authorities. It would have to be done somehow.

1200. Would you advocate a labour yard being opened by the guardians?—You mean whether the expense should fall upon the rates or charity? I don't see why it should not be done together.

1201. (*Chairman*): How would you propose the machinery?—That is a matter for the guardians—they work quite in harmony with the Charity Organisation Society in St. George's. I see no insuperable difficulty in arranging machinery.

1202. (*Mr. Allen*): Would you advocate that, in times of exceptional distress, free dinners should be given to the children and no assistance to the parents?—It is just the same difficulty that arises as when you are dealing with the adults. You cannot tell whether the child's parent is unemployed or not.

1203. Do you know that scheme that was tried at Stoke-on-Trent; it is a long time ago; I think in 1836?—I have heard of it. They opened a labour yard and gave relief in food.

1204. No; those who said they were destitute had their food in the house, but had not to sleep there.—I am not sure that that would not be better than the labour test, which is an interference with the labour market, and you cannot get the people away; you can't get rid of them; they won't draft off. In St. George's, labour is so abominably paid that I believe that any labour yard you would open would be more profitable to them than working at ordinary pay.

1205. You could give it them for a certain time—you may allow a man three weeks, or three days a week?—If you got 100 men at first, and the number rose to 200, the yard would have a tendency to become permanent; but I admit I have no experience of labour yards.

1206. (*Mr. Allen*): In our labour yard in St. Pancras we have no difficulty about it.

1207. (*Mr. Loch*): I suppose you think that one object of good administration would be to prevent the crowding of cases at a given point—such as the office of a Central Committee. The fewer number might then be properly dealt with?—Yes.

1208. With that object would you advocate a very clear public statement, showing what persons would not be assisted?—Certainly; but with illiterate people I do not think you would find that it would have the slightest effect. We had large notices stuck up.

1209. Then you would have to make your arrangements privately?—Yes; if you go out into the streets with your pockets full of sovereigns, and have it advertised that you are going to give them away, there is no end to the applications you will have to deal with. As an instance in point, just round the corner, from our office in St. George's, there is a little court, by no means the poorest in St. George's—I believe that almost every single inhabitant applied. They are all very poor, but a great many of them were no poorer than they always are. This shows how an advertisement brought in applications.

1210. Then the rule of privacy in almsgiving which holds good in regard to ordinary charity would apply to exceptional distress?—Yes; unless the exceptional distress became gigantic.

1211. But take last year as a test?—I think it was. I think the people would have got through; they would have pawned more things. I don't believe that there was starvation going on.

1212. Having created a large number of applications, you could not apply a workhouse test for very shame?—That is so. I do not think our instructions would have warranted it—at all events, it was not done anywhere.

1213. You mean outside St. George's-in-the-East?—I don't think it was done anywhere.

1214. It was not done, I suppose, because people had not thought about it?—Well, I don't know; I thought about it, but considered it impracticable from the reason you suggest.

1215. You say you gave a great deal of money in rent; did not that go to the landlords?—Well, no; because most of the people we relieved were a sort of

Mr. T. MACKAY.
July 9, 1886.

sub-tenants. We generally in paying had a sub-landlord to deal with. The landlord and the tenant often both applied.

1216. Was the relief given mostly in doles?—I think not in every case; we might have given in an exceptional case a few pounds. All these people are very poor people. It is a puzzle how they live. I suppose they never earned more than 10s. a week. You say they must necessarily be in distress, and you give them something; but they are not worse off than usual.

1217. Was the sewing test given to women?—Well, they had to work for their relief.

1218. Did you find that serve the purpose?—Yes; I believe the ladies who managed it were very well satisfied. It would be going on still, I believe.

1219. (*Chairman*): You said there would be a great difficulty in applying a stone yard test on account of the low rate of pay? On account of the intermittent state of labour. What is to prevent a man doing three days' work in the stone yard and three days' work at the docks?

1220. You don't mean that work is harder and more poorly paid at the docks?—Some of it is. Some make large sums, I believe; but there are different sorts of work. I think for ordinary men it is 3s. a day; but it is a good hard day's work, and it is not regular—that is the point.

1221. (*Mr. Allen*): 3s. 4d. a day is the dock labourer's pay.

1222. (*The Hon. and Rev. A. C. Stanley*): Did you give three or four pounds to one person?—I did it, but not frequently. When I got what I considered a good case, I considered it best to set the man right up again, taking his things out of pawn. I was informed that some men so relieved spent the money in drink; I therefore stopped giving money entirely, and, unless I had good reason for it, gave the relief afterwards in tickets only.

1223. What was the smallest amount you gave?—I don't think I gave less than 5s. Generally what I gave was 15s. in three tickets—that is, 5s. a week for three weeks.

Mr. T. W. MARCHANT, examined.

Mr. T. W. MARCHANT.

1224. (*Chairman*): You are the Chairman of the Charity Organisation Committee at Deptford, and you come here to represent the Mansion House Committee at Deptford?—Yes; they were in communication with the Rev. Brooke Lambert, and he was to form a Committee for Deptford, Greenwich, Lewisham, and I think Lee. He convened a meeting from the surrounding districts, and formed Sub-Committees. We met at Greenwich from time to time to discuss questions of policy, but the distribution was left to ourselves.

1225. You are fully acquainted with what went on in Deptford? Did you receive instructions from the Mansion House Committee?—No; from Mr. Lambert.

1226. They were Mansion House instructions?—Yes; there were rules as to labour test—3s. as the amount for single men, and so on.

1227. How much money did you have in Deptford?—£1,250.

1228. And how much did you spend?—We spent the whole of it except about £50 expenses, and a balance in hand of £10. We spent in round numbers £1,200.

1229. How many applications; can you give me that?—No; I have not got that. Our Secretary said that the returns had all been sent in to the Mansion House Committee. I should say that the average of each individual relief was 5s. on each occasion.

1230. Have you any idea how many were relieved?—That would give it you approximately. They had on an average weekly relief for about three weeks. It would give about 1,600 cases relieved.

1231. In what way did you get so many applications?—In the first instance, bills were issued stating that applications for relief might be made at certain places; the Lecture Hall, Deptford, was one of them. We gave notice that we were not relieving chronic cases, but cases out of work. We met Mr. Lambert at Greenwich on Wednesday, and held our first meeting at Deptford on the Friday evening, at which I was not present. I was there morning and evening afterwards daily during the whole week, and we were fairly besieged. The people used to come in crowds, and we had police outside to keep some sort of order, and the applicants were let in one by one. There were two or three committees in different rooms, and they came in and told their tales. In the main I think at first there was not much investigation.

1232. But upon that point—at first the people were relieved on the spot?— Yes, but not without some preliminary form being gone through. The Mansion House Committee in London suggested a form of inquiry to be made in each case. We had these printed in large numbers, and we had persons to see the applicants, so that, in fact, the circumstances of each case were filled up by a clerk.

1233. By the person himself or under his dictation?—Under his dictation. After the first day or day and a half—if any relief was given at once it was of a temporary character—the case stood for inquiry, and each paper was referred to some visitor to get the information.

1234. When you had made the inquiry, did it embrace communication with the employer?—Yes, we asked for all that. The name of last employer, we stipulated for that, but we did not actually refer or make inquiries of the employer.

1235. Any previous address?—Yes, and the number in family; how long in residence; what was their last employment and rate of wages; what amount of pawn tickets they had, and the last employer and some person who could recommend them.

1236. When this paper was entirely completed and inquiry made, what would it have contained beyond the impression of the visitor at the visit, which would be the knowledge of some person living in the district?—They were referred as far as possible to persons living in the district. We had a large committee composed of the clergymen, principal tradesmen, and so on; and eventually we settled into a tolerable system. We ceased after the first week to see applicants personally. We had these forms filled in and brought in, and after the merits of the case had been discussed this relief was given.

1237. Then they were disposed of by the Committee, and not by the almoner? What was the composition of the Committee?—We had ministers of religion; we had district visitors and men of that class, and we were fortunate in having one or two foremen at Braby's and Penn's works, and they were very useful. We had to meet in the morning and take down the cases, and we met in the evening to decide upon them.

1238. Where is the stone yard?—It is in Greenwich.

1239. Were you able to satisfy yourself that the same men who worked there were not relieved by you?—We had a list of the stone-yard cases before us.

1240. Was it your opinion that there was much exceptional distress in Deptford?—There is a good deal of distress now. The whole of the ship-builders are out of work. The trade seems to have left.

1241. So that there was exceptional distress?—Yes. Another cause of distress was that Penn's closed their works and threw out of employment a very deserving class of men.

1242. And did you find that this superior class of men were got in by your inquiries?—Yes; we were able to pay up their clubs for them; they did not apply in the first few days.

1243. Do you think that your money reached the proper quarter?—I have no doubt that it went to relieve cases of distress. There may have been some mistakes, of course—a lot of dock labourers and people undeserving.

1244. If you had time to make your arrangements, should you make them as before?—I should avoid the system on which we worked at first, of allowing all these people to come to us. The idea had got about that there was this large sum of money subscribed at the Mansion House; and when people saw this distribution going on, if it had not been done publicly they would have suspected some fraud was going on. However, we soon found out that the first arrangement would not do.

1245. You heard the evidence of the last witness, in which he expressed an

Mr. T. W. MARCHANT.
July 5, 1886.

opinion adverse to a public fund as compared with one administered by existing institutions or private individuals?—No doubt about that. Good is done by stealth—if the money had been collected privately, and distributed without this notoriety, it would have done many times as much good.

1246. (*Mr. Allen*): Are Penn's works closed altogether?—No; they are keeping their plant in order, but they have no contracts on hand.

1247. And in the next winter, the working people of Deptford will probably be as badly off as ever?—No; the workmen will get work elsewhere; and though Penn's have not the contracts, Maudeslay's have got contracts, and the Arsenal at Woolwich ——

1248. In the event of exceptional distress next winter, are you in favour of a labour test if it were possible?—If you could put men into work. If a man is starving, you must give him something at once; subject to that, the best thing is to give him work.

1249. Mr. Vallance has mentioned a test to be applied to all these people—to make them sweep the streets.—Mr. Lambert brought forward that plan before the District Board of Works for Greenwich. They were asked to organise it. I don't know if there was any disinclination on the part of officials, but it never came to anything. In Lewisham, they cleared and embanked a part of the Ravensbourne; and, in Lee, a hill was levelled; and in the neighbourhood of Deptford employment was given in making ornamental gardens.

1250. Was that in connection with Lord Brabazon's Society?—Yes.

1251. Deptford is not a suburban Union, and, therefore, you would not be able to give the same amount of work as Greenwich?—We are part of the Greenwich Union.

1252. Then employment might be found for people in the suburbs, like levelling ground?—Yes.

1253. Did the guardians give outdoor relief in Greenwich?—Yes, they do.

1254. Do they do it freely?—No.

1255. Judiciously?—It is chiefly confined to old persons over 60. I don't think they are extravagant in giving it.

1256. Did you find many persons come in from the country?—No; we relieved no one not resident.

1257. No, but who came to reside there on that account?—No, I did not find that; its operation was too short.

1258. You managed to keep the people for as long as three weeks?—Some had relief as many as five weeks—the cold weather continued such a very long time. It was the greatest cause of distress. A large number of people, unemployed during the winter—painters and such classes—found they had to hold on five or six weeks longer than usual.

1259. Did you find it possible to distinguish between chronic cases and real cases?—Yes; ultimately I think we could have worked it pretty well.

1260. And the amount that you had—was the amount sufficient, or was it merely a drop?—We did not want any more. They offered us more and we did not take it.

1261. (*Mr. Loch*): You said superior men in the end came in on account of one man telling of another?—Yes; it was very much the case.

1262. Then gradually you got touch of that class through the foremen you mentioned?—Yes; and through the district visitors. Many of the people had resided in their lodgings for many years, and the people in Penn's had been reduced to overwhelming distress.

1263. But that you learned not from their own applications but from the knowledge that people already had of the distress?—Yes; that was so.

1264. And at any future time such a plan in the district might be trusted to again?—Certainly.

1265. Then these inquiries you had made, was the inquiry made by a volunteer?—Entirely.

1266. Did they get to know the facts of a case?—Yes; we were all educated by our experience.

1267. And did you find that you gave not merely an allowance, a sum down, but relief adjudicated to the wants of a case?—Yes; in some cases we went beyond the Mansion House Fund. We gave some as much as 10s. a week. We went further by paying the club, and took things out of pawn; when they showed that they were in work we helped them in taking their things out of pawn.

1268. If there were to be a recurrence of distress, could the public rely upon somebody in Deptford being able to draw together certain leading men who would have touch of the best artisan class?—Yes, to a certain extent—not perfectly—but tolerably.

1269. Were the cases in Committee taken at a great rate?—At first, but afterwards with fair deliberation.

1270. You think it is better that you should not see the applicants personally?—In some cases we allowed them to come and see us, but the most respectable class did not care to come.

1271. Is the work as well as the labourer in the neighbourhood?—The dock labourers live with us, but their work is the other side of the river.

1272. But still they would be the paupers under the Poor Law?—Perfectly true.

1273. Are you not liable to this everywhere, more or less?—Very soon we ceased relieving dock labourers. They had to shift for themselves every winter, and were no worse off than usual.

1274. Do they apply to the Poor Law?—Some of them, but no one knows how they live. In the summer these men can get £2. 2s. a week.

1275. (Mr. Allen): It is those who carry the timber. Most of them live on their wives and children, I think?—Possibly. When Mr. Fuller was on our Committee, some attempt to organise some provident system among them was made, but nothing substantial was effected.

1276. (Mr. Loch): At any rate, this attempt had no permanent result?—Quite so.

1277. Was there any attempt made to make the relief tend to providence and thrift?—Only so far that we encouraged those who showed they were thrifty; those in clubs had favour shown to them.

1278. Did you pay rent?—No; none whatever.

1279. That is distinctly contrary to the previous witness?—Yes.

1280. Your reason?—I suppose our connection with this Society. It was due to that.

1281. Are there not a large number who sublet the houses in your neighbourhood?—There are a great many, but not in the poor class.

1282. Was the relief generally in kind?—No; about two-fifths in kind. Where we found deserving people whom we could thoroughly trust, we gave in money, because our impression was that it would go as far again.

1283. The more you could trust the people, the more you would give in money?—Yes.

1284. So that the relief in kind would be the test to show doubtful cases?—That is it.

1285. Would you propose—supposing another public fund—anything like a direct statement of the classes which you would approve of as classes for relief, and classes that you would like to exclude?—Yes; I think it is a desirable thing—very desirable.

Mr. W. HEALE, examined.

1286. (Chairman): What district?—Wandsworth and Clapham.

1287. You were on the Mansion House Committee?—Yes, and was Hon. Secretary for the three Committees of Battersea.

1288. Did all the money that came pass through your hands?—Yes, all three divisions.

1289. How much money?—Well, I have not got it, but I think it was about £1,700 for Battersea.

1290. Was that under the supervision of one Committee?—No, three Committees. One had £700, another £600, and another had £400. £100 and odd was returned.

Mr. W. HEALE.
July 9, 1886.

1291. Can you give me the number of persons that applied? I think No. 1 Committee had about 700 ; No. 2 Committee had 1,300 ; and No. 3, 1,200.

1292. How many of those were relieved?—About 75 per cent.

1293. Had you instructions from the Mansion House?—We started very early. We drew up a code of rules which the Mansion House adopted.

1294. Those are the rules we are acquainted with?—We adhered to those very closely. We had a rule that if a person had resided in the parish less than three months—no, six months—they got no relief. We got them all to come to the Committees. They had forms which they had to fill up, and the inquiries were carried out in each case. The clergymen and others examined each case in his own district.

1295. After they had made their inquiries, did they send in their reports?—They came back to the Committee with the forms, and the Committee decided upon them. After the first time the condition of relief was decided by the visitor.

1296. In the first instance the visitor?—No ; in the first instance the Committee decided the case ; when the forms were brought back after inquiry, the Committee decided how much he should have. Then relief was given week after week, but that was decided by the visitor.

1297. What points were the inquiries directed to? Were you able to communicate with the employer?—No ; in the district in which we lived many belong to the building trade—stonemasons, bricklayers, and so on. The men work all over London ; we could not get at the employers at all.

1298. Was a reference seen in most cases? We had no references. We had to take the visitors and clergymen, who reported after visiting in their own districts.

1299. Your impression, so far as you can form an opinion, was that the information you got was sufficient to enable you to come to a correct decision?—No, I am afraid not, but in the short time it was the best that could be done.

1300. Did it go to the right quarters, do you think?—Some went where it should not go, no doubt.

1301. You have heard the last two gentlemen give their evidence ; do you agree with them that so much publicity is undesirable?—Well, perhaps it was, but we did the other way. We got overflooded with people, and it was quite a week or ten days before we could attend to them. I am inclined to think that publicity was the best thing for it. If it had been given in a private manner we should not have found out so many deserving people - these people who have been relieved. The very first sum that was sent was sent to the clergy, and that was administered worse than afterwards. I don't think too much publicity could be given in a matter of this kind.

1302 In fact, you take an opposite view to that taken by these two gentlemen?—Yes, we found many cases that were deserving, and many that were not, by inquiries in the neighbourhood. One would tell us, 'He ought not to have it ; I saw him in such-and-such a house ; he is a drunken man,' and so on. We have streets of poor people, and the clergy know them well ; and we got all the clergy and dissenting ministers, and they went about together, and each case was visited.

1303. Is there a stone yard in your neighbourhood?—We knew that there was a great deal of distress. We were building a workhouse, and we determined to utilise the labour and not open a stone yard, but to make them dig sand, which would be better than breaking stones—dig out the sand and put in the foundations—and give them 2s. 6d. a day. The Mansion House Fund Committees sent up the people. The money was to be paid by the poor rates ; and we gave the Mansion House Committees the means of testing their cases.

1304. Did the Committee avail themselves of the offer?—We said the first two days we could take on 200, and we got 300 ; then we got to 250, and after six weeks we got back to 95.

1305. You consider that experiment a success?—I am sure of that. I saw the men at work and found many men there whose hands were bleeding with the work—men who had never handled a spade before.

Mr. W. HESLE.
July 9. 1886.

1306. Did you get good work out of them?—We did not. We did not expect it. We thought it better to get sand which we could get rid of, and we thought, if we did lose a little, it would be better than stone breaking. There is a knack in breaking stones.

1307. (*Chairman*): Yes, I have tried it myself and don't like it. It requires some geological knowledge to break a stone properly.—We have spent some £1,200, and have only lost £30, so that the poor rates have not suffered.

1308. In your part of the world, as in other parts, is outdoor relief——?—We don't give outdoor relief, except to widows and children, and a few aged people. We are a young parish; we have no old people. We have a lot of young men come down there, and they have perhaps died off and left their widows and children, and these we take in hand.

1309. (*Mr. Allen*): There was great distress, you think?—I am sure of it.

1310. Do you think, as a guardian, you would have been able to cope with it?—We were preparing for it. We saw a lot of it. I was living in the midst of it myself. We got the relieving officers to report some weeks before whether there was exceptional distress in their district, and they reported that there was.

1311. Most of the Unions reported that there was not?—I am inclined to think that the fault lay with the relieving officers. It is their habit to report that there is not more than usual of distress, because they only go by the applications on their books, and there are many people who never apply to the relieving officer.

1312. If there was this exceptional distress, would they not apply to the relieving officer?—Never.

1313. You think that was the only ground on which the relieving officer made his report?—We told them to go and make inquiries. If you take a relieving officer's word, he will say, 'I have no more applications this week than last.' There are hundreds of working men in our district who are above the workhouse and would rather starve.

1314. Your district is inhabited by a better class?—We have not the real ragged pauper.

1315. You have no slums?—No, none whatever.

1316. They are all working men?—Yes; men earning two or three guineas a week.

1317. Were those men working at the sand? Were they clerks?—Yes; clerks I think. There were some thirty or forty out of employment. We made it a rule; we put a ganger on, and told him that, if a man was not accustomed to the work, to work him lightly.

1318. You advocate a labour test—that you think is an absolute necessity?—Yes.

1319. And would you advocate another Mansion House Fund being raised?—Not administered in the same way.

1320. Would you advocate it?—Yes; I don't think we could get money otherwise. The administration was what was bad.

1321. And you think, with the experience you have had, you would be able to administer it very much better?—I am afraid we should not administer it much better, because we have not time to make proper inquiries.

1322. But suppose you had got your machinery in form a month beforehand?—They are simple volunteers; they have to take what people say.

1323. The men live down there, and they work in all parts of London?

1324. (*Chairman*): Did it ever occur to you that you might make the inquiries by letter?—We had thought of that: we had two clerks at work.

1325. Would it not have been well to have more clerks? I had to manage an operation of the sort, and the employers answered wonderfully well.—A great deal more might have been done if we had time.

1326. (*Mr. Allen*): You don't think that, in the event of there being exceptional distress, there would not be proper time to make proper inquiries?—No; the rush is too great. When you get 300 or 400 rushing into a room every day, it is impossible. You could not do much in two or three hours.

1327. You say you would object to money being raised privately?—I am afraid the wrong people would get it just the same.

Mr. W. Heale.
July 9, 1886.

1328. Would you suggest that a federation of charities such as the Charity Organisation Society and the Mansion House Fund, to relieve distress, &c., would work together?—Supposing they could get the funds.

1329. Supposing the Lord Mayor made the application to the people to pay their money to them?—I think it would be much better.

1330. Under these circumstances it would be better than having a Mansion House Fund?

1331. (*Mr. Loch*): You said that you relied upon publicity to check the applications?—Not to check the applications, but to check the giving of relief.

1332. But if your inquiry had been what you would have wished, then the need of publicity would be less?—Quite so.

1333. But under the circumstances you found there always will be great pressure?—Yes.

1334. And that pressure makes sufficient inquiry impossible?—What I consider sufficient inquiry.

1335. Then does that not point to the great undesirability of a fund?—Oh, yes, I don't agree with a fund administered as it was last time.

1336. And it is difficult to administer a large fund any other way?—Quite so.

1337. Then the question comes again, if we are to do justice to the applicants, in the administration of such a fund we must deal with comparatively few?—Quite so.

1338. Would you state that such-and-such cases would not be assisted?—We did in our district.

1339. Persons who had not resided three months, and who had been out of work for six months, &c.; and conversely also you said that those who had made a good struggle for themselves would be assisted?—Yes.

1340. So far you are satisfied with the programme you have got?—We were not very liberal.

1341. You say guardians are to deal with destitution?—Yes.

1342. Yet there was comparatively little pressure on the Poor Law?—Yes.

1343. Then the Poor Law did not perform its function?—Yes; the Poor Law could not deal with the poor except on application.

1344. Apart from application being made to the Poor Law, the destitution would not be relieved by the Poor Law?—It never is. You mean to say that a large amount of destitution was not dealt with by the guardians?

1345. Yes; and the reason for not dealing with the destitution through the Poor Law Guardians was what?—Because the poor do not apply.

1346. Then there are two classes of persons who want work and will not apply to the Poor Law—what one may call the respectable and the idle. Did you reject the latter?—Oh! a large number.

1347. Referring them to the Poor Law?—Oh! a large number of doubtful cases which the Poor Law would not relieve, except by the workhouse, applied to the Mansion House Fund and were sent to the labour-yard test. Some would not accept it.

1348. How did these people live?—We see them standing at the street corners all the year round. I think their wives must get their living at the laundries about.

1349. Then, owing to the labour of the wives, the Poor Law is not wanted for their destitution?—We cannot alter the Poor Law.

1350. We will take the other class; the Poor Law does not affect them, because they will not apply. Is it to be taken for granted that, under these circumstances, we are to have relief funds created by charity?—I think not. I think poor people can always tide through the winter as a rule.

1351. You think it was an exceptional winter?—I am quite sure.

1352. And with an exceptional winter like this, we must be prepared to have funds—special funds?—Well, I don't know if one could be prepared with a fund waiting. But I think we shan't get such a winter again for some years.

1353. Is not trade very bad?—Yes, I think I mentioned that; but I found from some I applied to that they had a lot of things in pawn and are redeeming them.

1354. Does not that show that that will recur next winter? You think that there is enough flush of work to enable them to recover those?—Yes.

1355. You say many builders out of work—do you mean the whole of them?—Yes, right through.

1356. Are there any who would emigrate?—Very few. Two applied in the whole district—one at Putney, and one at Clapham.

1357. And do you think the building operations are carried on with the same vigour?—Yes; large districts of small streets are being built now.

1358. And they can get local work and do not care to emigrate?—Just so.

1359. You had several working men in connection with the Mansion House Fund Committee?—Yes, some 12 or 15.

1360. And you found that you heard from them of people in distress?—No, whether people were deserving.

1361. Did you find that they knew of people who would not apply publicly, and who ought to be helped?—They did not mention it.

1362. Then what was said just now by Mr. Marchant would not be applicable to Battersea?—Not to our district.

1363. Under circumstances like last winter complete information is desirable in regard to the state of the labour market?—Yes.

1364. You made inquiry through the relieving officers?—Yes.

1365. As to the amount of distress?—Yes.

1366. And you gave them instructions to go and find it out?—Yes, that was through my asking the relieving officer whether there was not more than ordinary distress, when he said, 'Oh, no, no more than usual.' I then made inquiries for some few weeks, in consequence of which I moved that we should give the relieving officers instructions to go and inquire at the houses, and not rest satisfied with the reply, 'Oh, we have no more applications than usual.' The result was that they found that the people would not apply; but they said there was a lot of distress after they had inquired in the neighbourhood.

1367. This is a most vital question. Would you send in future years, not as a guardian, but as an individual; would you write to employers, or in any way, early in November, learn how the tide was going?—You might get where trade was brisk; but I think each district should be visited, and in each district each street. It is quite easy to know. The neighbours can give you the name of every one in the street who is out of employ. We should test the cases. But when we made it known that the Mansion House Fund was coming, the people were able to give me the names of cases all down the street.

1368. Would you be able to distinguish between winter chronic out-of-work cases and exceptional cases?—There is nothing the poor detest more than these chronic out-of-work cases.

1369. And you would suggest some such previous investigation as that?—Yes.

1370. (*Chairman*): One more question. You say that there was a great deal of distress in your district, though the relieving officer's books showed no increase of applications. It is true, I should imagine, taking the building trade as a starting point, that the same circumstances would have applied to a lower class?—You cannot get even the labourer in the winter to apply to the workhouse. They say, 'We break up the home, and we come out in the spring worse off than when we went in.'

1371. There are a certain class who won't apply; but is there not a class who will apply—a much lower grade? By the circumstances that would bring the higher class down, the lower class would also be pinched, and they would apply to the workhouse?—But the very worst men, if able bodied, won't apply to the workhouse.

1372. (*Mr. Loch*): Would it be practicable to apply such a test as was applied at Stoke-on-Trent, where the people came to the workhouse for their meals, but did not sleep there? At that time there was a very severe local crisis from lack of work; this test was applied, and it answered in a wonderful way; the applications dwindled down quickly, and there was no disturbance of the labour market by the creation of unnecessary works.—Did wives and children come in?

1373. Yes; wives and children all came in.—We could not feed all the wives and children of those that would apply.

Mr. W. HEALE.
July 9, 1886.

1374. The question is the validity of the test?—I think the stone-yard test is a very hard one, because the man works for ninepence a day, and gets half of that in kind.

1375. (*Chairman*): The respectable artisan who never applies finds it very hard to break stones, whereas to the loafer it is very easy.—I don't like stone-breaking.

1376. (*Mr. Loch*): Would you not be prepared to fall back on cleaning the roads?—That is all done by contract. That would be putting money in the pockets of the contractors.

1377. I am trying to find a way out of the difficulty you suggest.—We find we were under great difficulty in finding some employment for the unemployed, and we could not do it because of the contracts. If the Clapham district had been their own scavengers, we could have done it very well.

1378. Taking this view of the question, that it is desirable to give other labour than the stone yard, would you be prepared to carry out earthworks at a comparatively low rate of wage or would you pay the contract price?—No, not more than half contract prices; the work is not worth half-a-crown. If you have a ganger there, some people are worth 2s. Some people don't do. You have to put up with half work, because, if a man has never wheeled a barrow before, you could not expect him to do it.

1379. That was his incompetency, and not laziness?—Just so.

MISS M. M. GEE, examined.

Miss M. M. GEE.

1380. (*Chairman*): You have had some experience in Deptford?—Yes.

1381. What you are going to tell us now is not particularly about the Mansion House Fund?—I had something to do in it, but I had to give it up.

1382. Were you a member of the Committee for Deptford?—Yes, I was in the commencement, and acted in the work later on, and helped them with the inquiries.

1383. You were present when it was mentioned what was done as to the applications made in the first two or three days?—I think they were improperly dealt with.

1384. Could you have suggested an improved way? Did they come by three or four hundred a day, being seen by sub-committees, and was relief given on the few inquiries that could be made? Were you present when that was going on?—I was.

1385. Several improper persons must have been relieved?—Yes.

1386. When you got more into swing, were you still a member of the Committee?—They were just getting into swing when I left them.

1387. They never saw the employer?—I investigated in a few cases myself, according to the directions of the Committee, and found it most unsatisfactory.

1388. How far did you push the inquiry?—I was first told to go to the home and question with regard to the work. I was not obliged to go to the employer. Later on there were relief works under the Kyrle Society. I made inquiries. I asked for letters; they were brought by the applicants; but I could test whether they were genuine. They had them principally from the foreman of Penn's works.

1389. So far as your observation goes, did the relief that was administered by the Committee reach the genuine cases?—I think it was a mere chance whether it reached cases of genuine distress or whether they were chronic cases, or cases where work was given up to get at the fund.

1390. Do you think there was distress which it failed to touch?—I am sure of that.

1391. Some witnesses have expressed the opinion that the fund itself was a failure. Can you suggest that, if benevolent persons had sent their money to local societies instead of the Mansion House Fund, it would have been better?—I should have thought that the branch of the Charity Organisation Society would have done better.

Miss M. M. Gee.

July 9, 1886.

1392. You would suggest that a large subscription to the Charity Organisation Society would have answered better?—Yes.

1393. Are you a member of the Society in that part of the world?—Yes.

1394. Had they anything to do with the administration of the fund? The Committee of the Charity Organisation Society helped with the Mansion House Fund Committee, but not officially.

1395. Were their offices made use of?—Not at all.

1396. You have experience as a rent collector, I think?—Yes; Miss Hill is working down there, and I am under her. I only collect from six houses, but I have to do with some of the other houses, and sometimes was asked to do what was necessary in regard to sanitary operations.

1397. Did you practically find that your tenants were much more in arrear than usual?—Yes

1398. Were you able to apply your severe rules to these persons?—In some cases. I think now only one of my own tenants, who form a very small part of the whole, has increased her arrears. All the others stand as they did last winter.

1399. You don't know if any were able to hold their own by assistance from the Mansion House Fund?—The only one of my own that I got assistance for disappeared in the middle of the night.

1400. Are you able to speak as to the general distress in the district—as to the distress being exceptionally great?—Only as far as the cases coming before the Charity Organisation Society; and also, I believe, there was an increase of applications to the poor house.

1401. (*Chairman*): I think the contrary is the case.

(Mr. Loch read an extract as to the fact of there being fewer applications.*)

1402. That was the reply sent by the Board in February to the Local Government Board?—I cannot speak with any confidence about it. We heard that there had been an increase of applications.

1403. Was the Charity Organisation Committee of opinion that there was exceptional distress among the class that applied to them?—We thought there was more distress, but we could not prove it by our own books.

1404. Was there more distress among your tenantry?—Yes, in March and April.

1405. (*Mr. Allen*): Should you be in favour of a Mansion House Fund being raised again in case of a severe winter?—Yes, if it were distributed by the Charity Organisation Society.

1406. Would you call an Official Committee, composed of the Charity Organisation Society and the Almoners of the Society for Relief of Distress, and some of the clergy, a body of administrators you would approve?—Yes.

1407. Do you think the publicity of the Mansion House Fund a good or a bad thing?—I think it did harm.

1408. You would be in favour of funds being raised privately instead of publicly—that the Lord Mayor were to ask the public to strengthen the bonds of private societies?—Would it be given over to a local Committee?

1409. The question which I wanted to know from you was, whether you would strengthen the hands of existing charitable institutions in Deptford rather than appeal to the Lord Mayor?—Yes.

1410. (*Mr. Loch*): You attended the Committees at the Mansion House for the first fortnight or three weeks?—

1411. Could you in any way describe the way in which, actually, decisions were taken—was it done very fast?—Done very fast indeed. First of all we had two clerks writing, and forms were filled up, simply from the statements of the applicants, and they were handed in and judged of by the Committee. There was investigation as to second applications afterwards.

1412. Judging from special cases within your own knowledge, do you think

---

* The Clerk to the Guardians, Greenwich Union, 17th February, 1886: 'There has not been recently any unusual increase in the number of applications for out-relief, which are now rather less than in the corresponding period last year.... No exceptional arrangements appear to be necessary at the present time to meet the distress, with which they have to deal.'—*Return, Pauperism and Distress, 8th March*, 1886.

Miss M. M. GEE.
July 9, 1886.

that harm was distinctly done—that people were degraded by the relief?—I think so. Those who deserved least were helped.

1413. The people that you went to were people who required to be raised up, and some character to be put into them?—Yes, they wanted energy and increase of self-respect, and this rather decreased it.

1414. Could we arrange to get such information in your district as to enable us to judge of the amount of distress in your neighbourhood before coming to such a pass?—I don't think we have any organisation for such a purpose at present.

1415. As to the collection of information as to the amount of distress, could they get better information than last year?—I don't think they have any means of obtaining it.

1416. There is no single person in Deptford who could do it?

1417. Did you inquire into these cases?—A few of them.

1418. Did you find it possible with other work on hand to do it at all thoroughly?—I did at first. I was asked afterwards to go to the homes and make inquiries. In some places I found them very comfortable, and in one case I found them sitting down to a meat dinner. I went sometimes in the daytime and sometimes in the evening.

1419. And the greater distress was in March and April?—In my own experience.

1420. That is to say, the distress became felt—the results of the pressure showed themselves?—I think so.

1421. Did you find somewhat later that there was distress owing to the severity of the winter and out of work?—In many cases the distress has continued to the present time. It is almost as severe now as in the spring.

1422. What is being done now for the people?—Nothing on any definite plan.

1423. So that practically we only dealt with a crisis, which we, so to speak, created in our imaginations?—I think so.

1424. Is there anything that you would suggest that would touch the radical evil that is going on now? Are these people likely to find work?—I should think emigration or supplemental labour.

1425. But practically there is a great deal of out-of-work which is not being helped now?—Yes.

(*The Committee then adjourned.*)

FRIDAY, JULY 16TH, 1886.

Present—THE HON. AND REV. CANON LEGGE, in the Chair.

Rev. BROOKE LAMBERT,
Mr. A. G. CROWDER,
Rev. W. CURTIS HAYWARD,
Mr. J. H. ALLEN,

Hon. and Rev. A. C. STANLEY,
Dr. G. B. LONGSTAFF,
Mr. E. PETERS,

Mr. R. HEDLEY, attending on behalf of the Local Government Board.

Mr. C. S. LOCH, *Secretary*.

MRS. AVIS, examined.

Mrs. AVIS.
July 16, 1886.

1426. (*Chairman*): You reside in Walworth, I believe, Mrs. Avis?—Yes; at 5 Refferton Street, Weston Street, Old Kent Road.

1427. And are there any special points that you would wish to be examined upon?—Not that I know of. I have known the district for the last twenty years, and there is a great improvement in the people in St. Mary's, Newington.

1428. And you consider the condition of the people is improved?—Wonderfully, especially within the last few years.

Mrs. Avis.
July 16, 1886.

1429. You think there has been a tendency for the better-to-do people to move further off?—Yes.

1430. And that the population is of a poorer class?—No; I find the people whom I have to work with move away as soon as they are better off. We have new people continually coming in.

1431. And the process is a process of improvement while they are there?—Yes.

1432. Were you connected with the Mansion House Fund when it was going on?—Yes.

1433. And in your experience was there more distress or less distress than usual in the winter?—Something after the same—not more than usual—and the general condition of the people was better than it had been.

1434. That is in consequence of their own improvement in the way of thrift?—Yes; I think there is a very great deal of improvement, and the temperance movement has done a great deal of good. We have a working men's club, and there are the different lodges of temperance.

1435. Do you think that there was any special occasion for the Mansion House Fund?—Yes; I know many cases in which the homes would have been broken up but for that.

1436. Were those cases which would not have occurred in previous years?—No; it was slackness of work. I know two cases where the homes would have been broken up but for that fund.

1437. What are the details of those cases?—One was a case that came from Newcastle, and one was a man who was out of employment for four months, and his clothes got so shabby that Miss Grogan advanced him money to get clothes, and then he got employment again.

1438. What was his employment previously?—A salesman.

1439. Is that a man who is employed by others?—Yes; the cause of severance was the failure of trade. They had to reduce their staff.

1440. What particular trade was he concerned with?—The boot business.

1441. And you consider that there was more slackness last winter than in previous winters?—Yes.

1442. Was that before the winter came on?—Yes; and I am afraid of another like it.

1443. Suppose we go back to the winter of 1884-85, would there have been a special fund in that winter?—No; Mr. Praed was exceedingly kind that winter. The distress has been gradually coming on for the last five years.

1444. And it reached the worst point last winter?—Yes.

1445. Under these circumstances, do you consider that there should be another Mansion House Relief Fund?—That is a question I could hardly answer.

1446. Have you any idea in your own mind how to meet the cases of distress?—I have heard that there are a few pounds left from the Relief Fund, and I think it ought to be reserved for the coming winter.

1447. What plan was adopted last winter in your district for the distribution of the fund?—On No. 1 Board, I think there were eleven members appointed, and out of the eleven there were two or three working men to investigate the cases.

1448. A committee of eleven, two of whom were working men?—Yes.

1449. They all knew the people very well?—Yes.

1450. In what form was relief given for the most part?—Money, and tickets for grocery, meat, coals, &c.

1451. Were there a very large number of applications?—Very great; we did not relieve all.

1452. Could you give me the number?—I think, by what I could judge, there were between three and four hundred.

1453. And how many did you relieve?—Mr. Golds relieved fifty, I think, through my help.

1454. That was in that ward?—Yes; No. 1 Ward.

1455. Now, in the case of those fifty who were relieved, you have told us of one case; would most of them be similar cases to that?—Yes. There was a

Mrs. Avis.
July 16, 1886.

case of the name of Broad. They were very destitute, and were relieved to the amount of £3 or £4. And another case in Townsend Street, Kent Road— they were relieved to the amount of £3.

1456. If fifty were relieved out of three or four hundred, that would leave many who were not relieved—why were they refused?—I don't know that they were refused.

1457. But I suppose there were undeserving cases in the ward?—Yes; we had to use our own judgment.

1458. Was careful investigation made?—Yes, we investigated all; there were Mr. Golds, Mr. Lafone, and others.

1459. Were there any guardians on your Committee?—Yes, several of them.

1460. Were you in communication with the Charity Organisation Society?— Yes.

1461. Were any members of the local committee of the Charity Organisation Society members of your Committee?—Mr. Gardiner used to attend the local committee.

1462. Did you refer any cases to the Charity Organisation Society for investigation?—Yes; to Miss Grogan.

1463. Do you consider that next winter the distress is likely to be as great?— Yes; emigration is a most difficult question. They don't like to leave.

1464. And there has been no signs of revival of trade this summer?—Not any.

1465. Supposing there were the same amount of distress next winter, you said that there was a certain sum over which should be reserved to apply in the way of relief?—Yes.

1466. Is that surplus sufficient to meet your wants?—No.

1467. Then you think it would be desirable to raise another fund to carry people through the winter next year, or as long as the fund lasts? And with regard to the manner of administration, would you propose it should be administered by Committees as last year?—Yes. There were some discontented people, but, as a rule, we found them very satisfied.

1468. Which do you consider best, money or kind?—They all prefer money, but it is not well to give money at all times.

1469. Under what circumstances would it not be well?—Sometimes they make a bad use of it.

1470. Did you inquire into the character?—Yes, and if the character was good we would give them relief.

1471. You mean that in some cases of relief given the persons relieved were not the very best characters?—No. But some don't lay out the money properly. If they have to get provisions, they don't make it go as far as it might be made to go.

1472. Would it not be well that they should learn by experience how to spend money?—Yes; but it's a hard task.

1473. I suppose they think they would be able to do better for themselves?— We can't make them understand that.

1474. You mean they do not make it go as far as possible?—Yes.

1475. With some of them you were acquainted before?—Yes; I have lived so long with them—in amongst them all.

1476. Have you had applications from classes you would not have expected them from?—No; very few indeed.

1477. This is a state of affairs that you think now is chronic in your district?— Yes.

1478. Is there anything that you suggest that would relieve the distress, apart from the Mansion House Fund—to improve their position?—No. It is a thing I have often thought of and studied, but I can't do it. You may lead them sometimes by being kind.

1479. But by being kind you don't necessarily employ them?—No; there is no employment now starting. In a few weeks we shall lose many; they will be going into the country harvesting and hop-picking.

1480. But they will come back, and be again on your hands?—Yes; they will come back, no doubt.

1481. What is the trade in the district?—Costermongers and labourers, and brush drawers.

Mrs. Ayre.
July 16, 1886.

1482. And there is slackness in the trade?—Yes, in the brush trade especially.

1483. You mentioned bootmakers?—Yes, and they are slack also.

1484. Then I suppose the only thing would be to go elsewhere?—Yes; they are paid so badly for their work.

1485. That is another reason for going elsewhere, to be better paid?—They cannot find it; that is the difficulty.

1486. (*Rev. Brooke Lambert*): You spoke of the class of people having improved—you mean by reason of the generality of them belonging to clubs?—No; they are improved in themselves; they are cleaner, much cleaner.

1487. They take better care of their money?—Yes, some of them.

1488. Do you like to get them to belong to clubs?—Yes; we have an Investment Society in Green Walk; we have 2,000 members in it. The money is divided at Christmas, and it begins the first week in the new year, and they go on for fifty weeks, and that entitles them to 25s. I cannot get many to do it. They let their children put their pennies and farthings into it, because they have a share which provides them with boots for the winter.

1489. Or you give interest?—Yes, £1 for every share, with 1s. 6d. added and last year they shared 26s. 8d. each share.

1490. Do you ever find them going into the Post Office Savings Bank?—Very few indeed.

1491. The people who keep 28s. 6d. in the whole year, they cannot be the costermongers?—Oh! they could do more than that if they liked.

1492. Do not they take it out to pay their rent?—There's a good many of them do that.

1493. You have mentioned those two special cases. Were those two special cases of the class you ordinarily have to do with?—No; of a better class.

1494. As regards your own people, did many of them come to the Mansion House Fund?—No; very few of them.

1495. How was it when the distress was so bad that the ordinary people did not come?—No; Mr. Praed was very kind, who gave me money to help the people that I knew, and also Miss Praed.

1496. Then the Mansion House Fund was a supply outside the charitable resources of the district?—Yes.

1497. Then you said that one of these cases had lately come from Newcastle?—Yes.

1498. Have you had many coming up to London?—No; this man married one of our girls in the district, and trade was so bad that he took her down to Newcastle, but there he found he did no better, and so he brought her back to London.

1499. You have not heard people say they prefer London?—No, they prefer the country if they can get work.

1500. Then the other case. You said this salesman had been out of employment for four months, and, in consequence of the badness of his clothes, he did not get work. What was the ordinary work which he would have done?—He met with an accident and had been helped before. We had to give him the amount of 7s. a week. He hurt his knee-cap and was attended at the Surrey Dispensary for months. He had to give up a good situation because he could not kneel to fit on ladies' boots. He got this other situation, but, owing to the slackness of trade, they had to discharge him.

1501. Is he a saving man?—Yes; they are very careful people.

1502. You hoped the fund would be reserved to next year; if people knew that, would not people who would be trying to get away stay on that account?—You must think, then, that they are impostors?

1503. It takes a great deal to move people from their native place, and the existence of a fund would perhaps tend to induce them not to make an effort to go?—I think so.

1504. With regard to those people who you said were relieved with meat and grocery and coal tickets because they could not be trusted with money, were

H

Mrs. AVIS.
July 16, 1886.

they cases that would never be treated by the guardians?—They don't like the house, and they won't go in. They don't care for breaking up their home.

1505. They were able-bodied men?—Yes, there were just a few elderly men, but they could work.

1506. You said something about your belief that tickets must be given. Have you heard of cases where, when they had a ticket and took it to the shop, they had the ticket taken off their bill instead of getting goods?—No.

1507. And you never met the statement that when no money was brought to the shop they got the worst goods?—No, I know that Mr. Emery in the Old Kent Road gave them of the best.

1508. Have you heard a complaint made that among the small shopkeepers, those who brought relief cards were imposed upon?—Yes, I have heard of one case where, at a chandler's shop, they sold tenpenny butter for 1s. 4d. a pound.

1509. Have you heard of tickets being sold?—No.

1510. (*Mr. Crowder*): As regards inquiry into character, how do you do that?—I am so well known in the district, I can go into almost any house; but you have to win their confidence, and then you can talk to them.

1511. We will take a special case not known to you. What course would you pursue? You would judge from the house, and the cleanliness, and so forth?—Yes.

1512. But, further than that, as to inquiry from the last employer, were you able——?—No, I never went to the employer; I went about in the neighbourhood; and I knew the caretakers in the buildings, and they could generally give me information.

1513. Would it be possible, under your system, for a man to be relieved while at the time he might be at work? That would be possible, I suppose?—Yes, and I have found it so in several cases. But still you have to work very cautiously indeed to find that out. I have visited as late as 10 o'clock at night in order to find it out.

1514. Well, then, in regard to the guardians; this gentleman asked some question with regard to guardians dealing with some of the cases in which you were not quite satisfied, and the guardians only offered the workhouse?—Some of them; they said, 'You can come in.'

1515. But in St. Saviour's there is a labour yard?—Yes, they have one generally.

1516. That would be outdoor relief?—Yes, and some of them won't do it. We came across several men that grumbled at it.

1517. This gentleman appears to have made a remark worth considering. He says, 'Why not let the guardians deal with these rather undeserving people? If they are offered work in the labour yard, and receive relief on account of that work, it will not break up their homes'?—Yes, but they won't accept it. One man said he would rather starve; and I said, 'Well, you will have to starve.'

1518. Was that case relieved?—No, sir; we would not relieve him.

1519. And he did not lie down and starve?—No, he is alive now.

1520. When that sort of talk goes on, you are not quite so frightened as with a quiet person?—No, we know how to deal with them better.

1521. Do you know what sum you received from the Mansion House?—No, sir, I don't. It was through Mr. Lawrence.

1522. Do you think that a less sum than you received from the Mansion House would have been sufficient?—No, I don't think so.

1523. Have you any almoner for the relief of distress in your neighbourhood?—Miss Grogan acts for that now. I used to act for Mr. Praed and his sister. Miss Grogan took it up, and I help her.

1524. Was the relief given through Miss Grogan?—Yes, for the St. Mary's district.

1525. Not for you?—No, not for No. 1 Ward. It was Miss Grogan that helped this man with his clothing, and the man Short.

1526. (*Mr. Hedley*): Who is Mr. Praed?—The banker.

1527. Your Committee have not thought of any special way of dealing with distress next winter?—I have not heard of anything. I could not answer that question. I know Mr. Garner was very good, and Mr. Lafone. He knew the people, and he knew them so well.

1528. (*Mr. J. H. Allen*): Did you act on the Committee yourself?—No, I used to visit, knowing the district.

1529. For how many weeks did you give them assistance—three or four weeks?—Oh, more than that; I think some as long as six and seven weeks.

1530. And what sums were given them per week?—We used to give 7s. in coal, and sometimes 4s. or 5s. in money.

1531. Did you ever pay back rent?—No; but we paid up clubs to enable them to get their out-of-work money.

1532. (*Hon. & Rev. A. C. Stanley*): You spoke of the improvement of your district, and I rather gathered from what you said that the improvement was a moral one—that they behaved themselves better?—So they do, sir.

1533. But at the same time that there was this improvement, work has been getting worse?—Yes; for the last six years.

1534. So that people are better off through better management? Yes; better off in spite of want. I have known people who have not had a chair to sit upon——

1535. Do they drink less?—They are teetotallers; that is the secret.

1536. Do you think that temperance has made considerable progress in your district?—Yes.

1537. (*Dr. Longstaff*): When you have been among them, have you heard them give any reason for trade being bad?—No

1538. They say it is bad and cannot account for it.

1539. Do you know what sort of brushes the brush-drawers make?—All kinds.

1540. Do they make such things as blacking brushes and scrubbing brushes?—Yes; there used to be a deal of contract work, but that is not so now.

1541. These men did not tell you why the contract work was bad?—No, I have never asked.

1542. Have you heard of a large factory that has been started at Hackney, where they make the brushes from beginning to end by the introduction of an American patent? I happen to know that they are doing a very good trade.—No, I have not heard that. I know there are some places where the bristles are punched in instead of being drawn through.

1543. I know that these people had orders six months ahead and could not execute them.

1544 (*Mr. Crowder*): I think what Mrs. Avis has said explains that.—They draw them with the wire, the common sorts, and the fancy hands have a small wire to work with. You cannot talk to me about brush-making but what I can answer. I worked for Miss Nash for 24 years.

1545. (*Rev. A. C. Stanley*) You have said that the Mansion House Fund did good in many instances. Have you heard of cases in which it did harm?—Yes; people neglected their work to go to get it. There were only three that I could mention.

1546. In the majority of cases it was good?—I never heard of more than those three cases, and I think they thought that they would get more.

1547. Did you in any case have money entrusted to you where you thought it ought not to be given?—I never had money from anyone but Mr. Praed.

1548. And you always gave it?—Yes; if we found they were genuine cases we could give it. I have had as much as 30s. to give to people, and have not given it because I knew it would be spent in the public-house.

1549. You say that people managed their money better than they used to do. Did you find the worst management with people of the best class?—No, those who were worst off.

1550. Such men as this salesman?—No; they always had a very comfortable home.

1551. Generally speaking, in cases of distress, would you expect to hear that the man earned £1 a week, or 30s.?—We found more with the 30s. than with the £1.

1552. Many of these people go hop-picking; I suppose they earn a good deal of money while they are at the work?—I don't think they earn a great deal. Some save it and some spend it.

Mrs. AVIS.
July 16, 1886.

1553. Do any of them have a jollification when they get home?—That is generally the case. Some save it and some spend it. It is no matter where you go, you will always find that kind of people.

1554. (*Mr. Peters*): There is one point upon which I wish to be quite clear. Do you think that people had less money to spend last winter?—Yes.

1555. And that process has been going on for the last six years?—Yes.

1556. And you think that a good remedy for that is to distribute money amongst them?—Yes; but you must use your own judgment in giving it. It requires a great deal of forethought in giving. I have been deceived myself. I thought I was as sharp as a good many of them, but I am free to confess I have been deceived.

1557. (*Mr. Loch*): Mr. Peters has just asked you about giving. It appears that the real cause of the distress is lack of work, and that want of work is due to the fact that other men are supplying the market with brushes; and therefore is it not true that we may keep a certain amount of distress away for one winter, but we cannot go on doing that?—No.

1558. Do you think that any of these people would emigrate?—No, sir; they don't like to leave; they would rather stop here and starve.

1559. So that it comes to this, that they are forcing the hands of the public, and saying, 'You must relieve us here, because we won't go; and we won't go into the workhouse'?—No.

1560. And they put us into the difficulty owing to their lack of energy. Could you make any suggestion, as they are in this difficulty, by which we could make them understand their position and help them out of it?—No; it has been a very hard lesson to me. I cannot make them understand.

1561. There are only one or two trying to put it to them in this way?—No, sir.

1562. You mentioned that Mr. Praed was giving you money. I think there were other distributions of charity at the same time—at the Priory, I think?—Oh, yes; Father Nugee's; that would be in the New Kent Road.

1563. Were there other distributions going on like that?—Only that. Mr. Olney used to give bread away twice a week, but that was principally to his 'mothers' who attended his mothers' meetings.

1564. There were other people who were giving in other directions?—Yes.

1565. Could you trust to the local people to give what help was required?—I don't know anyone that came from without; we had no very bad cases of starvation in our district; they were all visited.

1566. It almost seems that your evidence points to the fact that, if there had been distress, there would have been enough money without the fund?—No; it was a great stress upon them as it was; but through the people interested——

1567. A great number of the cases that you relieved were of a very exceptional kind?—Yes, there were exceptional cases. I know several that never had relief before.

1568. In making these inquiries did the brunt of making the inquiry fall upon yourself, and one or two others?—No, there were several. Mr. Garner was very energetic in visiting.

1569. And those were people who could be relied upon under any circumstances?—Yes; they were gentlemen we knew, and who were connected with the men out of employment. It was not like having a stranger coming into the district to work.

1570. If a certain sum had been placed privately at the disposal of such gentlemen as that, I suppose the distribution would have been worked better?—I don't know that. It would have been worked more privately. It would have prevented a great deal of trouble and some imposture; but still you might have overlooked some. It is a most difficult thing; unless you are living amongst the people you are very apt to be deceived by them.

1571. Do you think that the mere publicity of the fund brought out deserving cases that you could not have reached in any other way?—No, I don't think so.

1572. How was it ascertained that people were not in receipt of Poor Law relief?—We made inquiry of the relieving officer. He sat on the Committee for Newington and for Bermondsey.

1573. So that you asked him in every case?—Yes; the gentleman who sat for Bermondsey was a very nice fellow.

1574. (*Rev. A. C. Stanley*): I gather that Mrs. Avis had nothing personally to do with the relieving officer, but that the inquiry was made by the Committee?—That was so; and if they were not satisfied, I went to visit.

1575. (*Chairman*): In what capacity are you working in that district?—I have worked for Mr. Praed privately for seventeen years.

1576. He employs you as his visitor?—I have got another district now—Red Cross Street, in the Borough.

1577. (*Mr. Loch*): And you have a room?—Yes; I have a class of girls at my house twice a week.

1578. And do you do any parish work for Mr.—for anyone down there?—No, sir; I work with the Rev. Mr. Snape.

1579. (*Rev. B. Lambert*): Suppose this salesman had come in an ordinary year—what would you have done in an ordinary year?—Mr. Praed would have helped him.

1580. (*Mr. Loch*): That is the point.

Mrs. Avis.
July 16, 1886.

Mr. F. J. DOVE (of the Firm of Dove Brothers) and Mr. R. ROBERTS, examined.

1581. (*Chairman, Rev. Brooke Lambert*): Where do you reside, Mr. Dove?—Halesworth Lodge, Hornsey Rise.

1582. And it is the building trade in which you are engaged?—My place of business is in Theberton Street, Islington.

1583. I think you have been very largely employed in the building trade?—Yes, we have.

1584. And you also, Mr. Roberts, I believe?—I am also a member of a large building firm in Rheidol Terrace, Islington.

1585. The Committee are very anxious to find out a few things that would help them about the exceptional distress. They want to know the extent to which it prevailed last year, especially last winter, and if you could give them any information with regard to the number of men that have been employed latterly, and the rate of wages as compared with former years. Now, as regards the first point—the number of men employed—have you been employing a very much smaller number of men?—(*Mr. Dove*): As far as my own experience goes, we are not employing a fifth part of the men we employed ten years ago. I think it is rather exceptional in our case, because a great deal of our work is of an ecclesiastical kind, and that has been especially dull of late years. I may tell you that we have built of ecclesiastical edifices about 400.

1586. In the course of how many years?—In the course of thirty years.

1587. Would your experience be the same, Mr. Roberts?—(*Mr. Roberts*): Yes, it is diminished; but I am a little doubtful whether, in our case, our trade has diminished heavily, owing to the diminution in volume of general trade, or because we are unable to do the work at the price at which it is being done. We are being swept out by keener competition, although the volume of trade is somewhat diminished as well.

1588. Is your trade in dwelling-houses?—Mansions and dwelling-houses mostly. We have been in business forty years.

1589. And you are undoubtedly employing a very much smaller number of men?—I am a little doubtful how far that is so. Some part is owing to less volume of trade; some, that we are unable to meet the competition.

1590. The answers have especial reference to the metropolitan area?—I should say that the amount of our wages was two-thirds less than three years ago.

1591. You are employing about one-third of the number of people?—Yes.

(*Mr. Dove*): If you would allow me to make an observation, I concur in the

Mr. F. J. Dove and Mr. R. Roberts.

Mr. F. J. Dove and Mr. R. Roberts.

July 16, 1886.

view which he takes about the undue competition. That competition has been brought about in a great measure by the creation of a great many more masters than there were.

1592. So that the actual amount of building going on in the metropolitan area is not very much less?—(*Mr. Dove*): Not a very great deal, but still it is less.

1593. There are more who want work?—Yes, I suppose so.

1594. In your own case, when you have a contract, do you employ persons living in the immediate neighbourhood, or do you import men from a distance?—(*Mr. Dove*): We have done a great deal all over England. When we go a long way afield—to Yorkshire or Lancashire—we, as a rule, take down a great many London workmen, and they lead the way for the other workmen; and if we pick up good hands there, we bring them to London. That is how the best hands are found in London at the higher wage. I have been president of our Central Association. I occupied the position for three years, and I can therefore judge as to how the wages go. I object to lowering wages.

1595. I was coming to that point presently. I should like to ask you a question. I gathered that there is a steady influx of the best workmen into London. The good ones you take away would come back again. The inferior ones would not get work because better workmen had been imported from the country?—(*Mr. Dove*): The last three years are the only three years for the space of fifteen years when the wages have been higher in London than the provinces.

1596. (*Dr. Longstaff*): I did not quite understand that.—(*Mr. Dove*): In London the wages have been kept up, and in the country they were actually paying $10\frac{1}{2}d.$ an hour; they have now dropped down to $8d.$ and $7d.$, while London is keeping up its wages.

1597. (*Chairman*): So that there is the attraction of the higher wage to London.

1598. (*Dr. Longstaff*): But previously it was not the case?—Yes.

1599. (*Chairman*): Sometimes a builder from a distance gets a contract; when he gets the contract, does he employ London men or import a large number from his own district?—They often bring up a large number, because they bring them at the lower wage—many of the bricklayers, the masons, and the carpenters that they have employed come up with them, and run the risk of the trades unions interfering with them; but after they have been seven or eight months they require the same wages as the others, because of the trades unions.

1600. That is one reason why you are unable to compete with those at a distance?—Yes, at first blush; but generally the provincial masters have had enough of it in a few years, and retire again.

1601. But this has the tendency to increase the number of hands, though the work may be decreasing?—I should think, according to my judgment, that London has been particularly favoured in that way, more than other parts of England. But there is less depression in London than in other parts.

1602. But it has been on the increase in proportion to the number of men that come up. Is that your view, Mr. Roberts?—(*Mr. Roberts*): Yes; and we find the men follow a particular foreman. A man will get attached to a foreman, and the men will follow that foreman from London to the country; and the men in the country who prove themselves capable, are anxious to come up, and they will follow the foreman back again, and go to London. I should be sorry to see a lowering of the wages in London. I believe it would enormously affect builders such as Mr. Dove and ourselves; it would throw the work into the hands of reckless competitors. My feeling is that, the higher the rate of wages, the better for the good firms; that really the lowering of the wages would only make the competition still keener.

1603. I think you said $9d.$ per hour, Mr. Dove?—For about nine hours a day; and extra working would be paid for at a higher rate. That depends upon the character of the firm. It is $9d.$ an hour for nine hours or a little more, but if they work on for three or four hours they expect more.

1604. We were comparing the number of men employed now with the number ten years ago. What was your rate of wages then?—8½d. I am not quite sure whether it was 8½d. or 8d., but still it has crept up in the last thirty years. It has crept up from 6d. per hour to 9d. in the thirty years, sometimes by a leap of a penny, and sometimes of a halfpenny.

1605. (*Mr. Peters*): Never going back?—No, never going back.

1606. (*Chairman*): And the rate of wages is lower in the country?—Yes. If it would afford you information, I shall be pleased to send you a tabular statement of the wages all over England.

1607. It would be very useful. Mr. Roberts's opinion and yours is that by keeping up the rate of wages, you ensure a better class of work?—Yes; the London builders who want to be paramount for work.

1608. Do you consider that during the last winter there was a larger number of men engaged in building out of employ than usual?—Yes; that is my experience. About ten years ago we were paying £1,500 a week for wages; this last winter we only paid £300.

1609. I think you were connected with the distribution of the Mansion House Relief Fund?—(*Mr. Roberts*): Yes, in Islington.

1610. You got some experience of the labouring classes?—Yes, my experience was that the tendency of the fund was to drift to the relief of the permanent poor. Do what we would to avoid it, we could not help it drifting. And I think it was to some extent owing to the fact that the Committees were composed to a large extent of clergymen and district visitors; and the charity went to their own particular set; it went to the same set as are relieved by the chapels and churches. I believe that many of the clergy honestly tried their best to avoid that, but as the matter was in their hands these people came. As a rule the mechanic does not go to church or chapel.

1611. Do you think it a good thing that the Mansion House Fund was publicly known, or would it have been better to have had some private fund?—I think it was necessary to advertise it; and my own view was that the organisation should not have been allowed to drop: that in each district a small office should be opened, controlled for the most part by laymen sitting every evening.

1612. Had you many guardians?—We had one or two guardians on the Committee. The relieving officer refused to relieve some cases, and sent them on to the Mansion House Fund, and in some cases they passed their old cases on.

1613. Did you co-operate with the Charity Organisation Society?—No.

1614. With the Society for the Relief of Distress?—No.

1615. Were they represented on the Committee?—No; I think Miss Sharpe used to attend, but I think there was rather a feeling that the Charity Organisation Society was not a very successful distributor of charity. We had a good many enthusiastic charity givers on the Committee, and any cold water was objected to.

1616. Had you a very large number of applicants?—Yes; they increased with the way the relief came to be known. The last applicants were very much less worthy of support than the first.

1617. The more you advertised, the worse class you got?—Yes.

1618. Can you give me the total number of applicants?—No.

1619. Could you give me the proportion of those relieved to those who applied?—Yes; I think almost every one who applied was relieved.

1620. Was any investigation made?—Yes, by means of the district visitors and others. All were in distress, and that was considered sufficient ground, whether they came within the Mansion House lines or not. If anyone made a remark, the answer was, 'the man was in trouble.'

1621. Did you send any cases to the Poor Law?—No; I believe at my particular Committee we did not.

1622. But they sent cases to you?—Yes.

1623. (*Rev. E. Lambert*): You had the Greenwich Seamen's Hospital, did you not, Mr. Dove?—Yes.

1624. Did you learn the state of trade down there?—No.

1625. There has been great complaint of want of trade down there. I suppose I am right in saying that the building trade has been less affected by machinery than other trades?—No; I should say that the industries connected

Mr. F. J. Dove
and Mr. H.
Roberts.

July 16, 1886.

with our trade are not greatly affected by machinery and by the importation of doors, and so on.

1626. Is that the case with you, Mr. Roberts?—Yes; but we do high-class work; an architect's plan has to be followed. We cannot get a dozen doors made to the same pattern. Even if trade is at all slack, each man expects to work the full nine hours a day; there could not be a distribution of labour.

(*Mr. Dove*): With regard to the machinery that we use, we put that on half-time; all the machine hands and the engine drivers we put on half-time.

1627. Then in one branch of your trade you can distribute labour?—Yes; but that is infinitesimal.

1628. I wanted to ask one or two questions about the fund. There were certain Mansion House Rules, but they did not even keep to those rules?

(*Mr. Roberts*): No.

(*Mr. Dove*): In North London we were rather more separate, and there was an enormous body of distressed people there. I was asked to go on the Committee, because I happened to be an employer of labour, and I thought it was my duty to do so to prevent imposture. I was made chairman of it after a short time, and we had a Sub-Committee, who investigated cases after the cases had been already investigated by the separate members of the Committee. Probably the people in Mr. Roberts's district did not do that. I or others looked over every case after it had been dealt with by the clergy, district visitors, and the members of the Committee referred to, and we rejected a great many of them. But at the same time there were a great many persons there—painters particularly, whose normal condition in the winter is always to get relief. These for the great part were rejected, but a great many came with such tales of woe and said that they were starving; and finding that they had not received outdoor relief, we assisted them.

1629. I understand you to say, and I agree with you, that there is a general distrust on the part of the better men—they would not go to a Society that was managed by the clergy?

(*Mr. Roberts*): I think it is so. I don't think it prevails now so largely as it did a few years ago. If a working man goes to the clergyman, he thinks he is bound to return the compliment by going to church or chapel, and he does not do it.

1630. I think you found later that it is part of a very common animosity in their class?—I think the old animosity against the clergy is gone.

1631. Is there, within your knowledge, the same feeling of not going to the Charity Organisation Society?—I think the feeling against the Charity Organisation Society is much stronger.

1632. Among the class of men who respect themselves?—Yes; because they treat the working man very hardly.

1633. If we had a few more working-men committees of the Charity Organisation Society, they would soon come round to us.

1634. (*Mr. Crowder*): Mr. Dove, with regard to the number who fell out of work last winter—comparing last winter with winters of equal severity and duration—should you say that there was such a lack of employment as to make you feel that some special fund was necessary—setting aside the severity of the weather?—That is a very difficult question to answer. For my own part, I thought the relief fund was a great mistake, because I am very much inclined, although I know it is contrary to political economy, to find work for the people. I am sure it is better to do that. At Holloway we pointed out to the parish authorities certain works that might be carried out—road-making and such things. It is better if that can be done, because we have always found, as to the artisan, that if he happens to be out of work for three months, he is never the same man again. He becomes demoralised. Even supposing we administered a fund like this as well as possible, the man will never be the same man as he was before. If you can find employment—not degrading, but with wages reasonable—if he has had 6s. 9d. and it gave 4s. 9d., it would do some good.

1635. In regard to these works undertaken by the vestries under the Metropolitan Board of Works, was it done by contract in the usual way?—Yes; road-making in the north part of London. There was a good deal of road-making to do, and there are rules as to the assessing the payment upon those who have to bear the expense, and it is a rule to get two-thirds of the money before commencing the work. The vestry passed that by and ran the risk of getting the money after the roads were made.

Mr. F. J. Dove and Mr. R. Roberts.

July 16, 1886.

1636. (*Chairman*): The rate of wages paid by the District Board was the same rate as usual ?—Yes.

1637. (*Mr. Crowder*): ' These works ' were tendered for ?—Yes. I must observe that, after we had made these efforts to get this special employment, many of the fellows exhibited themselves in their true colours, and threw it up.

1638. I think you said your experience was that a great many loafers apply ?—Oh, yes.

1639. In fact, the people who are accustomed to receive charity ?—Yes, and the men who are continually relieved by clergymen.

1640. And your belief is that fair wages paid by a vestry or committee would be a fair test—that it would act as a test ?—Yes, that is exactly my feeling with regard to next winter. I look to it to be more severe. I think in all probability the work will be in a less flourishing state in the coming year than it is now.

1641. I should like to ask Mr. Roberts what he considers with regard to the distress, whether he thinks a public fund necessary, or whether he thinks these cases might have been dealt with by existing societies ?—I think they would have been better dealt with by the existing societies. Perhaps I am looking back to the Mansion House Fund, and thinking it did mischief. I agree somewhat with regard to public works, and the demoralising effect of want of work upon a man. A painter's is a season-trade—they are out in winter and employed in summer, when all men not shifty or not distrusted are in constant employment. The number of painters out of work relieved in our district was very large, and the excuse for coming was that the trade was so bad in the last summer that they did not have so much work as usual.

1642. Some save in the shape of furniture ?—Yes; and some take other work in winter.

1643. Has anything in the shape of a labour test connected with any work that required doing suggested itself to you ?—(*Mr. Roberts*): The labour test is the best test. If you put a labour test at a lower rate of wages, they won't accept it, for fear of bringing down the rate of wages permanently. I think that is their objection to taking it rather than that it is a small amount for them at the time. I should say public works should not be less than at the standard rate of wages. They should not take advantage of the distress.— (*Mr. Dove*): I don't quite agree with that. After awhile, everything would become public works, and you would get a certain amount of healthy enterprise done away with that exists at the present time. There would be no inducement to seek a higher rate of wages.

1644. (*Chairman*): Then the work was paid for in the usual way, only it was not so much as they could earn in the building trade ?—It was put into the market at an earlier date than it would otherwise have been.

1645. (*Mr. Crowder*): Supposing that there should be exceptional distress next winter, can you suggest any plan that would be better than the Mansion House Fund ? which, I think we all agree, was a failure ; that it did a great deal of harm if it did some good. We cannot possibly expect that all those who have this world's goods may withhold their hands. Can you suggest how it could be better distributed ?—(*Mr. Dove*): The difficulty in that matter is to get one of what we call our real good artisans to degrade himself to come and receive charity. I really don't believe that up in our neighbourhood, in the number that came for relief, there was one thoroughly sterling, honest, straightforward man in the whole lot, judging from examination. Perhaps I am overstating the case, but I could not put my finger upon one.

1646. Could you suggest anything that we could propose to the public less objectionable than the Mansion House Fund ? We should have some people coming forward and ready to give.—Nothing occurs to my mind, excepting what I have just stated, that something should be thought of in time, by which workmen can go and find employment—something that will add to the comfort, or

Mr. F. J. Dove
and Mr. R.
Roberts.

July 16, 1886.

happiness, or health of the people without its being remunerative—a public improvement of some kind—such, for instance, as a scheme for making new roads through certain parts. In our own parts there is a scheme for carrying a road from Hornsey Rise to Hornsey proper, which would be a boon to the neighbourhood. There is an enormous traffic there ; and I think it behoves all parishes, as far as they can, to be alive to these facts, and so that they can put their hand to start something of the kind—infirmaries, wards for epidemics, &c. To a certain extent everybody can turn his hand to digging. I should not mind it if I were in distress.

1647. Suppose you had to deal with tailors, shoemakers, silversmiths, and people of that description ?—I should give them that kind of employment. Those very men that you speak of—the best of them—look upon it as a treat to do their allotment gardens, and why they could not employ themselves at a little heavier strain I don't know ; and if you induced a dozen or two to take it, others would follow.

1648. I doubt if you could get the Londoner to dig ?—Perhaps some could not do it.

1649. (*Mr. J. H. Allen*): I understand they are works to be paid for by local funds. You wish each local district to take upon themselves the execution of works to be paid for for a local purpose ?—Let every parish obtain a loan for carrying it out ; they can get it from the Consolidated Fund.

1650. Do you think it right to raise a loan, chargeable for a long series of years, to relieve immediate distress ?—Yes, I think so. That is taxing posterity to some extent.

1651. (*Mr. Hedley*) : There must be a time when this road-making must cease ?—I don't know. The question of where the money is coming from is another thing. I have felt in this matter that unless rich and poor pull together, we shall get into an awful mess. I am sorry to say that the workmen are men who won't go to the churches or chapels ; but they are better educated than they were, and are better able to combine.

1652. (*Mr. Crowder*) : By education you mean reading and writing ?—Yes.

1653. (*Mr. Hedley*) : Mr. Roberts, so you share Mr. Dove's opinion, that more men are likely to be out of work next winter ?—Yes, I think so. I think from the recent elections there has been a great migration of workmen from London ; having found trade so bad they have gone away, and I hope they have left for good, many of them. I hope they have found trade where they have gone to. My notion is, as to public works, I should rather have preferred if offices for relief were opened in all the districts—a multiplicity of them, and two or three gentlemen, employers of labour, and one or two working men, and that the representatives of churches and chapels should come once a month and compare their cases, &c.

1654. (*Mr. Hedley*) : That is just what the Charity Organisation Society are trying to do ?—You want them in much smaller districts. The organisation is often at some distance from the working classes ; you want them in the centre of poor neighbourhoods, and local people to serve on the Committee.

1655. When you found a case of distress, what would you do to relieve it—in the shape of work ?—If possible in the shape of work, and I should prefer money to giving in kind. I think the giving in kind is a very mischievous system in itself, and frequently I have found that a system of terrorism was exercised.

1656. Do they give a large quantity of outdoor relief in Islington ?—Yes ; I think rather more freely in Islington than in some places. I have not heard any complaint.

1657. Is there a labour yard in Islington ?—Yes, I think there is—breaking stones.

1658. Was it largely used last winter ?

(*Mr. Dove*) : That is a degrading thing.

1659. (*Mr. J. H. Allen*) : Why is stone-breaking degrading ?—Because it is a sort of thing you put the lowest of the low to do. It is like picking oakum. It is in a degree useful, but it is infinitesimal in its use.

1660. What harm is there in it ?—I am not speaking about the loafers.

Do what you like with those. Make it as abhorrent as possible to those. I am speaking of men like carpenters and joiners.

1661. But then I am a guardian in St. Pancras, and we have none of that class of men in the labour yard—no carpenter. It is solely painters and loafers.—Just so; a man worthy the name of a mechanic won't ask charity; he will rather die first.

(*Mr. Roberts*) I think you ought to bear in mind with regard to these matters—I think that the good artisan is not in actual want. If a man is a really good fellow he can make some scheme to get a living, and it is the loafer and inferior workman who resorts to charity. If a man is a capable man he looks about him.

1662. That is a very important point. You don't think that at the present time there are any mechanics who want charity?—Not the best of mechanics. Those in want are often mentally and physically incapable of being good mechanics.

1663. The trades unions—they would help a good mechanic?—They have not that system. The Amalgamated Society of Engineers have such a system, provided they took care that the men are good workmen in the Society. If the societies would weed out the bad workmen, the trades unions would be a good thing to the trade, but I fancy some of them won't allow them to support men out of employ.

1664. The Plasterers' Society does that, I think?—(*Mr. Dove*): The strongest one of all is the Masons', which does not support anyone out of employ, except on strike.

(*Mr. Roberts*) The Society of Engineers does support men out of employ.

1665. (*Dr. Longstaff*): You two gentlemen are more concerned in the better class of building work. Though you both do the better sort of work, you must have a good deal of knowledge of the inferior branches of the trade. Are the inferior branches of the building trade as much depressed as your own branch, or more, or less?—(*Mr. Roberts*): I should say more so. You notice in the suburbs those houses that are built by a sort who represent the great volume of London trade—speculative builders. That is a class of work in which there is neither architect nor builder; but, judging from the number of empty houses, I should say that that trade has suffered more than ours.

1666. As you do high class work, I suppose the majority of the men employed would be the best class of men.—(*Mr. Roberts*): Yes. (*Mr. Dove*): We don't take any except at the best wages. The speculative men may get them from $6\frac{1}{2}d$. an hour, except they take task work and earn 10d. an hour. If they take an undue amount of work for themselves, they will have to suffer for it afterwards.

1667. These speculative builders employ a great many men as artisans who are little better than labourers, who don't know their trade?—(*Mr. Dove*): Yes, that is especially the case with bricklayers. (*Mr. Roberts*): I agree. (*Mr. Dove*): A carpenter, to a certain extent, must have a knowledge of his trade. He has more tools to use.

1668. But still there are a great many men who are little better than improvers?—(*Mr. Roberts*): Yes; a man and his family will take a job. There was a case of painting the outside of a house; we were asked to give a price for it. A man took it perhaps at half our price. I saw the work going on. All three, a father and two sons under fifteen, were painting this house. We cannot compete against such men. That is done to a great extent by speculative builders. A man begins building a little house, and he has his son and his brother-in-law to help him, and they run it up together: they build simply with a notion of making money.

1669. Yes, there is a system of small contracts, I believe. Is that system getting more common?—Yes; they let it for the lump sum so much a house; and in fact I have heard of people building 'graves' in walls, leaving hollow spaces where there is no brick at all, so that there was a risk of its coming to pieces.

1670. Mr. Dove stated what is more or less generally well known to men in the building trade, that their wages have increased 50 per cent. in thirty years.

Mr. F. J. Dove and Mr. R. Roberts.

July 16, 1886.

Are these men steadier than they were, do you think?—Well, I must confess that as far as my judgment goes, the artisan is now far more respectable than formerly. Every man in our shop is rather a gentleman to what he was thirty years ago. It was the rule to find these men keeping Saint Monday, and Saint Tuesday too. Such a thing never occurs now, and they go out with their black clothes. They have given up their fustian and corduroy. The better class of men never think of wearing fustian.

1671. Is that your experience, Mr. Roberts?—Yes; I never hear a foreman now swearing at and bullying the men. You can notice the improvement in their dress too. There are no paper caps now. They are more courteous to their employers, and the employers are on better terms with the men. We have men who have been with us since before I was born.

1672. You both of you admit that your own business has shrunk considerably of recent years. You would naturally reject the inferior men, and would so have naturally a more select class and high wages. Do you think this general?—To a certain extent it is so. Those we weeded out were those we had least respect for, but still there were many that we should have liked to retain; but even as to the character of the men, the trade itself has tended to elevate the men. None of the carpenters have to work in the slavish sort of manner that they used to do. All the planing and preparing the work for the bench—with trying planes, and jack planes, and smoothing planes—that is all done by machinery. It is rather now a scientific adjustment of material.

1673. You have anticipated another question. Though machinery has not affected the building trade as much as other trades, it must influence the number of carpenters; you would not now have to employ so many joiners?—The introduction of machinery has rather alleviated the heavy work. After all, the work is only prepared for them; the men proceed with their work in a more leisurely manner, and consequently the saving by machinery is not much.

1674. And you think that is compensated for by the faster work of the machine. You all make use of the sashes and doors coming from abroad?—No. Speculators do.

1675. How long has that been the case?—(Mr. Roberts): I should say not more than ten years. (Mr. Dove): I think it commenced about twenty years ago, and has gone on increasing, but the singular part of that is as to the commonest doors: we get the doors over here nearly for the same money that we can get the wood. They use inferior wood, and if we import the timber, by the time it is sawed, it comes to as much as the door itself.

1676. Then if the door is bad, it is not really cheaper?—Yes; they don't put any glue in the joints.

1677. But although this has been done more or less for twenty years, it has been done very much more recently?—Yes.

1678. That must have thrown a great many joiners out of employ in the trade?—(Mr. Roberts): Yes.

1679. Your committee, Mr. Roberts, seem to have been possessed with a passion to give?—Well, perhaps it was, looking at it a little hardly. Ours is not like the Dock and Stepney District, so that we have not such a very large area to spend our money over; and when the distress was here, the Mansion House Fund lines were not much considered.

1680. Was the district visitor likely to be imposed upon, do you think?—I don't know that; but the people who get at the district visitor are the permanent poor; they cannot go out of the set.

(Mr. Dove): I found that in my neighbourhood we have got a very excellent Scripture reader there; but I could see as clearly as possible that his sympathy ran with the cases who came to him at the mission room on a Sunday to hear him preach. He could not help it. I dare say I should have done the same.

1681. (Mr. Peters): I think you said the chief cause of slackness was the excessive competition, that would cause the work to shift from you to others, and not due to depression?—That is quite right.

1682. And do you think that those people who took the work would employ the same class of workmen as you?—Yes; but the work would suffer in the nature of the material, not the labour. I don't think they have opportunity of reducing wages much. They take the work contrary to all the contracts—it is let to the lowest contractor—and employ a lower class of men.

1683. What is the cause of this increasing competition among those employers who compete with each other?—I have not given consideration to that. These things grow upon us so gradually; you hardly know of it till it is right upon you.

1684. It has never occurred to you it is on account of the capital going on accumulating in few hands beyond its necessary point?—It seems to me that several of our men come to grief by being taken by the hand and set up on their own account; they go on for a certain time, and sometimes do not. Many of our very best men are shocking bad financiers, and know nothing about it.

(*Mr. Roberts*): I can confirm that by a case in our own employ. A workman set up as a speculative builder. He got money advanced to him. He lives well, keeps three or four servants, keeps a carriage, and in a few years he makes an offer to his creditors: no difference in his expenditure. We have men who worked along with him, and they compare their position with his, while he is well dressed and living stylishly, and ask why they are still there, having their two or three pounds a week. I think it is the abundance of capital in the country which demoralises these men. There is a bitter feeling in the minds of the men who have worked alongside them. They are not connected with social influences, and if they have to compound, they go on again.

1685. (*Mr. Loch*): I should just like to ask Mr. Roberts if we could have any good system of obtaining information of the actual state of want of work from employers and others who could know the actual facts at any precise moment? There may be a sensation, and then there is a rush; if we could know beforehand and speak with certainty as to the actual facts, one might get the thing done deliberately and well?—The only way would be to send circulars to employers. If circulars were sent through the Builders' Society and other societies, they could give you facilities, and they would be able to tell you if the trade was diminished.

1686. That might be undertaken, with a probability of meeting with support?—It can hardly be done by a society like this.

1687. I was looking to the difficulty, if possible, of next winter. I suppose you would say, with regard to the labour test you would put men to, you would accept a division of classes, and you would not flinch from letting the loafing class go to the labour yard, and the better class to the scheme you propose?—(*Mr. Dove*): Some such scheme I should propose.

1688. I suppose you would say we have come to this plight, that competition creates a special class of workmen, and those are the people who press upon the charity funds. In distress we let charity go to people whom we ourselves create?—Yes.

1689. Then it is a question whether by any means we can make the quality of these workmen better, and prevent them coming down to this class which charity touches. Taking the fact, do you think they could be taught to do other work than they do?—We find that in the entirety of men who take to painting; we find that omnibus drivers and conductors have been painters and everything else. As to knowing what to put such men to, that is difficult. There are very respectable men among painters and decorators, but four-fifths of the people who call themselves painters are clerks and others who have been turned out of offices.

1690. Speaking of the real artisan who is a painter, and who suffers from the season, can you suggest any way out of the difficulty—could you, from your knowledge of trade, propose anything that he could turn his hand to? Is there any form of trade work or carpentering which is done abroad now to which their hands could be turned?—These are questions which cannot be answered off-hand. If you would propose the question on a piece of paper and send it to me I will be happy to consider it.

1691. I infer that it comes to this: that the success of the administration of a local fund depends upon the time taken in preparation for it. In Islington, could you get a muster of those who would know the people to deal with the

Mr. F. J. Dove and Mr. R. Roberts.

July 16, 1886.

Mr. F. J. Dove and Mr. R. Roberts.
July 16, 1886.

matter as you suggest, Mr. Roberts ?—I think we could. There is a fear creeping among the people that something will have to be done.

1692. Taking next winter, could you get a list of fifty or sixty people to whom you could say, ' We will entrust you with this work on certain lines ?'— I think we might. We should have a considerable number of ladies.

1693. When you deal with the chronic class of poor—'the permanent poor'—if you adopt in regard to them such a line as will exclude them, while you also keep out the intruder and the lazy fellow, would you not be driven into the same position as the Charity Organisation Society, and considered somewhat harsh in dealing with this difficult class?—Yes ; but if we had large bodies of local people, they would know the majority of the leading cases and be able to justify their action. My own impression of the Charity Organisation Society is that it is too much centralised.

1694. If we could arrange more sub-divisions, you would say it was the best thing to do. Have you thought of the desirability of giving piece-work in connection with the public works, which you suggested, so that the lazy man may be spurred to do rather more than he otherwise would do ?—(*Mr. Dove*): Are you referring to general work ? If they were works for purposes of improving the neighbourhood, or railways, or sewage, I should say yes.

1695. As regards the Poor Law, the guardians would do very little, you think ?—(*Mr. Roberts*) : Yes ; the Poor Law administration is too much in the hands of the shopkeepers, and working men know very little about it. I don't know whether the vestryman or the Guardian in Islington is looked upon with the greater contempt. (*Mr. Dove*) : I think Guardians are rather too much tied by the hands by the Local Government. It prevents a healthy kind of emulation between the parishes.

Miss F. R. WILKINSON, examined.

Miss F. R. Wilkinson.

1696. (*Chairman*) : You are landscape gardener to the Metropolitan Public Gardens Association ?—Yes.

1697. That Association has laid out a good many gardens last winter?— Yes.

1698. You took up more work than usual because of the distress ?—Yes ; for the last two winters.

1699. It is difficult, I suppose, to say how many have been employed this last winter?—I believe Captain Thompson has the numbers ; if you ask him he will give them to you.

[The Secretary read an extract showing the extent of the work and the rate of wages for the work, done by the Society.]*

1700. And then, supposing you were going to lay out a garden, what is the mode of procedure ?—Sometimes the local vestry sent the men. The Self-Help Emigration Society sent some men. At Stepney Church, the Mile End Mansion House Sub-Committee sent the men because they supplied part of the funds; and others were sent by the local clergy.

1701. Does your society employ foremen ?—Yes, we have foremen, and gangers if there is a large number of men.

1702. Are the foremen employed by the Society ?—The foreman is engaged by the Metropolitan Public Gardens Association, and the ganger is selected from the men. The foreman puts them all on to work, and sees how they do.

1703. In regard to character, there is no investigation into the character of a man ?—We suppose it is done by the people who send the men. We don't do it.

1704. If they are found to be good workmen they are brought in ?—Yes.

* 'At the present time (March 6, 1886) the number of men employed daily in laying out churchyards and other open spaces for the benefit of the public, and being paid for by the Association, is about 440. . . . The men are engaged from the neighbourhoods in which their work is found, and in some cases are paid at the rate of 4*d*. an hour for five hours, two gangs being thus employed daily, and a fourpenny meal provided for each man before he commences his labours ; while in other cases, when no meal is provided, the men are employed at 4*d*. an hour for eight or nine hours daily.'—From the Monthly Statement of the Metropolitan Public Gardens Association. *Charity Organisation Review*, March, 1886, p. 114.

Miss F. R. WILKINSON.

July 16, 1886.

1705. And the rate of wages 4*d*. per hour, and 4*d*. for dinner, for a day of five hours' work?—Yes, generally five hours.

1706. What is an ordinary rate for private work?—I have had to give a man 3*s*. 6*d*. or 4*s*. a day; then they worked 10 hours.

1707. Supposing you are employing these men at 4*d*. an hour, do you get 4*d*. an hour work out of them?—No, I don't.

1708. They are not first-rate workmen?—No; there were men of all trades.

1709. And when paid this lower rate of wages, they don't give much work for the money?—No, and those men to whom we have given 6*d*. a day more, we have got better work out of them.

1710. So that in your opinion the higher rate of wages would really secure more work in proportion?—This winter we have got very much less work done than the winter before, when we worked eight hours.

1711. The less you pay per day the less work you get done in proportion?—Yes; in Stepney we had very great difficulty. We could hardly get the men to work at all. They began by smoking, and down in Drury Lane we could not get men early in the morning. They would not come to work early.

1712. And did some go off after half a day?—Yes; at Drury Lane we only wanted six men, and we could not get them at seven o'clock in the morning. That was in April.

1713. You were carrying this on in the winter?—Yes.

1714. While the Mansion House fund was going on?—Yes.

1715. Did that keep them away?—I cannot say from experience; though I have heard it.

1716. Do you think that the fact of the Society employing a certain number of men was a benefit to some of those men?—I have known one or two cases where they have gone back to their own work in the spring, and are doing well. A good deal of the money was Mansion House money. It all was paid through the Society.

1717. It was work that would not have been done otherwise?—No, we made a good deal of extra work.

1718. When you say extra work?—More digging. It was all by way of improvement. It was all work we should not have had done if we had not had this money to spend in giving work to the unemployed.

1719. Did you know a man's former employment?—Yes, whenever I made inquiries; it appeared they came from all classes.

1720. Had you anything to do with the grounds laid out in Marylebone?—No, I had not; the Association paid for the labour there. All work is stopped now. We shall not have any more gardening again till October.

1721. You had £1,500 of the Mansion House fund, and you will get about £1,500 more?—Yes, I suppose so.

1722. Do you think that is the best way of relieving distress in London?—I should not like to give an opinion.

1723. It is a good way you think?—I think it is a good way to give labour, but very unsatisfactory as the work was done.

1724. Why not make some inquiry?—How can I? It is not part of my work for the Association. The antecedents of the men are supposed to have been inquired into.

1725. It is done to supply work to respectable working men?—They are supposed to have been inquired into.

1726. (*Mr. Allen*): Can you tell me why the Association thought it necessary to give a fourpenny meal in addition to the wages?—They did not want to interfere with the labour market, and decided to pay 5*d*. an hour five hours' work, and to give a meal.

1727. Did it appear to the Society that there was any difference in giving food?—I don't know the reason.

1728. Suppose you were asked your opinion, would you recommend the meal and raise the rate of wages?—I think the meal is a very good thing in many cases, because the men are often half-starved.

1729. Perhaps that was one of the reasons for giving the meal before they started?—Yes.

1730. Supposing you were beginning again, what rate of pay would you

Miss F. R. WILKINSON.
July 16, 1886.

recommend?—Not less than 4*d*. per hour for eight hours, and I should like very much to have two classes of workmen.

1731. So that you could promote a man into the better class? Yes.

1732. (*Mr. Loch*): With regard to the payment of wages, we have evidence that there are two classes of workmen—the loafing class, who will not work, and the better class. I understand that in spite of the inquiry which takes place a great many of the loafing class come in?—Yes.

1733. Do you think that by making a selection and grouping them according to industrial power and energy you could set them to piece-work with good results?—I should think it might be done.

1734. There would be certain advantages, would there not? I have had no experience, but I should think it might be done.

1735. Taking the cost and comparing it with the contract price for that amount of labour applied to similar work, what would be the difference, do you suppose?—We spent four times the amount it could have been done for by contract.

1736. (*Chairman*): That was the result of employing cheap labour?—That was not the object. The object of the Metropolitan Public Gardens Association was to give work to the greatest number of men.

1737. (*Mr. Loch*): But a great many might have been at the stone yard?—Yes.

1738. And it would have been better for the others, as they make each other idle?—Yes.

1739. (*Mr. Peters*): What effect upon loafers has it, do you think?—I got rid of some. With this large number I could not know all the men.

1740. May it not be possible to do harm by paying them a low rate of wages?—I should think they might be——

1741. (*Mr. Loch*): You would not propose to go on in this chronic fashion, supplementing lack of work by these means? Could these men be turned into emigrants?—I believe a great many have emigrated.

1742. You don't know how many—what proportions? Could these works be so carefully managed, *e.g.*, as to make the man who came in as an indifferent labourer a good ground worker?—I should think so. I know several made capable under a good foreman.

1743. And if you were to clear out those who were labour-yard cases it might be done so as to divide the classes, and take those who have good stuff in them, and make them better?—Yes.

1744. I gather from your explanation that the men are sent to you from various people, more or less selected. You have a pay-sheet filled up by the foreman?—The foreman fills it up, and one of the men signs it, to show they have received the amount.

1745. Did that work well?—Yes; I have not heard any complaint.

1746. Were there a great number of dismissals?—I could not tell how many were dismissed, and how many went away of their own accord.

1747. Do you know why they went away of their own accord? Was it in March or April?—No. They could go away at an hour's notice; they were paid daily.

1748. So far as this was a permanent means of support during difficulties or distress, it did not act in that way for a great number?—No.

1749. With regard to dismissals, do you suppose Mr. Collie would be able to tell us?—Yes, he would be able to tell.

1750. Did you find at all that things of this sort were said: 'We have such a great many to work, it does not matter whether they are bad or good. We must keep them, and say nothing about it'?—No, I did not hear that.

1751. The plan of employing two gangs of men was not very satisfactory?—No; the men only just got into the way of working when they had to go. In a letter to Captain Thompson, Mr. Lovegrove, Surveyor to the Hackney Board of Works, said he had found the plan of only working the men five hours to have worked much better than he expected, and that he was continuing the plan, only doing away with the meal and paying 5*d*. an hour for five hours' work.

1752. (*Chairman*): One of the gentlemen who was here just now, largely engaged in the building trade, said he found nothing so demoralising as for a good man to be out of work. Now your Association would, in the case of good men who are employed in such work, by employing them in such work as yours in the winter months, save them from this demoralising influence?—Yes.

1753. The Association would prevent them from being idle?—We did begin to employ painters this year very early.

(*Dr. Longstaff*): The gist of the thing lies in the Association making strict inquiry into the cases before it gives the work. I cannot see why there should not be strict inquiry made.

1754. (*Mr. Peters*): As to taking on the painters very early?—Their busy time does not come on till quite the end of April, but we began with them in March.

(*The Committee then adjourned.*)

FRIDAY, JULY 23, 1886.
Present—MR. PELL, in the Chair,

Mr. E. PETERS,
Rev. W. CURTIS HAYWARD,
Dr. G. B. LONGSTAFF,
Mr. A. G. CROWDER,
Mr. F. J. S. EDGCOMBE,
Mr. J. H. ALLEN.

Mr. HEDLEY, attending on behalf of the Local Government Board.

MR. G. COLLIE, examined.

1755. (*Chairman*): Mr. Collie, will you give us your address, and say what business or occupation you pursue?—I live at 18 Fawcett Road, Rotherhithe, and am a gardener by occupation.

1756. What do you desire to tell us upon the subject you know we are inquiring into—the distress last winter, and the way in which it was met? We should like to have your views generally. First of all, were you a recipient or a distributor?—I was a foreman in the employ of the Metropolitan Public Gardens Association, and superintended the men.

1757. Indirectly you were a recipient and paid to workmen?—The Association received money from the Mansion House Fund, and it came to me. I had the paying of the men.

1758. Did that money go into hotch-potch with the money of the Association?—That I do not know. It was only the unemployed that I had anything to do with.

1759. You know you had some money to pay among the unemployed; that money you believe to have come from the Mansion House Fund through your Association?—Yes. I believe so.

1760. How much did you pay away?—This last spring?

1761. Of this Mansion House money?—I cannot say exactly. I should think between £400 and £500.

1762. Were you paying away other money—the original funds of the Association—for the same workmen?—That I cannot answer.

1763. Were you paying more than you usually would pay away?—Yes; we were paying twice as many men to do the work as could have done it.

1764. Before this money was sent to the Association—what is the Association called?—The Metropolitan Public Gardens Association.

1765. Before it was sent to the Association was there an unusual number of applications for employment?—The unemployed were those we employed before from our own fund.

1766. About when do you think this fund began to be increased by the contribution from the Mansion House Fund?—About the middle of February.

1767. Did your Association put out any public intimation that more men could be taken on owing to this money?—Yes; the Association took men from the vestries of the different localities where works were going on, as soon as they knew they had the means of paying.

1768. Would you take any men except the men who came from the vestries?—None.

Mr. G. COLLIE.
July 23, 1886.

1769. What vestries were they that supplied you with men?—Bermondsey vestry supplied me.

1770. Any other?—No, not me.

1771. Not your work that you were overlooking?—No.

1772. The selection—did you feel yourself bound to take any of the men on that your vestry sent you? Were the inquiries made by you or by the vestry?—By the vestry.

1773. You set them on?—That was all.

1774. Was the result of setting these men on satisfactory to you as an overlooker of labour? Would you like the job again as a foreman of labour?—I would not object to the job again.

1775. You thought you got good men, who gave you no trouble?—Some were good, others middling, and others bad.

1776. Do you think business was conducted on satisfactory terms when the master compels you to pay such a mixture, and leaves the foreman no power of dismissal?—Oh, but I had power.

1777. Did you dismiss any?—Very few. The men as a whole appeared to be a decent lot of men. I had about 125 of them.

1778. You mean, they were not disinclined to do their best?—There were very few who were actually lazy, but they were not accustomed to the work, and did not earn the money that was paid.

1779. Then as far as a useful application of the money you have not much to say for it?—I think it was of very much use to the men employed.

1780. If you had had the £500 to spend, you would have got more labour if you had selected the men yourself? Would you have got double the labour?—Yes, quite that.

1781. Had any of the work to be undone afterwards?—No, sir.

1782. What was the sort of work they did?—The work we did was the graveyard round St. James's Church, Bermondsey. We removed nearly all the tombstones in the ground to the sides, and then laid out the space as a garden.

1783. You levelled it?—We made the ground into a park-like garden.

1784. How big a piece of ground?—Two acres.

1785. Have you seen the ground of St. George's-in-the-East?—No, I have never been in that ground; I expect it would be the same kind of work.

1786. You put the gravestones back?—Not to their places; but put them back to the wall, levelled the ground, and proceeded to turf it. It's a very pretty garden now, sir.

1787. I have no doubt of that. Now, what condition were the men in when they came to you? Were there outward evidences of want?—Yes; a great many of them were very poorly clothed.

1788. Did they look badly fed?—Well, there was no sign of starvation.

1789. And what classes of persons—what was their employment, could you tell?—A good many of them. A good many were waterside labourers—river men. A great many of them were casual labourers, ready to do anything they could do.

1790. Any tailors, do you think?—Yes. I had two or three tailors, sawyers, hatters, and so on.

1791. Had you any healthy men among them, who said that putting them to this work would disable them for their particular industry—the regular employment they would pursue if they could get work in it?—No. I had no such complaints.

1792. You really were nothing but the overlooker of the work, and you got the most you could out of them?—Yes, sir.

1793. And you saw that they did what the Association desired should be done on the ground?—Yes, sir.

1794. What caused the work to be discontinued—did they leave? What time did they go off?—As soon as the work was nearly done.

1795. And you exhausted the money that had been subscribed?—I believe we did, sir.

1796. Can you tell me what time of year—was it April or May?—A great many of the men were paid off after four or five weeks; then the rougher part of the work was done; then I kept the more useful and handy men to finish up the work with.

1797. Was it the intention of the Association to have executed this work before the Mansion House fund was heard of?—Yes; I know they intended to do it.

1798. How should you have proceeded to do the work if you had not had the exceptional distress and the fund?—When the Association did work they always employed the unemployed, and paid them at the rate of 4d. per hour.

1799. Did they select their men?—Well, when the men were taken on we could not tell till they were tried whether they were useful; and if they did their best we tried to keep them on.

1800. Would you have completed this job without the extra help?—Yes; but with it we did the work more quickly.

1801. Did you say that you had been in the habit of paying 4d. an hour?—Always the same, 4d. an hour.

1802. Did you say—I understood or inferred that you did not get so much work done for 4d. by this body of men as out of the men you usually employed?—No; because in time of distress there were actually more men employed than could be looked after properly.

1803. Am I right in saying that you were actuated by other motives than the completion of this garden—namely, that of putting money into the hands of men who were very much in want of it?—Yes.

1804. (*Mr. Peters*): You gave them 4d. an hour; how many hours?—When we began this we gave them eight hours a day. The Association last year employed them nine hours a day at 4d. Then, after we had been at work about ten days at St. James's, it was arranged to take on the men in gangs, and to work each gang five hours, so that they had only 1s. 8d. a day each man. They began work at half-past six in the morning; they were allowed 4d. to have breakfast at nine, then they worked up to twelve o'clock.

1805. Was it not very dark at half-past six in the morning?—No. In the middle of February there is a good deal of light at half-past six. Then the next gang were taken on at twelve. They were allowed 4d. also; they did not get the money, but a meal, which they had at two o'clock.

1806. And you estimated that meal as worth——?—Fourpence.

1807. (*Rev. W. Curtis Hayward*): Then in fact they only got 1s. 4d. and a meal?—No; 1s. 8d. and a meal.

1808. (*Chairman*): Oh, did they have a meal besides?—Yes; it was not given as part of the money. It was not considered part of the wages, but a gift by the Association.

1809. (*Rev. W. C. Hayward*): I was not quite sure of one fact—were you employed by the Association as a foreman before the Manson House Fund?—Oh, yes, sir.

1810. In the early part of the winter?—Since March, 1885.

1811. For how long were men content to work for you at that rate? Did you have the same men?—I had no difficulty in keeping the men on as long as I liked.

1812. Do you think the plan of giving a fourpenny meal was a good plan?—It would do very well for a single man who was in distress, but was not much good to a married man. Nine hours would have been preferable for a married man, even without the meal.

1813. Supposing the secretary of the Association in the beginning of the next winter were to give them 2s. for the five hours' work, or 1s. 8d. and a meal, which would you recommend?—Oh, the meal.

1814. Why?—For the class of men employed. You would be certain of their having one good meal.

1815. Do you mean they would drink the 1s. 8d. instead of eating it?—Some, no doubt, would prefer drinking it to eating it.

1816. (*Dr. Longstaff*): Did any large proportion of the men throw up the work of their own accord?—No; I don't recollect one throwing up work except he had got a better job.

Mr. G. COLLIE.
July 23, 1886.

1817. (*Mr. Crowder*): What opportunity had they of looking for work in the regular way? Did you cease to employ them after 12 o'clock?—Yes; they had all the afternoon to look for work, but they said that then it was not much use to look for it. We made shifts. One week one set of men were the morning gang, the next week they formed the afternoon gang.

1818. Did any number of them get drunk in any part of the day?—That scarcely ever occurred. Very little indeed; wonderful little.

1819. (*Mr. Edgcombe*): What is the market rate for such work as these men were supposed to do—the open market price?—Not less than 5 *l.* an hour.

1820. Would you be able to get men to work half a day at that rate?—A good man might expect 5½*d.*

1821. What was the work?—Spade work principally.

1822. They were sent by the vestry?—Yes.

1823. You don't know if there were any who would have liked the work who did not get it?—Oh, hundreds came from different parts round. I always sent them to the vestry-hall.

1824. Those who applied were *bonâ fide* men out of work?—Yes; the greater part of them were. A very few came merely to get the money, and did not like the work.

1825. There was a certain percentage of men you got rid of because they would not do the work?—Yes.

1826. (*Mr. Allen*): Where do you live—in Bermondsey?—No, Rotherhithe.

1827. Do you think there was much more distress last winter than usual?—I cannot say with any authority—with any certainty. The men said there was.

1828.—You could not say it of your own knowledge?—No.

1829. Were these men the class of men who are always out of work between January and March?—There is always a certain class of men out of employment in the winter. The great majority of them were, no doubt.

1830. Then supposing Lord Brabazon's Society did not exist, these men would have had to come to the parish?—Just so.

1831. If they had, would it not have been a good plan if the guardians had opened a labour yard?—Yes.

1832. If they are always out of employment in the winter, these men, instead of being paid out of charitable funds, would have been assisted by the parish? Is there a labour yard at Bermondsey?—I believe there is.

1833. Why did they not go to the labour yard, then?—I believe there is stone-breaking at Rotherhithe, and men were employed there.

1834. Why did not these men go there?—I was told that the money there was only a shilling a day, and the labour was very hard to men not used to it.

1835. Then they preferred charity money?—Yes.

1836. But there is no doubt about the fact that if there had been no Lord Brabazon's Society they must have gone to the parish?—I don't know what else they could have done.

1837. Then there would have been no help?—No.

1838. Did you make any inquiry about the class of men you took on? Were any inquiries made as to character?—Well, the people at the Bermondsey vestry knew most of the men that were taken on.

1839. Knew them to be men of good character?—Men who were not loafers.

1840. There is just one other question about the waterside labourers. Don't they earn very large money in the summer?—When work is plentiful.

1841. They are men who carry timber, and they earn large sums of money, and they drink the greater part of it?—I have no doubt a great many of them do.

1842. And, consequently, during the months of January, February, and March hey are always out of work?—Yes, the greater part of them.

1843. (*Mr. Loch*): Did you make any special arrangements for looking after the men while they were at work, so as to distribute the men—the industrious men with the idlers?—When I had a lot of men like that, I had always one or two picked out whom I knew before, who had been with the Association before. They were given a little larger money to assist in overlooking; the men were therefore either under my own eye or under the eye of one of them. If the men were well conducted and appeared to be useful, they were selected as men to be kept on when we were obliged to slacken hands.

1844. Did you take care to sort the men so as to put the good with second rate?—Oh, of course. If I had half a dozen good men with forty or fifty indifferent ones, I set them on with the awkward ones.

1845. With regard to payment, did you try paying them on any other system than 4d. an hour and a meal?—No.

1846. What do you think of a system of paying them by the piece?—I think it would be difficult to arrange with work of this sort. For one thing, if you set men on to work by the piece—say, to trench a bit of ground—a good many of them would have no idea of what you mean by trenching, and I do not think it would be any good to themselves. They could not do it.

1847. But, generally, the men get to be more handy?—Yes, some of them.

1848. It would be a better test if you could apply the piece system?—Yes; but I don't think it could be done. It would be a good plan to adopt a scale of wages.

1849. That is what I am driving at. How would you arrange it?—Well, some would be dear at 1s. 8d. a day for any good they did.

1850. You might estimate the wage-worth of the men and pay by that?—Yes; but the incapable workmen could not live on that.

1851. But might it not be better to let these men go to the labour yard?—Yes, I should say they might.

1852. If there had been a distinction between labour-yard men and other men, would not the garden-work have sped better?—Yes, very much. There appeared a very strong feeling against going there. I don't know anything about the labour yard by experience.

1853. (*Rev. W. C. Hayward*): If they got 1s. a day only, how could they live?—No; how could they?

1854. (*Mr. Hedley*): Remember that in the labour yard they are paid according to scale and according to family.

(*Chairman to Witness*): You don't know much about the labour yard. The Committee admit that in addition to the shilling a day which the men would have by going to the labour yard, there would be something more given, on a scale having reference to the number of the family—that the shilling a day was not all they would get. That is the Committee's opinion, not that of the witness.

1855. (*Mr. Loch*): At other times do you admit people to these works without inquiry?—No.

1856. What sort of inquiry do you make?—Formerly the men had to go to the Memorial Hall in Farringdon Street.

1857. What is meant by formerly?—1885.

1858. You mean that the year before it had been the custom of the Association to send them to the Memorial Hall for inquiry?—Yes; and to Collier's Rents, Borough.

1859. You left the inquiry afterwards with the vestry? Did you find you had a better set of men before?—There was very little to choose between them.

1860. (*Chairman*): You have told us one thing, that it was reasonable that men should have the morning to look for work—would it have been a better plan not to have commenced the work till nine or ten, and left the men to look for work?—Oh, yes. It was the intention to relieve as many men as possible, and on that small piece of ground there could not be so many men employed in one gang as could be in two, therefore we employed twice as many men as we could otherwise have done on the ground.

1861. When did you close for the day?—Half-past five.

1862. Did you not tell us that the men of the neighbourhood earned very large wages in the summer, with the certainty of being out of work in the winter?—Yes, it is the case. But I believe this last summer, and also this present summer, labour has been very short all through.

Mr. G. COLLIE.
July 23, 1886.

1863. Therefore you think that the origin of these men coming to your society for assistance and work in the winter was due to their not having been so well employed in the previous summer as previously?—I believe the work along the river-side has been very slack in the summer of 1885, in the winter, and now.

1864. (*Dr. Longstaff*): Have you any personal means of forming an opinion as to whether there is likely to be great distress next winter, or otherwise?—Yes, I hear people speak of it. It appears to be the opinion of the men themselves.

1865. I suppose you are still working as a gardener in some way?—The Association not being prepared to go on with more new work at present, my services, as foreman, of course are not required.

1866. Then you have not come in contact with men otherwise than in connection with the Association?—No; except what I have heard—hearsay.

1867. (*Chairman*): What particular class of workmen are you acquainted with yourself—with gardeners?—Yes, sir, with gardeners.

1868. Would you tell us whether they are receiving less wages now than they were last year?—I don't know, sir. My work as a gardener was in private situations, so that I do not know.

1869. You must have made an acquaintance with gardeners. Have no men whom you know come and asked you, 'Can you put me on to work, for I'm afraid we are going to have a bad time of it?'—Oh, yes. Jobbing men I cannot say about.

1870. You find more men out of place who have been in gentlemen's service?—Oh, yes. Establishments reduced; wages not so good.

1871. Are they making a fight to keep up wages? Could they get work at lower wages? Is there a little struggle going on on that point, whether they will take less wages or stick out and try to get the same as before?—Oh, I think they would accept less wages, certainly.

1872. And still they cannot get employment?—Many cannot.

1873. (*Dr. Longstaff*): Really good men, of good character?—Oh, yes; competent men; excellent in every way.

1874. And you think such men would have got employment a few years ago? You don't think them incapacitated by age?—Oh, I know men in the prime of life, men out for a long time, working in nurseries for very small wages, lower than 4*d*. an hour; men who have been getting over £100 a year.

1875. (*Chairman*): That you know yourself?—Yes, that I know; but that is a different question altogether to London employment.

1876. But it shows the general depression.

MR. G. T. WESTBROOK, examined.

Mr. G. T. WESTBROOK.

1877. (*Chairman*): You are good enough to come to tell us something about the distress last winter. Do you live in Limehouse?—Yes.

1878. How many years have you lived there?—Thirty-nine.

1879. And what is your employment?—Shipwright.

1880. Working for whom?—For Lester & Perkins, Albert Dock, till to-night.

1881. Had you anything to do with the distribution of charitable funds last winter?—Oh, yes, sir.

1882. How were you engaged—with Mansion House money?—I saw Mr. Maltby, the agent of the Charity Organisation Society Committee.

1883. About what time of year—middle of February?—It was at the commencement of the Mansion House Fund. Mr. Maltby gave me a letter of introduction to Mr. Jackson. He is a member of Toynbee Hall.

1884. And what did you do with Mr. Jackson?—He took me on to see the cases as they came in.

1885. And he engaged you to do what?—To do the general work of the office.

1886. At Limehouse, for the Mansion House Fund?—Yes.

1887. Was your work confined to indoor work?—Very nearly all the time.

1888. Perhaps you will tell us how you spent the day?—I got there at nine in the morning. I had a desk; I entered the cases that had been done the previous day. I entered them into a ledger, and then entered them into alphabetical books of reference. After I had done that I went out and visited some of the cases.

1889. Some of the cases to which money had been awarded?—To which nothing had been awarded.

1890. You went on a tour of inspection and inquiry as to some cases?—Yes.

1891. And what revelations did you get upon the cases? Was there evidence of great distress?—Yes; and evidence of great imposture, too.

1892. And some evidence of idleness, I suppose?—Yes.

1893. Which was most abundant, imposture, idleness, or distress?—There is a difference between the classes of people that I visited. Some I visited were hard working people brought down to distress; others were chronic paupers.

1894. And some opened their mouths because they thought something might be put into it?—Yes.

1895. Then the people who were hard working—honest distress—what class were those?—They were mechanics generally.

1896. About what would be the rent of the houses they were living in?—Unfortunately, the houses down there—the houses are six to eight-roomed houses, and they are let out in apartments.

1897. And these people you are speaking of were people renting a room or two?—Yes.

1898. Did you find that they had pawned much of their goods?—Yes.

1899. Did you find them sitting without fires in their rooms?—No; not particularly without fires.

1900. And to what did they attribute their distress - to work having stopped on the river at the time, or to something having happened to the trade in the summer?—It has been slack these last three or four years - a general depression.

1901. Were they people who were likely to have had money in the savings bank?—Yes, sir.

1902. Did they tell you that they had sold out?—I knew possibly that they had drawn out. And people in building societies had been obliged to part with their shares for common necessaries.

1903. How were these cases treated? Leave the imposition out. How did you deal with the honest cases? You found a man poorly off, who had drawn upon his capital; you reported to the Committee, and what was done?—They relieved him.

1904. With money?—No; not with money. There were several cases, first of all, we relieved with money. That was before we got fairly into working order, but very little money went out.

1905. Do you approve of money?—No, I don't.

1906. What was the better system that you adopted when you had to do so?—Tickets upon different tradesmen, not one particular man, but selected tradesmen.

1907. People who would supply them with goods, and not swop them for money?—Oh, yes

1908. Upon the whole, do you think that the Mansion House fund was of service?—It was of great service.

1909. What would have happened to these people but for the Mansion House Fund?—I believe they would have gone to the Poor Law guardians.

1910. After all, was there money enough placed at your disposal to prevent any of those deserving people from going, or had they some still to get?—I think it tided them over it very well for the time.

1911. Now, we have got to the end of July; does the depression in business still continue?—I can only answer for one—the shipwright—that is still continuing. The shipwrighting trade has gone from London.

1912. (*Mr. Allen*): It has gone for the last ten years.

1913. (*Chairman*): Are these men hanging on to a business that is exhausted?—They cannot get anything else; there is such depression. A great many have gone to other trades.

Mr. G. T.
WESTBROOK.

July 23, 1886.

1914. But there are some who won't do that?—There are some who can't; it's not to be got.

1915. Not in Limehouse?—If I could get away from shipwrighting I would to-morrow. The trade is done. There are so many of us that the trade is done.

1916. Then you think you may have the same sort of distress next winter that occurred last winter?—I am afraid so in our trade; I can't answer for other trades.

1917. Well, now, don't you think it is possible that these men are hanging on to a decayed industry because they think that during the winter they may get some relief from bounty?—Oh, no, sir.

1918. I don't want to trap you in any way, but I want your opinion. Take your own case, and those of men with whom you are acquainted. Suppose that they knew absolutely that there would be no Mansion House Fund, do you think they would remain at Limehouse, where they are, if they felt for a certainty that they could not calculate upon some bounty in the cold weather?—Necessity would compel them to remain there. Not calculating upon any relief, they would gladly go, if they could better themselves.

1919. Then may we not gather from that that men are being kept there to their detriment by the hope of some bounty coming to them in the winter, and that it would be better to make an effort now?—That is so, probably.

1920. (*Chairman*): I asked him whether, if these men could feel certain that there would not be bounty coming to them next winter to meet this depression, would they or would they not stay there? Is there still virtue enough left in the trade to enable him to live through the winter, or does it require some bounty like the Mansion House Fund to enable a man to go through the twelve months?—That is the condition of our industry now.

1921. Would they stay?—They would have to stay, simply for the reason that there is nowhere else for them to go.

1922. That is your opinion, but there is a map of England.—How are they to go?

1923. (*Mr. Allen*): The shipwrights, as a matter of fact, have not had much work for the last ten years?—Yes.

1924. But a large number have moved off?—We were 2,000, and now we are about 1,300. There have been a number of apprentices coming into the trade.

1925. The wages are the same as ten years ago?—Seven shillings a day.

1926. Is there a labour yard at Poplar?—I cannot answer.

1927. Are you not in Poplar Union?—No; in Stepney Union. There is no labour yard there.

1928. Supposing there had been a labour yard there, would they have gone in?—Not if they could have struggled on without.

1929. I think you have said that they were almost reduced to starvation?—Yes, several. I should have thought that they would have gone into the labour yard. I could not say whether they would or not.

1930. Would it have been a hardship to them to go there?—Yes, sir.

1931. Why? Would it injure their respectability?—Yes; it would lower them. They would feel it so.

1932. Do you remember, a number of years ago, when a great many went to the Poplar workhouse?—Yes, a number went into the labour yard.

1933. That was about fifteen years ago, and the labour yard was quite full. The shipwrights went in then; then why should they not go in now? Among the men that you visited were they all connected with the shipping trade?—No.

1934. What trades were they connected with?—There were some bricklayers, and some moulders and engineers.

1935. The engineers are allowed ten shillings a week by the Union. They would not be in destitution?—No, sir; but I don't see why that should debar them from getting it.

1936. Still, they would not actually starve?—No.

1937. You know Lord Brabazon's Society?—I have heard of it.

1938. Do you know at Stepney a large number of people were offered employment and would not take the work?—I didn't know that they refused the work, but then the question is what did they offer them?

1939. Only small wages, but 'a small loaf is better than no bread.' Would they be suitable for emigration?—Yes.

1940. Do you know that they would be willing?—I know several young fellows in the Shipwrights' Society would like to go.

1941. Good men?—Yes, good men; not loafers.

1942. Young men?—Yes.

1943. Single?—No, married men.

1944. (*Mr. Edgcombe*): With reference to the distribution of the Mansion House Fund, I understand the relief is only given to deserving persons?—Yes, sir.

1945. It was only given in kind, I understand?—Not in money.

1946. Why was that?—In case it should have been made a bad use of. We found that where they had had the money they had spent it in drink.

1947. Did not that show that the investigation was imperfect?—Yes.

1948. If he was deserving why could he not be entrusted to spend his own money? You confined the relief to persons whose characters answered inquiry? Five shillings would have gone further than five shillings' worth of tickets? We gave the tickets 'on any grocer.' When the first order came we had to name the tradesman, and we thought that by altering it to 'any grocer,' or 'any baker,' the man could go to any shop—general shop—where they kept butter and cheese as well as groceries, whereas if we named a grocer, he could only get groceries.

1949. Supposing you are quite sure as to class and character, it is less trouble to you and more agreeable to him to give him cash?—Yes.

1950. It was only because you could not trust your own investigation that you hedged yourselves in this manner?—We thought we would give it all in kind. The Committee sent down that there was no rent to be paid, and we thought if we gave cash it would go for rent.

1951. (*Mr. Crowder*): What was the nature of the investigation?—I went to the house. At first they came there before the Committee, who took the case down. Afterwards we made the rule for them to leave the address and then there was a visit. The number of children I saw, and whoever they referred to—the landlords of the house—I went to see if they were indebted to them—backward in their rent. We had no employers' reference; we found out we must insist on that before we could grant them relief.

1952. So that we have the visit to the home, reference to the landlord, and then to the employer?—And then we wanted a reference to someone local as to character.

1953. And when you said you distinguished the deserving from the idle and the impostors, did you mean depending on your impression on the visit, or on the whole investigation?—The whole investigation. I was so thoroughly deceived by them I could not believe them.

1954. Well then, in Limehouse, what was your rule with reference to the class who are never in regular work—the casual labourer—do you know whether the Committee had any rule sent down to them with reference to that particular class who were never in regular work?—We relieved them.

1955. Mr. Freemantle sent down a letter saying that that class was not to be relieved, and I understood that that was carried out in Stepney?—We did not relieve the casual labourers if they were not in regular work. One half of the applicants in the Limehouse district were dock labourers.

1956. Was any inquiry made of the relieving officers with reference to these people being in receipt of parish relief?—Oh, yes; every case paper went to Mr. Jones, the relieving officer. He knew one or two cases that I had reported well of, and he could tell me what had happened for some years.

1957. On the whole, considering that the number of applicants was large, and the work hurried, and the staff small, were you satisfied with the method you adopted, on the whole?—Yes, at the latter end.

1958. And do you think upon the whole that it did more good than harm?—Oh, yes; it weeded a lot out who would have been relieved if there had not been a strict inquiry.

Mr. G. T. WESTBROOK.

July 23, 1886.

Mr. G. T.
WESTBROOK.

July 23, 1886.

1959.—I meant did the fund do good? Did the good outweigh the harm?—Yes, I think so.

1960. Now, take a shipwright, an artisan, a man whose wages are seven shillings a day, a man who does not drink, a good mechanic, a man living respectably in every way, what would be the effect upon the independent feeling he would have, of having to lean upon a fund of this sort?—Very few put themselves on. If I had not pressed them they would not have gone on to a fund. One man whose case was brought before us, he begged that we would not let them know that his name was before them.

1961. What was the effect of breaking down that fine spirit by the fund? I am speaking of the good man. Do you think a fund like this would lower him at all?—I am afraid it would, sir. That is what I feel myself. I suppose it is human nature.

1962. (*Dr. Longstaff*): Then some of these men whom you had a difficulty in persuading to accept of the fund might, in case of a similar fund being formed, accept without much difficulty?—I cannot say that. If they thought it was public, because it was lowering them, they would feel it very much.

1963. But they would not feel the lowering the second time so much as the first?—No, their spirit would be broken, crushed.

1964. Now, I gather that you approve of the system of tickets on the whole. If you were asked to be one of a committee, would you approve of the use of tickets?—Yes, sir.

1965. Did you come across any instance in which the tickets were used for any other purpose—sold or converted into drink?—I know one case where they were sold for money, and the man got tight with the money. And another one of a person who had sold six shillings' worth of tickets for three shillings. My informant was behind her, and she said 'I have six shillings' worth of tickets, and I have got a pair of trousers and a coat in pawn, and I must get them out. You can have them for three shillings.'

1966. In that case it was not drink; it was converted into trousers. Did that often occur?—No.

1967. Did the Committee redeem things from pawn?—Yes, tools, clothes, and bedding.

1968. Did the Committee pay arrears of clubs?—Yes.

1969. Do you think that was a proper thing to do?—Yes.

1970. Did it give satisfaction to the artisan?—Yes.

1971. You said that at one time your trade numbered 2,000, and now only 1,300; are those the statistics of the union or your own impression?—I cannot say they are exactly the numbers, but that is what I take the number to be at the present time, from what I know of the society.

1972. You have a fair means of judging, then?—Yes.

1973. And it was considerably larger?—Yes.

1974. When did the number begin to diminish? How long ago was it 2,000?—Ten years ago.

1975. Has it been diminishing more rapidly lately?—We keep at a standstill now, because there are fewer apprentices to come in. There is a lot of these; though they leave the trade, they do not leave the society.

1976. They are driven to take work of some other kind?—Yes.

1977. They are still living in the place?—Oh, not all in Limehouse.

1978. (*Chairman*): Not the 700. Have the 700 left the district?—Oh, yes, entirely.

1979. If 700 shipwrights had left London, that would mean about 3,500 people altogether, counting women and children. Who is now employing these people where they live?—I have no means of judging.

1980. Have the wages fallen in your trade?—No, they are about the same now.

1981. But a man does not earn as much now in a month as before?—Nothing near.

1982. How many days' work is it common for a man to get now?—Men average about three days a week.

1983. I suppose eight or ten years ago he had five days a week?—Yes.

1984. (*Mr. Allen*): And overtime besides?—Yes.

1985. (*Dr. Longstaff*): You said some of your people would be willing to emigrate, is that to continue as shipwrights or to turn their hand to anything?—Yes, turn their hands to anything. We have one from Limehouse who has gone away this time.

1986. Would you be able to give the emigration department of this Society information as to proper persons for emigration? We have had inquiries about men to go to Australia.—I would be willing to try.

1987. (*Mr. Hedley*): Do you think that a man going into a shop with a ticket gets as good value for his money as for the money out of his pocket, as good value for your ticket?—I am afraid not, in some places.

1988. Is it not a matter of fact that the shipbuilding trade has left the Poplar and Limehouse district?—Yes, from the cheapness of production in the north.

1989. Had not strikes a great deal to do with it?—No, sir; perhaps it may be the overcharges of the employers.

1990. As a matter of fact, the trade has gone?—Oh, yes.

1991. (*Chairman*): But is it not also due to a very different class of ships being built?—Much cheaper in the north, because there is the carriage of the iron to London, a duty on coal in London; everything tends to make production cheaper in the north.

1992. (*Mr. Hedley*): Have you any idea where it has gone to?—At the present time I don't know, sir.

1993. If the shipwrights were inclined to get work, could you advise them where to go?—No; we are connected with all ports, and have advices that trade is very bad indeed everywhere. There has been a depression amongst employers. At the docks they are fairly overstocked.

1994. (*Chairman*): Are you talking of the London Docks?—Any docks.

1995. You mean lower down the river. The question put was 'the docks.' I wish to have it cleared up. Do you mean the new docks at Dagenham, that they are overstocked?—They are overstocked—with water. I was speaking of the old docks.

1996. (*Mr. Hedley*): You said that some of the dockyard labourers were unwilling to receive relief from the Mansion House Fund, that it hurt their self-respect?—No, artisans.

1997. Which do you think would take most of their self-respect, and deteriorate them more in the eyes of their fellow-workmen, their receiving something from the Mansion House Fund, or being known to go into the labour yard—which would prejudice them most in their character?—If a man fall down like that, I don't see it is against his character to receive it. They ought not to lose their self-respect.

1998. What would be their own feeling—that a fellow-workman would look down upon them for receiving money from charity, or from working in the labour yard?—I think they would feel it more going into the labour yard, because some of their own mates would have to pay extra rates for them on that account.

1999. (*Mr. Peters*): I understood you to say that very few artisans or shipwrights have recourse to charity in the winter?—Very few.

2000. How have they managed to get through the winter?—That is a puzzle. I have asked how I managed myself. I am an abstainer, and have a moderate share of work, but some of them have less than I do. I don't know how they managed.

2001. Has the possibility of getting relief made them stay on in the trade of shipwrights?—No. It is because they have not known what to do or where to go.

2002. (*Dr. Longstaff*): Do you know whether there is any difference of wages at the different ports?—Some of the very small ports have very small money—about 5s. I think.

2003. (*Chairman*): Five shillings for ten hours?—I don't know how many hours. In the north, and at Cardiff, and London, and Liverpool it is 7s. Only I heard they have lowered it at Sunderland; but Liverpool and Cardiff are the same as London.

Mr. G. T. Westwood.

July 23, 1886.

Mr. G. T. WESTBROOK.

July 23, 1886.

2004. (*Dr. Longstaff*): Some of the places in the north have dropped down a little?—Yes; I think it is 6s. 6d. on the Clyde.

2005. (*Mr. Loch*): You said there were a certain number of men who would go away if they could, and some would emigrate. Is there any way of dealing with those? What class would it be who wish to go and cannot? Are they men who are too old to go?—Oh, no; young men.

2006. Next, as to those who are out of work, but would not emigrate—what would you do with them? What is the cause that they cannot take up another trade?—Why they cannot take up any trade is the stagnation.

2007. These are youngish men?—Yes.

2008. In a time of distress you say there are two classes—the superior class of men who are out of work, and glad to do something, but who would not work in a labour yard; and those who would rather not work in the labour yard or do work of any other sort. Would you divide them, and give work in the labour yard to some and other work to others?—Yes.

2009. If you wished to give work to the other class, who were (*e.g.*) shipwrights, would it be well to give them work which would help to teach them some other trade?—I don't think it would be any good.

2010. You think there is no choice for them?—Any other trade is overstocked.

2011. There is no industry which we might do in London which is now done abroad?—Oh, yes.

2012. Can you name any?—That is the folly of free trade.

2013. That is another question. You had great crowds at your office?—Yes, sir.

2014. Would there be any sort of hardship in having cases sent from certain sources only?—I would make the suggestion that they should come through the trade societies, because our own society can tell exactly the amount of money a man takes in a year; the secretary by the cards can tell exactly how much work a man has done. He would be able to give you an idea of the amount of work they are doing. He could give you good cases.

2015. (*Mr. Crowder*): And can you depend on the truth of these cards?

2016. (*Mr. Loch*): Is there any way in which they could be checked?—Yes; I would say that he should produce a tradesman's reference, and also an employer's reference. Two men may be doing the same amount of work, and one may have a family and the other may have none.

2017. Would you seek benefit societies' men in the same way?—Yes.

2018. And in that way you think you would get a pick of cases?—Yes, a better sample than we had at Limehouse.

2019. (*Chairman*): With regard to shipwrights, how is the supply of this skilled labour kept up? Is a shipwright's son a shipwright?—No, sir, not now.

2020. Of your own knowledge, within the last ten or twelve years, have many men come from the country and turned to this business?—No, sir.

2021. You know something of the riveters?—Yes.

2022. You know a good many men came up from Ashford?—Yes. I know a man, a weaver, who is a first-rate riveter. Now we see the men's indentures.

2023. And your system of payment through the leading hands makes that sure. Do you take the materials from the hands?—No, we take the materials from the foreman.

2024. But that system of having a leader makes you sure to exclude men not belonging to the trade?—That is not my duty as a committee-man. I go and ask a man for his card. If he cannot produce a card, we give notice and he has to leave us.

2025. What is to prevent your employer keeping him in employment? Does that make him go away?—No, not at all. Then we leave.

2026. (*Mr. Loch*): In Stepney there is no outdoor relief, and there is no labour yard. You have only the workhouse and the medical relief. Was Stepney worse off this winter than Poplar and Mile End, where there was outdoor relief and labour yard? All this time, with all this distress, was there no real suffering caused by their having no outdoor relief?—I don't understand.

2027. In Mile End there was outdoor relief; in Stepney there was not. Did the difference of having outdoor relief in one union and not in the other make no difference in the amount of distress?—I am not acquainted with Mile End. I don't know anything of them.

2028. Take the question apart from the contrast, did outdoor relief make a difference in Stepney?—It would have made the Mansion House Fund better off.

2029. Would it have made the population better off?—Certainly, it must have done so.

2030. (*Mr. Crowder*): It was the able-bodied men with whom the Mansion House Fund had chiefly to do, not sick cases where outdoor relief is given. Outdoor relief does not touch the able-bodied men, except with the labour test; it is only the women and the sick people?—I am thinking myself, with those dock labourers, if we had had a labour test with them, many of them would have shirked it.

2031. Those are the people you would have put into the labour yard if you could?—Yes.

2032. (*Chairman*): If there had been some outdoor relief you said they would have been, certainly, better off; is that the opinion of the men, or your opinion?—That is my opinion—if they received out-door relief and Mansion House relief as well.

Mr. G. T. Westbrook

July 20, 1886.

Mr. G. DEW, examined.

2033. (*Chairman*): You live at Camberwell?—Yes.

2034. What is your trade?—A carpenter.

2035. What shop or master do you work for?—Mr. Love's, and I was working previously for Cubitt's for many years.

2036. Was there last year an abatement in the demand for employment in your particular industry?—Yes, there was a very great abatement.

2037. Did wages come down?—No.

2038. Why, if there was an abatement in the demand for labour, did not the wages come down?—Because the masters of London are different to many masters; they are very honourable.

2039. Do you think a grocer who is overstocked with sugar is an honourable grocer if he won't drop the price because he has too much sugar in his warehouse? Your idea is that there should be an arbitrary price. I wish I was in those happy circumstances myself. I am a farmer. You think there should be an arbitrary rule with regard to the price of labour?—Most decidedly. We must have a standard for average men.

2040. Have you been able to keep up the scale of wages?—Yes.

2041. Has not that beer, rather at the cost of some of those who were obliged to keep away from work because they could not get what they thought they ought to be paid for their services?—I don't think if the wages had been reduced it would have brought more work.

2042. Does that apply to painters as well as joiners?—Yes, I think so.

2043. My house wants painting, and I have an estimate of the cost of doing it. I am not going to do it. But if people came and offered me to do it for 30 per cent. less it might induce me to have it done.—When people want a thing done they have it done.

2044. You found there were less people employed last summer?—More particularly the winter. A severe winter tells worse upon the building trade than any other as regards outdoor work.

2045. But on your system of payment, if there is any merit in it, I think they should be able to provide in the summer for other times when work is not abundant?—If they can get extra wages we are pleased to see them do it. We are bound to fix an average rate, like the lawyers. We copy them to a certain extent, though we can't copy them as closely as we should like.

2046. Though circumstances of trade might induce a rise of wages, you would refuse a rise of wages; or does the rule apply only to a fall?—If we thought the rate too low, we should apply to the Masters' Association; we should try to talk the matter over, and see if we could arrange matters;

Mr. G. Dew.

Mr. G. Dew.
July 23, 1886.

but if we could not arrange, and still thought we were right, we should give them six months' notice.

2047. But as to workmen, not so enlightened as yourself, who are inclined to work for less money—and there must be some ready to do it if they could get work?—Well, I have had great experience that non-society men seem quite as anxious to get the full money as the others, and the men who will work for the less money are the bad men.

2048. Leaving that as it is, you find difficulty to get employment for the society men?—We were more successful with the society men than with those outside.

2049. And that left you with less of a fund to fall back upon in winter?— We had plenty of funds. I was on the local committee, not the Mansion House Committee—Mr. Powell sat on the Mansion House Committee— Secretary of the Trades Committee. He was a member of the Mansion House Committee convened by the Lord Mayor.

2050. Did he think it was a good thing?—He thought it had done a certain amount of good, though we are all doubtful as to the effect in the future.

2051. Do you think that it was indispensable—that you could not have got on without it among the people you are talking of?—I don't say that, but it was a sore pinch, and many men had been pinched so hardly, and had pledged a great many tools, and were not in a position to take work.

2052. You hear a great deal of the distressed condition and depression of the agricultural labourer. Would you be surprised to hear that there is nothing of this sort known among our people? May it not be the fact that the agricultural labourer when there is not demand for work goes off elsewhere for other employment? Do you find an influx of country people now?—Yes, we do. I am a countryman myself. I believe that two-thirds of the carpenters in London are from the country, and the labourers even more than that. A very large number of men come to take work on buildings and the like.

2053. May it not be owing to the fact, that country people think that London is paved with gold?—That is very probable.

2054. Would this not be increased by a distribution of a Mansion House Fund?—It may be so.

2055. That if the Lord Mayor should not have the Mansion House Fund next winter, and that it should be illegal to have money in that way, would that keep the extra hands from coming up?—It would have a good effect in that respect, and some may be expecting, and not making the same savings as before.

2056. You, as I think, mean that it may operate to prompt a man not to put his best leg first?—I have that fear.

2057. And though it may have been of some service in former cases, would you say that the operative does not derive, as a class, the benefit from such an attempt to relieve them?—I don't think he does.

2058. (*Mr. Peters*): You have fixed a minimum wage?—Yes, 9d. per hour, and 52½ hours per week.

2059. (*Mr. Hedley*): Have any foreigners come to London as carpenters?— Very few. There are a great many in fancy trades—cabinet-makers—but very few carpenters; not for strong constructive work; they are not up to much.

2060. What are they chiefly—French, German, Swiss?—Almost equal between French and German.

2061. (*Dr. Longstaff*): Does your trade suffer greatly from the importation of made up windows and doors?—Not so much as many think. As a rule, I don't think we suffer anything.

2062. You are free traders there?—We have many fair traders among us, but——

2063. But if a large number of doors and window frames are sent into London must not that cause less work for joiners?—But there are less of these doors in shops than are supposed. Any man in the country who wants a window frame or door, may go to the timber yard and buy it, but as a rule it is not general.

2064. Is not a good deal of that sort of material used in the inferior firms?—

No, I think not, even in the speculative building. Speculative work is done piecework, and the men engaged in that line can compete with any foreign work.

2065. If there were to be next winter any Mansion House Fund, can you suggest any different way of managing it than that you took last winter?—I should like to see some means of giving employment if it was possible.

2066. But supposing money was to be distributed, do you see any special defect in the system that was adopted?—No, I think it was as good as could be had I would give relief in money, but in food only when you know them to be drinking people.

2067. Would it not be as well that the drinking man should go to the workhouse?—Yes, but the difficulty is with his wife and children.

2068. What is your opinion of the state of trade at the present moment? Are you doing a large amount of work for summer?—We are beginning to get better now. Up to the present time it has been slack, but we have strong hopes of things improving ; and if it does, which I believe it will—all the workmen's trains now coming into the city are very crowded, and that is always a sure indication that trade is improving.

2069. You don't think there is special fear of impending distress next winter?—No, unless there is severe weather. I don't think there will be anything like we had last winter. There is one thing I should like to suggest from the society point of view. Should you decide to use the larger part of the money in finding employment, that it should be done by paying near the average wages, and employing men two or three days a week, and set them free on other days to look after themselves on those other days.

2070. (*Chairman*): Say three days to build and three days to pull down: it is all raised upon public money given by those who like to give it?—As far as the society is concerned. The society gives 10s. a week while out of work. If they meet with an accident they give £50. If they are permanently disabled the men get £100

2071. (*Dr. Longstaff*): There are a large number of carpenters, are there not, in your society?—A very large number.

2072. And even a larger number of good workmen who are not society men?—Yes.

2073. (*Mr. Crowder*): In your trade there are a great number of unskilled labourers?—Yes.

2074. They would be casually employed from time to time?—As a rule they are employed from week to week until they are discharged during the job.

2075. They would be a lower class, as a matter of fact. You are aware that for twenty years there has been no Mansion House Fund until last winter?—Yes.

2076. Supposing last winter had not been the severe one that you describe it, do you see any greater reason for such a fund as we had last winter than during certain other winters in the last nineteen years?—Well, I think work was very short. The severe weather aside, it was the worst that I remember for depression of trade, and it had been so bad all through the summer that those who were inclined to do the best they could had not the money. We had to have levies on to keep up the funds, and last winter was the first time we had to put levies on to increase the funds. We have had to put levies on for the purpose of keeping them up for unemployed benefit. 1s. 6d. a week for a long time.

2077. Did you not say that, with regard to the undeserving man, you would not object to his going to the poorhouse—but "how about his wife and family"?—Yes.

2078. Supposing the relief of the wife and family were offered on condition of the man going to the labour yard as a test? A man is suspected of being given to drink, and we say to him, there are your wife and children ; we should not like to ask them to go to such a place. We will relieve them for a week or two, and we will give you relief, as well as your wife and family, if you will come in. You would throw the burden of the sacrifice upon the man. 'You have nothing to do but to enter, and we will offer your family relief at once?—

Mr. G. Drew.

July 23, 1886.

Mr. G. Dew.
July 23, 1886.

It would be a good thing if you could get him to accept the relief on those terms.

2079. (*Mr. Edgcombe*): Did you see how the Mansion House Fund was spent last year?—Yes, a little.

2080. That it did not touch your society?—No, I did not say that. Sometimes men have been out so long that they are past our society. For twelve weeks they get 10s. a week, after that, for twelve weeks, 6s.

2081. So far as you were able to see, did the fund reach the right people?— Yes, I think it did. In Camberwell and that way they were chiefly the building trade that applied.

2082. Do you think it is at all likely there were high-class artisans whose distress was not found out?—Yes, I have heard of one since, a man whose character I can speak to. He is an abstainer. I did not know it then, but it appeared he had sickness and death in his house. He had been eleven weeks out of work. It was his foreman who came and asked me if we could do something for him.

2083. Can you suggest any means by which these men could be got at?— Only by having working men on the Committee. They are terribly afraid of the parson and the Poor Law guardian. They feel they will be too much humiliated, and will not go.

2084. (*Mr. Allen*): Was that man a carpenter?—No, a plasterer; but I don't think he was in the society.

2085. (*Mr. Loch*): Do you think that better arrangements could be made for ascertaining the actual condition of affairs in regard to distress? Last year there was rather a rush at one part. Would your society, and the sort of men you have referred to, be willing to let us know how matters stood, so that we might set to work with sobriety, and do it well?—Our society were very reluctant to let us have anything from this fund, and it has not been well received. We have means to provide for all our hands, and we don't care to have much to do with these Charity Committees.

2086. There is a distinct difficulty as to knowing what the extent of the distress is. Can you suggest any way of ascertaining? Would you suggest writing to employers to know the general extent of distress? You don't want to establish a fund before the time?—I don't know. If you were to send a written intimation round to the secretaries of some of the trade societies they would be able to give you some idea whether their members were very much pinched. If men have a difficulty in paying up their money, they can tell at once what the state of the trade is.

2087. Did the Mansion House Fund make that inquiry through you?— No.

2088. Do you think that one could test the matter in this way: by privately asking a few of the leading men in the trade to meet and talk it over?—Yes, I think it would be possible if you wrote to some of the secretaries of different clubs asking them to appoint a representative, and have a meeting somewhere.

2089. Privately, of course?—Yes.

2090. With regard to men who have been out of work; is there any other work to which carpenters could turn if they had instruction, which possibly is not within their reach now—fancy work, for instance?—That is the cabinet work; that is a distinct branch of itself.

2091. Would a man in your trade be able to take up the other?—As a rule that trade is nearly always overstocked.

2092. There is no other direction you can suggest?—A carpenter can turn his hand many ways, but as a rule, in the cabinet trade, they are worse off than we are.

2093. Do you know if carpenters emigrate?—Yes, many; we are evidently a little too thick to do any good.

2094. Where would you suggest that they could go?—We have several branches—America, Canada, Australia, the Cape; and if an offer was made of any considerable amount to them ——

2095. Would the societies help by advice to make it work smoothly?—Yes; we can, even with our own society, if our funds stood at £3 a member—we could give a grant of £6, but we have never been able to give that assistance.

2096. (*Mr. Allen*): You have never done that yet?—No.

2097. (*Dr. Longstaff*): If money were advanced for people to emigrate to the Australian colonies—money advanced on loan—would the branch of your society in Australia assist to recover that money to assist others?—No; I don't think we could impose anything like that upon our branch secretaries in the colonies. The people out in the colonies are not anxious to get the colonies overstocked, and that would tell against it. The only way you could do would be to send out *bonâ fide* men to act as your agents out there send them out with a gang.

2098. And you think a man like that would be forthcoming?—Yes, I think Mr. Acworth asked me if I knew anyone likely to go. We sent one man out, and that was one of the best bits of money that we spent. Mr. Acworth wrote to me and suggested a man for emigration if I could name him. We had had a member of our society and other societies—a provident man—and this man had been in and out of work; he was a staircase hand, the highest hand of the trade, and he had been fair hard up. He was a widower with four children. He wanted to emigrate; he could not see a chance of permanent work, and so we got up a concert, and Joseph Lester promised to take the chair; but it turned out a wet night and we did not clear expenses. Mr. Acworth took the case in hand, and I had a grant of money and sent him to St. Louis, in the United States. And since he has been there, I have heard he is doing well.

2099. (*Chairman*): What employment had he got there?—Carpenter and joiner.

2100. (*Mr. Loch*): You would suggest helping in that big way?—Yes, and by taking tools out of pledge.

2101. (*Mr. Crowder*): Only you must know your case.

2102. (*Mr. Loch*): And if you felt that you were spending in that fashion, much more care would be taken?—Yes.

2103. That would be a point in any future administration?—Yes.

2104. Was much given for rent last year?—Nothing was given for rent in the Camberwell district.

2105. Would you be inclined to use the Poor Law more in regard to cases that you did not help? Would you send the lower class right away to them?—I would if I could.

2106. You would simply send them? If they did not go it would be their responsibility?—Yes.

2107. Did you deal with people who would be out of work every year?—No, we did not deal with them so liberally as with others, when we found they were always asking relief. Some men try to hold on to a trade that has left the country.

2108. (*Chairman*): Now, Mr. Dew, there must be some cause for this distress somewhere or other, and men being in these difficulties. We must admit that all that the Mansion House Fund has done is to deal with the distress itself. It has not concerned itself at all with the cause of the distress. Would you be glad if the effort was made to get rid of the cause of distress by sending some of the people out of the country, or to join a co-operative undertaking? I am a great co-operator—distributive co-operation. Is not that what your view is, that the Mansion House Fund has dealt with the distress when it came? You would be pleased to see the money applied to remove the causes by getting rid of surplus population, and by teaching people to help themselves if they could, and you are not satisfied with the Mansion House Fund as an institution?—No, I hope people will not anticipate it.

2109. Do you think it would be well for us to repeat this caution?—I think it would be a good thing if something could be issued in the shape of a warning not to expect charity next year.

2110. (*Mr. Crowder*): And the more quietly the thing could be done the better. The publishing of it in the papers is, you will agree, an evil. If it could be done through existing societies you would approve of that way of doing it?—But I think people have not got confidence in these private societies. But if you could get a few working men to sit upon the Committees in each

Mr. G. DEW.
July 23, 1886.

branch of the Society, it would have a good effect and give greater confidence all round.

2111. (*Chairman*): You would like to see the best men in the masses shake hands with the best men in the classes?—Yes.

2112. (*Mr Hedley*): To what age do you allow a workman an out-of-work allowance of 10s. a week?—As long as he is earning full money at his trade, and after that they have to go on the superannuation fund.

2113. I belong to the Hearts of Oak, who give 4s. a week superannuation. We take very little part in the management of the Hearts of Oak.

2114. (*Chairman*): Do you think that speculative building is pulling up a little in London now?—No, I don't think it is.

2115. You think they are going on with it now?—Oh, yes, but nothing like it was. We think we make a little start, but street improvements will account for it.

2116. Is it the case that in certain towns—Leicester, for instance—that building is going on with great rapidity, and there is a great demand for workpeople?—No, we get reports of the state of trade all through England, United States, and Colonies. I don't know, except in the Colonies and States, where there is any demand for labour. All through England the return for trade this present month is bad. In one or two places they are fairly employed but the general run is bad.

(*The Committee then adjourned.*)

TUESDAY, JULY 27, 1886.

Present—MR. J. H. ALLEN, in the Chair.

Rev. BROOKE LAMBERT,   Mr. PETERS,
Mr. C. S. LOCH, Secretary.

MR. M. STEPHANY, examined.

Mr. M. STEPHANY.
July 27, 1886.

2117. (*Chairman*): You are a member of the Jewish Board of Guardians—the secretary?—Yes.

2118. Where do they meet?—13 Devonshire Square, Bishopsgate.

2119. Have you any other place of meeting?—No, sir.

2120. You are secretary, and deal entirely with the Jewish population?—Yes.

2121. How are the cases brought before you—in the same way as before an ordinary Board of Guardians?—Yes.

2122. Who makes inquiries?—The secretary and investigation officers. Applications are received by the secretary.

2123. How are they received?—Three times a week.

2124. Do they apply to the investigation officer?—No; they apply to the secretary at stated times.

2125. And then what is the form of proceeding? Do you take down their cases?—We take down their cases if they are known. If they are not known, they have a form of application which they have to fill up.

2126. What is the nature of your inquiry? Is it a very strict inquiry, or are you satisfied with mere outward details? Do you go very closely into the past history of the applicants?—Yes, as far as we can.

2127. (*Mr. Loch*): Have you a form of application with you?—Yes (*producing one*). That is the first application form.

2128. (*Chairman*): Well, then, all these questions being answered, are they brought before you or before the Committee?—Before the Committee. It is returned to me, and then handed to the investigating officer for inquiry, and brought before the Committee, which sits twice a week, except under exceptional circumstances.

2129. Who is the Relief Committee composed of?—All the members of the Jewish Board, thirty-nine in number, who are elected annually. Part are elected bi-annually from the United Synagogue. We receive a quota from the United Synagogue, and they have the power to send a certain number of delegates that are elected annually by the subscribers.

2130. You have a permanent chairman?—Yes, Mr. Lionel Louis Cohen, M.P. He has been chairman for a long time—for the past ten or twelve years. He was the first honorary secretary in 1859.

2131. How long have you been secretary?—Nine years, but I have been in the office twenty years.

2132. During the last winter did you find there was exceptional distress among the Jews?—Yes.

2133. Was it exceptional distress?—Exceptional distress.

2134. Brought on by what?—By lack of work, I think.

2135. In that particular part of London where the Jews congregate?—In the East End, where most of the poorer Jews reside.

2136. I believe most of their occupation is that of tailoring?—Tailoring, bootmaking, cabinet-making, hawking; a great many trades, which you will see here from the annual report (*produced*). They comprise a very large number.

2137. And you found there was distress last winter?—Yes.

2138. Have you any—of course you have a good many skilled artisans—was there any distress among them?—Well, we had a larger number of skilled artisans than before, but not very large.

2139. And were you able to deal with all the cases satisfactorily?—Yes, we were.

2140. That is temporarily relieved them?—We relieved them temporarily.

2141. I think you had some assistance from the Mansion House Fund?—Yes, we received £1,100.

2142. And do you think that was a very great benefit to the poor of your persuasion?—Yes, I do.

2143. It did a great deal of good?—I think it did.

2144. It did not do more harm than good?—In some cases perhaps it did. It brought a great many new cases to us.

2145. From the East End especially, or from all parts of London?—From the East End especially.

2146. Do you from your knowledge of the work in the East End of London expect that next winter will be better or worse than last?—As far as I see, I don't think we shall have so bad a winter, because trade is looking up. As far as my knowledge goes, we are not receiving such a large number of applications from working men as we did at this time last year; that therefore leads me to suppose that things will go on a little better.

2147. That is very satisfactory. Supposing there had been no Mansion House Fund, what should you have done? Should you have been able to meet the distress?—We should have issued another appeal to our community. Of course the funds of the Board are very limited; we can only work from year to year.

2148. Is the money collected then in the synagogues, or by general subscription?—An appeal is sent round to the Jewish community.

2149. And it is always pretty liberally responded to?—We must not grumble, although it will be seen from our list that we get almost from the same people over and over again.

2150. Supposing you had not had this £1,100, you would have had to appeal to the community; and if the money had not come in, should you have referred them to the Poor Law?—We could not; there is no outdoor relief.

2151. But supposing they are chronic cases of people who are always out of work between January and March, should you have recommended them to go to the parish?—No, I don't think we should. We never do. We always look after the Jewish poor. We certainly should not turn them away to the parish, whatever the consequences might be.

2152. What were those cases refused for—178 against 3,000 odd?—Because we found they were not cases worthy to be relieved.

Mr. M. STEPHANY.

July 27, 1886.

2153. (*Mr. Loch*): They are very few? That is, totally refused, not receiving any kind of relief.

2154. (*Chairman*): Do you relieve them in kind or money?—Kind and money.

2155. Do you give them any other kind of relief, such as sending children to school?—There are such cases; *e.g.*, cases of orphans or deserted children, if the parents cannot be traced in any way.

2156. Do you ever adopt the boarding-out system?—We have a few; those who cannot be sent to the Jewish schools.

2157. Do you find that works well?—Yes; we have not very many.

2158. Would you board out among people in the country?—We do not. In London they are only generally temporary cases, until we can trace the parents. If they are orphans, we send direct to the orphan school.

2159. But in these cases of desertion you do not always find the parents?—I am very pleased to say we have not so many cases of the children deserted. We have wife desertion; but it is hardly in the sense of the word 'desertion.' The wife is left here and the man goes abroad, and eventually the wife is sent out to him. They are all classed as deserted wives, because they have only what they get from us. On page 78—'the Emigration Committee'—you will see that twenty-three wives who had been deserted have now joined their husbands, with seventy-nine children.

2160. Of course your organisation is very complete, only you have fewer people to deal with than we have?—I think I may say our organisation is quite complete.

2161. These cases that you have emigrated, are they all doing well?—Yes, very well. We give them a printed form, asking them certain questions, which we ask them to return within two months after their arrival in the States or Austria. These are returned to us; and those returned are certainly very satisfactory; and we are in communication with the United Hebrew Charities of New York. They act as correspondents, and we hear a favourable account of those who go out. They are cases which are improved by emigration, all able-bodied persons and mechanics; and with each shipment a list is sent out to our correspondents on the other side.

2162. Have you ever emigrated any people on loan, asking them to repay back the money?—We tried that, but it did not answer. In this form we tell them it is expected that, if they succeed, they should return the assistance they receive. One case in Australia we have received something back, and we are in anticipation of receiving the whole amount. The case will be marked in red letters in our books.

2163. One more question. Referring back to the Mansion House Fund, should you recommend, in case of any exceptional distress—should you recommend a Mansion House Fund to be raised on the same principle as the last?—I think not.

2164. (*Rev. Brooke Lambert*): What is the average attendance of guardians?—The attendance of the Relief Committee is taken by rota. The Relief Committee sit every Monday and Thursday.

2165. Is the Chairman there?—No; he takes his turn with the others.

2166. The personal relief will depend on you more than on the members?—Well, the registers are always opened. We have our books in alphabetical order, and as each case comes in, full particulars are at the sight of the Committee at once.

2167. Do you relieve a large number—the same people year after year?—Yes, a very large number.

2168. Is the purpose of your relief to help their misery, or to try to make them independent of you?—Certainly to try to make them independent. I refer to people——

2169. What of those cases helped from year to year for many years?—They would be widows and chronic cases of sickness, and so forth. I was going to refer to page 60.

2170. What is your average expenditure in relief a year?—About £12,000 in relief of all kinds.

2171. I suppose that is——?—That is in shape of loans, sewing machines, apprenticeship.

2172. What do you think was the percentage of relief this winter above an ordinary winter?—Well, fully 25 to 30 per cent.

2173. (*Mr. Loch*): In your community alone?

2174. (*Rev. Brooke Lambert*): Were the applications very much larger after the Mansion House Fund was started?—Yes, we had a very large number.

2175. And I suppose some would have got it who would not have got it another year?—No; every case was investigated first. I must tell you a very large number of cases applying for the Mansion House Fund were refused a very large number.

2176. Do you know what was the percentage of rejections?—I could let you have it accurately by-and-by. I should not like to give it from memory. I have the correct figure at the office.

2177. In relieving these chronic cases of poverty, how much do you think would be a proper allowance for a single woman? As for a man and woman, what is your scale of relief?—We have no scale; we know them. According to the circumstances of the case.

2178. What do you consider a person can live on—7s. a week a woman?—The Board would not give a single case 7s. a week, because there are so many other societies among the Jews in which a widow would receive a pension. The Board would not grant 7s. a week to a single case.

2179. You know all the other societies that are relieving?—Yes, we are in communication with them all.

2180. A man and wife together?—What the Board would give? The Board would give, perhaps, 5s. or 6s. a week, part in kind and part in money. We make distinction in this way. If a case is out of the radius of the Society's books (our tickets are by contract), and if they are living out of the district, then we would give cash. Or, in a very decent case, where money would be better for them, we give cash. We have a special committee called for convenience the Investigation Committee. The case is recommended by the Relief Committee, and they go into it more particularly, the case being visited by an honorary visitor, who has that case under his charge for some years.

2181. And gives the money himself?—Oh, no; all moneys are paid at the office of the Board.

2182. Do you find any feeling on the part of your better artisans that they would object to coming to your office?—We find the better class of artisans will keep away from charity as long as they possibly can.

2183. You never knew of a case in which having to appear before the Jewish Board of Guardians prevented a man from applying?—No, because his case would be brought before us indirectly.

2184. And they don't lose caste?—Oh, no.

2185. You talked about the wife being sent to the husband—was that at your cost or their cost?—Partly at our cost. We require the husband to find part, say half of the passage money. If he cannot pay the moiety, but can pay it within a pound or two, they will always lend a hand where the husband is willing to receive his wife and children.

2186. Have you ever sent them out when the husband contributed nothing at all?—No.

2187. You have not found that that has acted badly?—No.

2188. Then you do a good deal of re-migration, and send a good many back to their own country?—Yes, a large number.

2189. What proportion do you send back every year?—You will see on page 33. In 1885 there were 583 sent back to the Continent.

2190. Do you know whether you sent more back last winter?—Yes; evidently by the statistics we sent 41 more.

2191. But that would not give the spring of this year?—No: this is to the close of 1885. I don't think that we had an influx of foreign poor owing to this fund.

2192. No, I did not think of that. What I was wanting to know, how far the number of those sent back would tell of the extreme distress?—583 last

Mr. M. STEPHANY.

July 27, 1886.

Mr. M. STEPHANY.
July 27, 1886.

year, against 542 in 1884 ; 419 in 1883, and 451 in 1882. That is 130, in three years, increase.

2193. But the distress was not felt here so badly in December as it was in February. I did not know whether you knew there was a greater number in 1885 ?—Yes, there was. That was owing to the law enacted in Germany expelling all the Poles and Russians from Prussian territory. That caused a great increase in immigration. Some had left Poland twenty-five years ago, and being aliens, they were expelled, and where we could induce them to return we got them to go back, but where they had left to avoid the military service, we could not do it. Most of them were very respectable cases.

2194. Should you say that the fact of its being known that you send people back to their own country tended to make them come over to England for a chance of work ?—No, I think it acts the other way. We don't know how many we send back on that account. We only send them, as a rule, as far as Hamburg, and they have to travel back to Russia, which is a very long way. In exceptional cases we certainly do defray the cost.

2195. You do defray the cost ?—When it is a special case

2196. Did you use work as a test in giving relief ?—No.

2197. You never do ?—No, we have not the means.

2198. Your sewing machines would be another way of doing it—not even in a time of pressure like last winter ?—We did not feel the need ; but we had not the machinery.

2199. (*Chairman*) : Supposing you had the machinery, do you think it would be a good thing ?—Yes ; in some cases.

2200. (*Mr. Peters*) : Do you include the children of widows left ? Would you send the widows' children to your schools ?—No ; we would be sending them there under the Pauper Removal Act. We generally make them an allowance. Those fixed allowances are brought before the Committee periodically.

2201. The correspondents in America, do you pay them ?—Oh, no.

2202. How long would the weekly allowances last—as long as the children are not earning money ?—Yes.

2203. And where able-bodied men come, how long would the weekly allowance be ?—Able-bodied men as a rule do not receive weekly allowances. If we gave it for two weeks, you would not call that a weekly allowance. We bring them constantly before the Relief Committee, and their case is considered.

2204. You have assisted by way of loan, do you get the loans repaid ?—Very fairly ; we have a paid collector for that object.

2205. (*Mr. Loch*) : Do you think it would be as well in a future year for the Board to combine with other charities to prevent overlapping, to meet the difficulty of exceptional distress better ?—Yes, I think so.

2206. In that case what has hitherto been done ? Other Christian charities would refer their cases to you ?—Yes.

2207. Do you find that there are a certain number—the lowest fringe—who try to make money out of both the Christian and Jewish ?—Very few indeed.

2208. Do you find that the plan of investigation that you adopted last year on those forms was sufficient ?—Yes.

2209. Did you have a large crowd ?—Yes.

2210. How many in a single morning at the most crowded time ?—Well, I suppose between 300 and 400.

2211. How many men did you put on to make the investigation ?—Three ; we had no volunteers. Those cases that were immediately known to us (I am taking all the cases together), would not require investigation, where others would require investigation.

2212. Because you happened to know some and not others ?—Yes.

2213. The employers you did not refer to ?—That inquiry was made by the investigating officer.

2214. Was that made in every case that you did not already know this winter ?—Yes.

2215. Was it useful ?—In some cases.

2216. It was worth making ?—Oh, yes.

2217. Did you pay rent ?—In very few cases, because our rule at the Board—

it is not written law—we make it a rule ; we say we will not pay rent because it holds out an inducement for landlords to let people get into arrears.

2218. As a matter of fact, I suppose a proportion went in rent if the people were hard up?—No doubt. We gave a great deal of relief in kind from the Mansion House Fund in chronic cases. Where we had a doubt, we would apportion the relief out in kind.

2219. The better your inquiry, the less the need for relieving in kind?—certainly.

2220. Practically you exclude no class of cases?—No.

2221. Take out-of-work cases, do you find that you are able to go on helping them ? Do they come back to you?—They come back perhaps every three or four weeks.

2222. Do those cases recur every winter ?—Yes.

2223. Then you are dealing with a proportion of cases that are out of work in winter ?—Yes ; among tailors and shoemakers. There are two months of stagnation.

2224. Do you ever help them in their trade ?—Certainly.

2225. Did you find you were able to do anything in that direction with this Mansion House money?—Yes, in purchasing tools for them. If a man required tools, if he had worked in a shop and had an opportunity of getting work on his own account, we supplied him with tools

2226. Do they pawn much in your community ?—Yes.

2227. And I suppose you help them in that way too?—No, we do not help to take things out of pawn.

2228 (*Mr. Peters*): Why do you not take things out of pawn ?—We do not, because as a rule they would put them back again.

Mr. M. STEPHANY, July 27, 1886.

MR. J. D. POWELL, examined.

2229. (*Chairman*): What are you, Mr. Powell ?—A carpenter.

2230. Are you the Secretary of the London United Trades Committee of Carpenters and Joiners ?—I am an operative, and not a paid official.

2231. You were a member of the Mansion House Committee ?—I was.

2232. And did you attend all the meetings of the Mansion House Committee ?—The whole of them.

2233. And you acted, in addition to that, as a member of the Holborn Committee ?—Yes.

2234. Did you take an active part ?—Yes, as visiting ; but I took the thing more in a general way, and visited different Committees over London.

2235. What Committees ?—Holloway, East End, and Clerkenwell occasionally.

2236. You went for the purpose of seeing whether the right people were working ?—Yes; and if I could have spared the time I should have spent the whole of my time in visiting committees.

2237. What was your opinion of the working of them ?—Some of them were working admirably. The only thing I should have liked to have altered was the form, which should have been made out more concisely. They should be asked what people had endeavoured to do in the past for themselves ; whether they had joined a society, or a club, or a penny bank—a thing like that—so as to produce some proof that they had endeavoured to help themselves.

2238. Should you have said that the general people that applied were artisans, or were they the chronic labourers always out of work in the winter ?—I should like to know what I am to understand by the word 'chronic.' Do you mean the men who are periodically out of work, or those who are lazy and habitually out of work ?

2239. I mean the class of people who are always out of work between January and March—like a painter.—Yes.

2240. Then the bricklayer, who is always thrown out of work in a frost ?—Would you include cases of that description ?

2241. I think I should, certainly ; but that is only a private opinion. Taking

Mr. J. D. POWELL.

Mr. J. D. POWELL.
July 27, 1886.

the cases of people that you know, were they first-class workmen that applied — first-class carpenters and joiners?—I think the joiners and carpenters were conspicuous by their absence. We make a point of looking after our own men. My object was to secure the money going into some right direction—that some of it should benefit deserving cases.

2242. Should you have known anything about carpenters who did not belong to your society?—Certainly.

2243. Did many such apply?—A vast number.

2244. Should you call them respectable working men—artisans?—Yes.

2245. Why is it that they don't belong to your society?—I could not tell you. A good many do not care to make any provision at all. Most of them pay from 2s. to 2s. 6d. a week to trade and benefit societies to make some provision.

2246. And do you think the Mansion House Fund benefited that class of carpenter—you speak of those who do not belong to your society?—Oh, yes; it benefited that class and also a few members. There are four carpenters' societies. Even with our rules, which are carefully drawn up, you cannot make anything to meet such a pressure.

2247. Supposing there had been no Mansion House Fund last winter, what would they have done?—I cannot tell you. We should not have assisted them. Why should we? Unfortunately we had a most unprecedented number of our own members out—4,000 men. That never took place before. We had a special levy to meet it. Each member of the 30,000 members paid 7s. 6d., besides 1s. a week.

2248. So that you could not have assisted any others?—We did get 30,000 seven and sixpences.

2249. Do not the working men assist each other very much when they are out of work, in distress? I am not speaking of men in your society.—Well, I believe they do, but I do not know much on that point; for I never subscribe to anything of that kind myself. I think it should be done through the general society.

2250. Then I understand it is your opinion that that distress was exceptional last winter?—Unquestionably.

2251. Do you find any signs of improvement at the present time?—Certainly; the number of unemployed is not so bad as it was last winter; but it is worse now than it has been for many winters.

2252. Do you see no sign of improvement?—No, the decline has been gradual for seven years.

2253. Now, Mr. Powell, what would be your idea of a remedy for such a state of things? It is gradually getting worse and worse. There must be more carpenters in London than are wanted?—But it applies to everything else. That applies to the depression of trade; when it gets to the lowest point it revives.

2254. As to whether these men would have emigrated if it had been put to them?—I believe they would. I think it is the best and most thrifty men that emigrate. You see if a man gets down to a certain point he is very little good for emigration, because he gets weak in physique, and his mind gets distracted, and he is not a useful subject to emigrate.

2255. That might be after a couple of years, but not in three months.—Quite so, but I have known this last winter; we have had men out of work who were never out of work before.

2256. Then do you think that these cases ought to have been assisted by the charitable public when they are out of work?—I should not make any proposal to assist a man unless he had tried to assist himself—anything—if he could only show me an old bank book. I think one of the best references I had was a bank book, which showed how carefully he had worked, and how he had dribbled out his savings to meet his necessities. I should consider that quite sufficient.

2257. What would you do with the others who had not made provision?—I should let them go to the Poor Law. It seems to be formed to meet their case. But I would not do it if he had made the smallest provision for himself.

I have no feeling with the society business. I should never ask a man to join it. I should consider I was doing him a favour by taking him into it. I should be sorry to see the Mansion House Fund got up periodically.

2258. Do you think it did more harm than good?—No, I would not say that, but I believe in many cases it was the actual cause of harm, and a large class were relieved who should not have been relieved.

2259. Supposing that the plan was adopted of having Committees in every Union next winter, do you think your societies would join the Committees?—No, sir.

2260. Why not?—Well, you see I would rather give you a qualified answer to your question. I think our leading men would aid in anything, but you must not expect a society to take official cognisance of anything in the charity way. As individuals they would serve, and give you good advice.

2261. That would be useful. But as an official would not sit on a Committee.—Only as an individual. I have come across several cases. I have gone and got tools out of pawn, and I have found them quite insufficient to enable a man to get a living.

2262. That would be from want of knowledge of the Committee.—I have remedied that, by telling the Committee what he would want to make him self-supporting by setting him up again. In that way we have been the source of permanent benefit to a man.

2263. (Rev. *Brooke Lambert*): You distinguished between periodical and chronic want in certain trades that have periodic want, like painters and bricklayers? You think that in the event of the establishment of a fund in the future, they should have relief when they have been earning good wages in the summer? Do you look upon them as entitled to relief in the same sense as other people?—Oh, no.

2264. You thought Mr. Allen was rather hard?—No. I wanted to understand what was the meaning of the word 'chronic.' I should get practical people to look into the cases and say whether they were proper cases or not.

2265. You would say that a man disabled by want was entitled to relief?—A man must expect to get old—he must provide for that by the superannuation fund. Every man can do something to help himself.

2266. Could you help us at all as regards a labour test? In the first place, do you think that a good class of workmen would accept a labour test?—No; emphatically no.

2267. Would he receive it as charity, as a gift, when he would not receive it as payment for work?—I don't say they would not receive it. I have found extreme difficulty in persuading people to let me interest myself, and I have had the aid of certain Committees in helping these cases.

2268. Then as regards these semi-respectable cases, half shiftless and half good, how about the labour test?—You would have to do something. If you had some good Committees you would have some practical knowledge of the trade. A carpenter is not like a clerk. He only goes where they have work to do. A man takes a job, and when it is over he goes somewhere else, and they get a thorough good knowledge, as a rule, of people in the society and people out of it.

2269. Do you think that emigration is in any instance a remedy for the evils of the want of work?—Yes. If you could get a proper place to go to : State-directed emigration I should like to see.

2270. How long do you think that would last as a remedy, if you thought of emigrating to Canada or Australia?—No, I think the remedy is in another quarter—the population question.

2271. Emigration is not a final remedy?—No, things are very good in Australia, but emigration is only a temporary remedy.

2272. Now I want to follow out that point about clubs. I sent round at Greenwich as to the club, and I could not get any cases to relieve. The Odd Fellows and the Foresters told me of one or two doubtful cases, that the Secretary would write to me about afterwards, but I never heard of them. Your clubs always help them as far as possible?—Yes, as far as possible, if they can be shown to have tried to pay. I have heard of a case of a gardener asked, 'Why do you not belong to anything?' He said he did, but he got hard up and

Mr. J. D. POWELL

July 27, 1886.

did not pay up. That must have been wrong, because the clubs have the power, and do frequently vote money, to pay arrears. There is generally a little fund of that sort.

2273. The fact of the establishment of a fund, or the recurrence of the establishment of a fund like the Mansion House Fund, would have a tendency to make people crowd to London to get it?—I am afraid they could not crowd in greater numbers than they do now.

2274. Was there a Mansion House Committee at West Ham? It applied for a further grant. Would you have granted it?—I think you will remember I spoke against it.

2275. Oh, it was you?—You could not compare distress now with distress in the winter. Even privations are not so bad in warm weather as they are in the cold.

2276. There is a good deal of strong feeling against the Charity Organisation Society among the better class of workmen. Do you think there is more feeling against that than against other charitable societies?—Yes, I think so; it is only on the principle of give a dog a bad name.

2277. You have not come across instances yourself?—Oh, yes. Dismissing cases too quickly, and prosecuting too close and too particular inquiries instead of assisting. But I would not say that that is a general thing.

2278. (*Mr. Peters*): In out-of-work cases where there is no thrift, would you think it a hard thing to offer a man to keep his family if he went into the workhouse?—I don't think you can make any such stipulation as that.

2279. The objection to the workhouse is that you break up the home; but with regard to a test that he should go into the workhouse for a few days, is that a great hardship?—I should not like to give an opinion. I should blame the man who did it. There are men who are so unthrifty, that it is bad. But I think the best way is to weigh and take each case on its merits.

2280. How would you deal with such cases then?—I think you ought to take a case with its surroundings. I am afraid you could not lay down any rule.

2281. You think it would be hard to lay down a rule to offer a man the house?—He must do something; he must not expect his neighbours to keep him.

2282. Has it ever occurred to you whether or not these periodical occurrences of distress are caused by our industrial arrangements, the way labour is worked by capital?—It may be, but I don't think you can investigate that.

2283. (*Mr. Loch*): With regard to one inquiry. Did you apply in any way in this last year the system which you have more or less indicated in regard to proof of any degree of thrift on the part of applicants?—As far as possible I did, and I had been in hopes that that would have come out with the final statement of the Mansion House Fund.

2284. It was done, but more or less informally?—Yes.

2285. There were large crowds at the door sometimes?—Yes.

2286. Do you think that there might be any system by which cases should be sent by people who already know them as friendly society's men, so that we might reduce the crowd in that way?—Yes, I think something might be done in that way, if you were not to draw a hard-and-fast line.

2287. But still you think something might be done? Taking the districts you know best, you could lay your hands on twenty or thirty men whose word would be worth having as to cases?—Oh, yes. The whole of the secretaries except three of the Carpenters' Societies signified their willingness to serve on Committees.

2288. If these men had been the introducers of cases, we might have got a good class of cases, and a certain amount of information?—Yes; if local workers had welcomed working men instead of choking them off. The first time I went to a Committee they tried to choke me off; but I am not easily choked off. At the first Committee I went to there were five clergymen, two Catholic priests, and four guardians. They looked at me as if I was going to garrott them.

2289. Do you think that there are plenty of workers in the districts who would be available, or would it have to be re-done?—At any future time there must be some central fund, and it must be done irrespective of this society or any other ; but don't appeal to the heads of any societies in the first place. The best way to do it is to get lists of officials of all the societies, and invite each one. You would then get plenty of Committee men—known, reliable men. Very nearly 100 volunteered this time. In one case, that of a secretary of twenty-five years' standing, they did not tell him the Committee that he should have served on till they sent him a post-card, saying that there was to be a meeting, which would possibly be the last : they kept him waiting three weeks. I won't say it was a general thing, but there was a disposition, when people were willing to serve, to choke them off ; and in some cases they were successful.

2290. Do you think that you could rely upon inquiries made by men—working men, and so on ? Ordinarily, do you think that they would know so much as to be able to speak of a case so that you might rely upon it?—Yes ; they would probably recommend cases that your system of investigation would reject.

2291. I am taking your own standard of what is required in the matter of thrift?—Just so.

2292. The condition of success would be arrangement, and plenty of time?—Quite so.

2293. With regard to periodic cases, would it be fair and right to make an arrangement by which those of the reckless sort should be sent to a labour yard, and if work is wanted for others it should be supplied by such an Association as the Public Gardens Association ?—It might be done in some cases, but you would have to consider the class of calling, like clerks ; what condition would a clerk's hands be in afterwards ? The jewellers and Clerkenwell men, they would ruin the fine touch of their fingers. The same thing would occur with violinists. It would be quite useless to put men like that to a labour test.

2294. Excepting those, there would be a residue that you could so help : would you keep them distinct?—Yes.

2295. Would you pay them at the rate of 4d. per hour?—I should pay them at the full price, and employ them half the time. I should give them the exact usual price, and give them half the time. I should rather say five hours a day, so that they might go and earn five hours' wages and have five hours to look for employment. Otherwise I am quite certain that there will be a tremendous storm—if a large fund is got up—if labour at 4d. an hour is carried on to any great extent. Lord Brabazon and Lord Dorchester's associations—there are a certain lot of nondescript men—they are not bricklayers' labourers, and I don't think it did much harm ; but if you are going to spend money, give the men proper money, and have proper men to do the work. I am afraid you would not get any of the best class to take 4d. an hour.

2296. As to another form of work, do you think that anything can be done in the direction of putting men on to work which would be useful to them in their own trades, but possibly in some kindred branch, or higher branch, work that would be educational ? I take it that a man may have three weeks out, and he might learn something that is useful to him in that time ?—Would you give him some payment for it ?

2297. Oh, yes.—I think in all cases of payment you should get something for your money.

2298. I think it should be educational and not directly valuable, and it would be relief in a special form.—You would teach a man something higher in taking up other branches of the work than that he had been doing.

2299. Suppose you had a gasfitter who could not do the turning ?—Yes.

2300. And then he could turn his hand to several things ?—Yes.

2301. If that was feasible, you would approve of it?—Yes.

2302. Do you think that there is any chance of any new employment being introduced into London as an alternative to emigration ? Do you see any remedy in the shape of other employment ?—No. I can't say that I can answer that question.

2303. (*Rev. Brooke Lambert*): Do you think that at any future Committee—if a

Mr. J. D. POWELL.

July 27, 1886.

Mr. J. D. POWELL.
July 27, 1886.

committee was started in my neighbourhood—should I be doing right to refuse to sit on it?—No; certainly not.

2304. You don't think that there is a general impression abroad on the part of the better class of the poor that the clergy rather give the relief to those who go to church?—I must say I found a little of the feeling, but I find in a number of instances that the clergyman has come in second and the man has come in first.

2305. (*Chairman*): Then you would recommend that the clergyman should be on the Committee?—Yes.

2306. You said there were five clergymen and two Roman Catholic priests on one Committee?—It was a large parish. I would have some evening meetings and have a larger Committee. Each clergyman and each of the priests had a right to be there, but I would have had the Committee enlarged and extended. It was a mutual admiration society as then constituted.

2307. How was such a large Committee to work?—By subdivision.

Mr. A. S. ANDREWS, examined.

Mr. A. S. ANDREWS.

2308. (*Chairman*): What are you, Mr. Andrews?—I am in a firm of coal merchants.

2309. What position do you hold?—A subordinate position, under the manager.

2310. A sub-manager?—Yes.

2311. Now, do you employ a great many men?—Yes, I think about 50. It varies a little.

2312. What is the work they do?—Unloading steam colliers from the north, and loading the coals from the buildings into vans.

2313. Your firm are not actually coal merchants, are they?—We are properly coal merchants who buy coals in cargoes, and we send them out not only in large wholesale quantities but in as small a quantity as a ton. We have 18 vans and 30 horses.

2314. Were you able to keep all the men employed last winter?—Yes.

2315. The whole of them?—Yes.

2316. Would it be the same among all coal merchants?—Yes.

2317. A severe winter would be your harvest?—Yes; I was going to mention that.

2318. What are the wages those men earn?—The fillers are paid piece-work. Some weeks they could earn £4 each man. The average through the winter would be a little over £3. In the summer they would not earn so much—perhaps £2.

2319. Were any of the men you know of out of work in your trade in last winter?—No, we saw no exceptional amount of labour available. We have Ratcliffe and Shadwell to one side of us, and Limehouse on the other.

2320. Did you have experience of the Mansion House Committee?—Yes; a sub-committee.

2321. Did any coalmen make application for relief?—I think not one. There were one or two carmen, but the greater number of those who came up for relief were not skilled artisans.

2322. So far as your trade was concerned, there was no reason for the Mansion House Fund?—No, certainly not.

2323. The time of the year that your *employés* would be out of work would be the summer?—Yes; we try to give them permanent work as much as possible—perhaps twenty men may be idle when we are not working cargoes of coal.

2324. The men who earn £4 a week, do they put by anything?—We have one gang who are thrifty men.

2325. And another who drink pretty hard?—Yes.

2326. So far as the trade is concerned, you don't know much about the distress?—Not in my own trade.

2327. Any other trade?—Only from my experience on the Committee. We had a very poor district. I was on another Committee—Newton Hall Committee. We dealt with all classes of cases.

2328. What classes were they at Mile End?—They were mostly people whom you would have got at any time of year.

2329. You mean dock labourers?—Yes; and the less competent artisans.

2330. Do you live down there?—Yes.

2331. Was there more distress down there among the other class of working men than you have known before?—Not to any large extent. I could see no signs of anything serious.

2332. Then there was no occasion, in your opinion, for a Mansion House Fund?—No.

2333. That was in the Stepney Union?—Yes.

2334. They do not give outdoor relief?—No.

2335. And at Stepney you had no labour yard?—No; the workhouse is at Bromley.

2336. The class of people that came would be the chronic class of people?—Yes, most of them.

2337. And they are always out of work from January to March?—Yes.

2338. That is the only time of the year we have to dread. If we can get over those three months, we are safe for another year?—Yes.

2339. That class of people—would you recommend that they should apply to the parish?—Yes, I think they were cases most of them that the parish would relieve.

2340. And should you agree with the last witness, that only those people should be relieved who have shown some signs of thrift?—Well, I thought it was a thing to be taken into consideration by the Committee—signs of thrift; but I don't know that you should absolutely refuse to help a man if he had not been thrifty.

2341. In case a man is unthrifty—I don't suppose that a man who has been a dock labourer all his life could show any signs of thrift?—Their work is so precarious that they have not much opportunity.

2342. Is the trade in Ratcliffe worse now than it has been in years past?—Some trades, certainly.

2343. Did the substitution of steam for sailing vessels do that? All persons connected with shipping must have suffered?—Yes, in this neighbourhood.

2344. Do you know much about the dock labourers?—We have a number of them about us—not a great many, but a certain number. Ours is the Regent's Canal Dock.

2345. Most of these people would have gone to the docks lower down the river, I should imagine?—Yes, that is their difficulty. They could at one time get the labour up here.

2346. Why don't they go down to Dagenham or Woolwich?—Well, I suppose they locate themselves in Ratcliffe, and live in a state of semi-starvation rather than move away.

2347. Do you come across sailors wanting assistance?—Very few cases.

2348. Then sailors are pretty well employed?—Yes, I think they are.

2349. What do you think about next winter? Do you think there is any chance or probability of an outcry for assistance?—The only thing would be the example of last winter. Trade is going on as it has been two or three years. I think there is a feeling of improvement.

2350. I think it has been mentioned by other witnesses.

2351. (*Rev. Brooke Lambert*): I don't think I have anything to ask you. Does your trade, though requiring a good deal of strength personally, require very much training?—No.

2352. Did you use it as a test when these men came before you?—We should have been putting other men out. We have regular men who hold on for us.

2353. Then your circumstances are quite different to ours at Greenwich. I was told by a coal employer that he had work if we had men to do it.—I had the same experience with dock labourers in two or three cases. I arranged for them to go to work with Liverpool steamers, and they did not turn up.

Mr. A. S.
ANDREWS.

July 27, 1886.

(*Chairman*): It is rather a difficult thing for a weak man to carry a sack of coals.
(*Rev. Brooke Lambert*): The men I sent were giants.
2354. (*Mr. Loch*): I want to ask you one or two questions about the guardians. Do you think that these dock labourers, of whom you relieved many, ought to have been sent to them?—I think they were proper cases.
2355. Would you have had the labour yard for them?—I think so.
2356. In the case of the absolutely thriftless would you make the labour yard the ultimate test, or would you make a distinction between the drunken and grossly improvident, and be content that they should go there? I think you heard a question asked by Mr. Peters, in which he suggested that a man might be referred to the workhouse, and the family kept outside?—Yes; I think that would have been a fair test. I don't like the idea of breaking up the home.
2357. You would say that charity was undertaking the Poor Law work?—Yes, it was.
2358. Did you think of getting permanent results from the relief?—We granted a number of sums for taking tools out of pawn and paying up clubs.
2359. Did anything you gave in the way of relief go in a wrong direction?—We had rather a sentimental Committee, who were anxious to grant as much as possible. That was the great difficulty to contend against. It was thought the public were clamouring for the money to be promptly divided.
2360. Did you find that the local people on the Committee knew the people?—Yes. I thought there were too many clergy, and in the case of one or two special cases I thought too many of 'our poor people' benefited.
2361. Did you find the employers of labour were on the Committees?—No; I think not in this case.
2362. Did the local magnates fulfil their local responsibilities?—With the exception of the clergy and one or two guardians, I think not.
2363. Supposing that there had been no fund, and local people had done their duty, would they have had breadth of back to bear it?—I think that half the money would have done all that was useful.
2364. And that half subscribed locally?—Yes.
2365. Did you approve of the plan I suggested to one of the witnesses, to have a reference in the first instance to the foremen in workshops as a start?—I think it good. My immediate chief was on the Committee at Ratcliffe. That was a small Committee, but that answered the purpose.
2366. How did you make inquiry?—Each one of the Committee. I took no inquiry cases. They each visited cases, and reported upon them; but we had two workmen in our employ, whom we kept to look after their own men in their trade.
2367. And used these two men to look after the cases of working-men?—Yes.
2368. Could that system be carried further?—I would not subdivide it too much. They pointed out many cases which we should not have known of otherwise.
2369. (*Chairman*): Would it cut two ways? Would not these bricklayers be inclined to favour bricklayers who came up for relief?—Yes, they might do that; we had an eye on that.
2370. Did you have a reference to employers in all cases?—No.
2371. That would have been a valuable thing?—I think it would be.
2372. Did you apply to relieving officers to prevent overlapping?—We had a guardian who took cases to the relieving officer to make inquiry.
2373. Would you approve of the opening of works in any shape, *e.g.* by the Public Gardens Association, for the men who ought to be relieved—men who would have satisfied inquiries?—We did that with Stepney churchyard.
2374. And put on men whom you had inquired about?—Yes, we made some inquiry.
2375. And parallel with the Stepney churchyard works had you the labour yard?—No.
2376. Do you think there are cases now which could be dealt with by means of emigration?—I fear that emigration would have been very little good. Very few people that any colony would have made anything of—not the sort that Mr. Peters would have asked.

(*The Committee then adjourned.*)

FRIDAY, JULY 30, 1886.

Present—Mr. A. PELL, in the Chair,

Hon. and Rev. A. C. STANLEY,
Rev. BROOKE LAMBERT,
Mr. E. PETERS,
Mr. F. J. S. EDGCOMBE,
Mr. J. H. ALLEN.

Mr. R. HEDLEY, attending on behalf of the Local Government Board.

Mr. C. S. LOCH, *Secretary*.

MR. NATHAN MOSS (SAUL MOSS & SONS, Curtain Road), examined.

Mr. N. Moss,
July 30, 1886.

2377. (*Chairman*): Are you connected with the furniture business?—Yes; it is conducted very largely in that part of London.

2378. Does the weather in winter prevent your people working?—Oh, no.

2379. Therefore your men are not like bricklayers, for instance, and do not have to lay by in summer owing to their having to leave off in winter from atmospheric causes?—No occasion for that.

2380. Generally, with respect to 1885, from the beginning to the end of the year, had you found men in your trade poorly employed?—Yes. Cabinet-makers were not as well off, I should perhaps say, because they were employed upon a cheaper class of work.

2381. Had they as much work as usual?—Yes, but it was of a character that did not bring in so much money.

2382. Were the wages which employers were able to pay insufficient to provide for the necessities and needs of the workmen?—No, I do not think that for a moment.

2383. They were sufficient for the wants of the labourers engaged in it?—Yes.

2384. But did not leave, I suppose you would say, so large a margin for luxuries and enjoyment?—Yes.

2385. Do you think the men had to deprive their families, owing to this lower-paid sort of work, of anything they might fairly claim?—Yes, I think so.

2386. Would you tell us from your experience what these subjects were?—I am hardly in a position to tell you that.

2387. Do you think they pawned their tools?—Yes, in many cases.

2388. How did they get on with their work if it was abundant and they had no tools?—In times of prosperity they get together a quantity of superfluous tools, and they pawn those they can do without.

2389. Were they worse clothed—short of greatcoats, for instance?—Not particularly.

2390. Do you think the theatres and places of amusement they generally resort to were less filled?—I really cannot say.

2391. Do you think public-houses suffered?—No, I never heard anything of that kind.

2392. Have any butchers' shops been closed?—I could not say.

2393. What leads you to say they have been badly off?—Because I know from my own knowledge that trade has been of such a character, and also because I know from my own knowledge that these men have suffered to that extent.

2394. But might not a good workman get more by making an inferior article?—No; a man who makes a good chair could not possibly make a bad one. He is taught to make a certain thing, and he must make it as he was taught.

2395. Are we, then, to gather that men who were engaged in making superior articles were not employed?—You will understand that a man who takes as long to make an inferior article as he does to make a superior one cannot earn so much as the man who has been engaged all his life upon inferior goods.

2396. Do you think that the men engaged in the better sort of work were, for want of that work, compelled to undertake work of an inferior quality?—I

Mr. N. Moss.
July 30, 1896.

think that was the case. I should say that we are not employers of cabinet makers—only purchasers from the men who make goods themselves to sell. Men suffered more during the depression by having to sell their goods at a lower rate.

2397. Do you think there was an amount of suffering among these men and their families which justified an appeal to the public on their behalf?—Well, I do not think there was, really.

2398. You think they had to go through great straits, but that they were not such as would wreck them or their families for the future?—I do not think so.

2399. Are things better now than then?—I cannot say they are.

2400. *(Rev. Brooke Lambert)*: You were treasurer of the Shoreditch Committee of the Mansion House Relief Fund?—Yes, sir.

2401. Every case was investigated?—Yes, I believe they were, as far as I know. Of course, it was done very hurriedly.

2402. Can you say how far the cases were investigated?—No, I cannot; I understand that they were.

2403. ' 2,858 cases were relieved at the Town Hall in the course of twelve days, besides a very large number of other cases relieved by the Ward Committees subsequently, and when it is remembered that every case had to be investigated, and the strictest precaution taken against imposture and fraud, rampant at such a time as this, some idea may be formed of the unremitting and indefatigable efforts of the Ward Committees, upon whose shoulders the inquiry work chiefly fell.' Do you think that is literally correct?—I cannot tell you to what extent those cases were investigated. I was not on those Committees.

2404. Well now, supposing that a new fund were raised, what alteration in the organisation of the Committee would you suggest?—Well, I am quite of opinion that it ought not to be left to individual efforts. I do not think that individuals and voluntary helpers in the various districts ought to be called upon to do the amount of work that has been done in this case.

2405. What would you substitute?—I think some organised body, composed of men of local influence, and paid inspectors——

2406. Paid inspectors?—Yes; investigators. I do not know anything much of the machinery of the Charity Organisation Society, so that I cannot say whether they would be a suitable body to employ.

2407. Did you use any labour test at Shoreditch?—Generally not, but the vestry of Shoreditch decided to open the stone-yards. They had a lot of waste granite, and they decided to pay men at so much per day; very small pay, I believe. The yards were soon full, and they had more than they could take in.

2408. Did you say that applicants were told they must apply at the stone-yard?—Yes, if they happened to be able-bodied men. In almost every case that was done.

2409. Did you refuse men because they would not go to the stone-yard?—I cannot remember that anyone was refused.

2410. Would you advise the establishment of a labour test another year?—I cannot say exactly; that is, I do not know what sort of a test you would apply to cabinet-makers.

2411. *(Mr. Edgcombe)*: You said that you were not very familiar with the work of the Mansion House Committee?—Yes, I was not present on all occasions.

2412. You attended a sufficient number to form a pretty good opinion of how the work was done?—Yes.

2413. The reason I asked the question was, that when the Chairman asked you what investigation was done, you did not seem to know.—That was because it was done by the Ward Committees; I did not attend any of these. I cannot say whether the inquiry was done successfully or unsuccessfully.

2414. There were no paid inquiry officers employed?—No; I think the only persons who were paid were the clerks.

2415. Such inquiries, more or less thorough, were conducted by the members of the Committees only?—Yes, tradesmen and clergymen. They might or might not have been familiar with the work.

2416. What work did they undertake to do?—It was very simple work they had to do: I do not know that it required very much knowledge. They had the address of the applicant and made inquiries, &c.

2417. I suppose of course that they went upon a regular system—visited the employer, and so on? In my experience it is a matter of skilled work, sometimes, to ascertain whether a man ought to be assisted.—I daresay there was some imposition.

2418. (*Mr. Allen*): Were the class of persons relieved chronic cases—that is, men who were always in difficulty?—I think they were to a large extent; yes.

2419. Supposing there had been no Mansion House Fund, do you think the Poor Law authorities would have been able to deal with the distress satisfactorily?—I can hardly answer.

2420. Were there many really good workmen out of employment?—I think there were.

2421. Would it be a large or small number?—There was a minority; I cannot say to what extent.

2422. Were you personally acquainted with any really good workmen who were at that time out of work?—Yes.

2423. Many?—Not many, but there were some.

2424. Half a dozen?—Yes, quite that.

2425. Do you think the Poor Law would have met chronic cases?—I do not think so.

2426. Do you think there is likely to be any exceptional distress next winter?—I hope not. I am rather of opinion that we shall have a better trade.

2427. Have you anything to go upon?—No, only the general knowledge that one acquires through seeing and speaking to people in the business. We generally know whether stocks are large or not.

2428. Supposing there was to be any exceptional distress, should you advocate the formation of Committees in the same way?—Not in the same way; I think it ought not to be left to voluntary aid. There should be employers of labour, guardians, and working men.

2429. Would you form a Committee of that description? Do you think it would be good?—Yes, with inquiry agents and one recognised system throughout the metropolis.

2430. (*Mr. Hedley*): Did good men go to the Mansion House Fund and get relief?—Yes, in several cases their tools were taken out of pawn.

2431. What makes you say you do not think the Poor Law would have dealt with ordinary cases satisfactorily?—I do not think they would have the means at their hands to deal sufficiently with them.

2432. But the Poor Law have the whole of the rates at their hands?—Yes, but by what I can understand the relief they give is miserably insufficient.

2433. (*Chairman*): Do not you know that the amount of relief is settled by law?—These men would do anything rather than go inside the workhouse.

2434. (*Mr. Peters*): Do you think the Mansion House Fund did more good than harm?—I think it did a great deal of good.

2435. But it had some pauperising effects?—I am not going to say there were not some cases of imposture. I do not see how it could be avoided.

2436. (*Mr. Loch*): You say the offices were very crowded?—Oh, yes, at the earliest part of it.

2437. And how many inquiries do you suppose you had at that time?—I cannot give any detail at all.

2438. Do you think it would be good if any plan of preventing such crowding in a future year were considered?—Well, if the thing is organised better probably that would be prevented.

2439. But if the crowding was very great, and the people overworked, the inquiries must have been superficial?—I should not like to say. The Committees were large, and they divided the work amongst them.

2440. Taking your last statements as a sort of standard of the amount of

L

Mr. N. Moss.
July 30, 1886.

work available in your trade, do you think it was much less than is ordinarily to be had?—I do not think it was.

2441. It was, therefore, different in kind rather than amount?—Yes, quite so.

2442. The consequence was, good workmen were wasting their powers on cheaper work?—Quite so.

2443. Do you think that in consequence of that there were workmen who ordinarily did cheap work who could get no work?—Well, I cannot quite say that.

2444. Then what it comes to is, there was a greater demand for cheap work than usually?—Exactly.

2445. And that a good workman had to lower his standard, and the bad workman had work as well?—Yes.

2446. Now, is that to be a permanent state of things, do you think?—I hope not, but I cannot say.

2447. It was extraordinary?—It has been the tendency.

2448. Do you think anything can be done to prevent a good workman becoming a bad one?—He may get a little slovenly in his work, but he cannot go very far wrong.

2449. At any rate he has to expend very much more labour to get a livelihood, or work longer hours for worse pay?—He has to work longer.

2450. (*Chairman*): How many men emigrated?—I have no doubt that many good workmen go to Australia and America.

2451. Is there a good field for cabinet-making in Australia?—I don't know. I rather think there is.

2452. (*Mr. Loch*): Is there no other department of labour, so far as you know, in England, to which the men could put their better talents—no kindred work now done abroad to which they could be put?—I don't think there is. In London trade is different to the country. In London generally, if a man makes a chair—so to speak—he cannot make a table; he must be kept at the particular article. In the country he can make anything you place before him.

2453. You think that trade is so divided in London that a man can only make a particular thing. Would it not be a great assistance to a man if he could turn his attention to making some other article outside his own trade?—It would amount to his serving his apprenticeship over again.

2454. (*Chairman*): He is a machine?—Exactly. If work different to the ordinary kind is given to nine-tenths of men, they can't or won't do it.

2455. (*Mr. Loch*): It is not worth the masters' while to teach the men other things. If a man can only do one sort of work, he has to go down hill directly the single form of industry is not wanted?—That is rather going to the extreme. It is taking a very extreme view of the thing to say a man must go down hill because he won't turn his hand to other things. I have known cabinet-makers to go down to Epping Forest and take to the 'three-sticks-a-penny' business when they could not get work; they have opened greengrocers' shops, and become carmen, and have given up their trade altogether.

2456. So far as the particular profession to which he has been apprenticed he is in that position?—Oh, yes.

2457. Would you be in favour of any technical education—say, teaching a man how to make two sorts of chairs well?—Yes; the technical colleges will do a vast amount of good in that way.

2458. Supposing a period of out-of-work affected a certain set of good workmen, in another year would you approve of giving relief on condition that they were taught to make other things than those they could already make?—That is another very big question. If you give relief while the men are learning another trade, it is rather a large thing: I should not like to advise as to that.

2459. The demand of the public is constantly for cheaper goods?—Yes.

2460. That is the reason so far of the degradation of workmen?—Yes; I hardly like to call it degradation.

2461. It gives rise to a lower form of work than before?—Exactly.

2462. Therefore eventually the trade falls into depression, more or less?—Yes.

2463. (*Mr. Allen*): I have just one question. Is the depression of trade in cabinet-making the same all over London?—I think so. Some of the large cabinet-makers in the West-End have gone completely out of it. Jackson & Graham have gone out of the trade, simply from the fact that the class of work is not required. People are going in for the cheapest thing they can get.

2464. (*Chairman*): Your works are in the City?—In Curtain Road, which is next to the City.

2465. A great deal of cabinet-work is done in the City?—I don't think so.

2466. In Eldon Street?—That is almost cleared away. It has all gone to Curtain Road.

2467. (*Mr. Halley*): Do you manufacture for the home market or the foreign market?—For both. The Cape and Australian are generally the best markets.

2468. For America?—Nothing at all, I don't think a piece of furniture goes there. They produce it themselves. They have the machinery there, and produce a different class of work.

2469. The import duties are too heavy, I suppose?—No doubt it has something to do with it. They have the wood almost on the spot, and have improved their machinery so much that they are sending furniture here, but the American work does not seem to find much favour in England.

2470. (*Chairman*): On the whole, Mr. Moss, may we say that you do not despair of cabinet-makers' fortunes—the workmen?—My opinion is that the state of distress is simply a chronic state of distress. The majority of men who have had relief are in the same state every year; that is just my opinion. From what I can gather, three parts of them are men who have work out of doors.

2471. Would you assent to the statement that three parts of them deserved to be in that state—that it was their own doing?—I should hardly like to say that. I should like to see more thrift. A great deal might be done by themselves, if they had the mind to do it.

2472. (*Mr. Hedley*): Was the distress last winter more severe than on previous occasions?—I don't think it was much more. The Mansion House Fund did a a great deal of good. I think we had about £2,300; that was distributed amongst the small tradesman in the parish for provisions, groceries, and various things required, and no doubt it assisted them very materially. There was great depression amongst the small shopkeepers. They had been giving trust to the people, and the ready money of the fund was of great assistance to them.

2473. (*Chairman*): It must also have encouraged them to continue the system of giving trust?—Of course another winter they would do the same thing if they thought it was probable that the Mansion House Fund was coming again. It was proposed this year that only three or four tradesmen in each district should supply the articles required. I suggested that every tradesman—no matter how small—should have a share. I knew they had been giving trust, and wished them to get some ready money. I paid something like 2,000 tradesmen's accounts. I should not care to have a task like it again.

2474. (*Mr. Edgcombe*): Was there any great objection to giving cash? Did you feel bound by your instructions to give tickets, or did you think it was a wiser course than giving money?—We thought it the better plan. We could not work it so as to give all the people money.

2475. (*Mr. Peters*): They would have spent it badly?—It might have been taken to the public-house.

2476. (*Mr. Loch* referred to the Board of Trade return for 1883—the last published, showing that the imports of mahogany were to the value of £494,110 for furniture, hardwood, and veneers, together with other wood imported for the same purpose, and set down as 'unenumerated,' to the value of £581,115. The return showed, he pointed out, a considerable increase on 1881 and 1882)—That is no test. You cannot tell by that. All our wood pretty well comes from abroad.

2477. (*Mr. Allen*): Very little mahogany is used now, it is going out of fashion?—They use it for the inside work.

2478. (*Chairman*): They have run so short of American walnut now that they are pulling up the old stock fences, that had been down there for forty years. I saw one curly root of walnut sold in the United States for £5. It was said that four years ago it would not have made 5s. I am told now that walnut wood is dying out, and cherry wood coming in.

Mr. N. Moss.
July 30, 1886.

INDEX TO THE EVIDENCE.

Able-bodied, No Outdoor Relief given to, 1089.—No Out-relief to except by the Labour Yard, 1167.—Paupers, increase of, 1062.—Should earn any money given to them, 1026.—Were offered labour test, 2409.—Relief of the, 1505, 2204; *see* also Labour Yard and Labour Test

Abstainers applying were received favourably, 213

Acworth, Evidence of Mr. W. M., 393

Administrators of the Fund, *see* Fund

Aged People past work not relieved, 583

Agencies, *see* Organisations

Andrews, Evidence of Mr. A. S., 2309

Almoners, Appointment of, 33, 35, 39 *et seq.*—Appointment of Sub, 28.—Clergy, the chief, 41.—Distributed Grants on their individual judgment, 44.—Insufficient, 302.—Isolated action of, 42, 50, 56, 139, 175.—Status of, 305 *et seq.*

America, Building Trade generally bad except in, 2117.—Furniture not exported to, 2469

American Work in Furniture Trade not favoured in England, 2470

Appeal for Fund, *see* also Fund.—Simply decreased the number of Applications to other Charitable Agencies, 134, 137

Applicants (*see* also Applications and Cases), Advisability of Trade and Benefit Societies sending, 2015.—Character of, 1894.—Class of, 942.—Crowd of, would be prevented by better organisation, 2439.—Deserving, generally mechanics, 1896.—Employed, Character of, 1776.—Employed, Description of, 1776 *et seq.*—Employed, were mostly of the class always out of work in winter, 1830 *et seq.*—For employment were *bonâ fide* out of work, 1825.—Fund created, 671 *et seq.*—Great number of loafers, 1638.—Great crowds of, 1181, 1231, 2014, 2210, 2286, 2211, 2437.—Had to fill up forms, 961.—Increase and worse class of, as Fund became advertised, 591, 1617.—Labour-yard should be offered to some, 2009.—Mode in which sent, 606.—Mostly irregularly employed, 1180.—Mostly labourers, 1028.—No instructions in the Rules of the Fund as to the character of, 108.—No really good artisans amongst, 1646.—Objection of, to go to the Clergy, 1629, 1630.—Object to inquiry, 637, 639.—Occupation of, 315 *et seq.*, 401, 1481; *see* also letter from Mr. Bramly, p. 22.—Proportion relieved, 472, 592.—Question as to length of residence of, 475.—Reluctance to go to the Workhouse of, 2434.—Required as far as possible to state case personally, 429.—Small knowledge of Clergy and Relieving Officers of great majority of, *see* letter from Mr. Valpy, p. 15.—So numerous that at first passive attitude only taken, 16.—Stated that they had to pawn more than usual, 1192.—Status of, 361, 362, 1094.—Suggestions as to sending, 2287 *et seq.*—Superior class of, 617.

Applicants—*continued.*
—Unthrifty, should be sent to the Poor Law, 2258.—Were almost all relieved, 1619.—Were seen by Committee and visited, 565.—When too numerous, told to fill up forms, 429.—Will not go to the Charity Organisation Society or the Poor Law, 633.—Worse for drink after receiving relief, 866, 1187

Application Forms caused respectable people to apply, 431.—Distributed by School Board and District Visitors, 432.—Evidence as to, 604.—Issue of, 558.—Necessary, 426.—Of no value, 981.—Sent in large bundles to the Clergy, 293.—Should have been more concise, 2238

Applications (*see* also Applicants and Cases) at first improperly dealt with, 1383.—Fund caused many new, 2145.—For relief, Fund stimulated, 135.—From common lodging-houses not assisted, 830; *see* also Lodging-houses.—Great number of, 1301, 1451; *see* also Applicants.—Large number of, refused, 2176.—Method adopted to invite, 18.—Mode in which, came in, 1261, 1262.—Mode of, 1181.—Mode of dealing with, 831 *et seq.*, 1184.—Mostly chronic cases, 992, 995, 2337.—Mostly personal, 1183.—None excluded, 2221.—Not increased by the Fund, 784.—Notice-board set up which attracted, 827.—Number of, 830, 858, 1230, 1291.—Of skilled artisans dealt with satisfactorily, 2140.—Ordinary, Percentage of increase above, 2173.—Stimulated by distribution of forms, 161.—To the Charity Organisation Society, 31

Artisans (*see* also Mechanics, Working Man, Workmen), Better-class, will suffer great poverty before applying to Poor Law, 906.—Distress among, not discovered, 2083.—Distress confined to, 1102.—Employment by speculative builders of inferior, 1668. — Employment should be found for better-class, out of work, 1688.—Fund benefited, 2247.—Fund did not reach better class of, 912, 986.—Fund regarded as more especially for, 148.—Good, not in actual want, 1662.—Good, will not degrade themselves by applying for charity, 1646.—Improved condition of, 1671, 1672.—Large number of, applied, 2244.—Might not be affected by depression in trade, 917.—Not a large number of skilled, applied, 2139.—Reluctant to apply to the Fund, 1961, 1997, 2183.—Superior class of, relieved, 1242.—Very few apply for charity in the winter, 2000.—Would not apply, 825, 1662.—Would not care to be seen cleansing the streets, 852

Australia, Field for cabinet-makers in, 2452, 2468

Avis, Evidence of Mrs., 1426

Battersea, Evidence as to, 1286

Begging, Large amount of, 1165.—More persistent in consequence of Fund, 388 *et seq.*

Benefit Societies *see also* Clubs, Friendly Societies, Thrift), Advisability of cases being sent by, 2015
Bermondsey Vestry sent men to be employed by Metropolitan Public Gardens Association, 1770
Blackmail levied, 332
Bloomsbury, Evidence as to, 200
Boot Trade slack, 1483
Brabazon, Lord, *see* Metropolitan Public Gardens Association
Bramly, Evidence of Mr. J. R. J., 273
Brickfields, Many applicants worked in the, 1094
Bricklayers, Wages of, 120
Brush Trade slack, 1482, 1540 *et seq.*
Builders, Scarcity of work among, 1355.—Speculative, do not employ foreign material, 2065.—Speculative, use material from abroad, 1675.—Trade of Speculative, 1666
Building, Decrease of, 1133, 1592.—Societies, Enquiry of, 912.—Societies, Increased membership, 330.—Speculative, not improving, 2115, 2116.—The principal trade, 318
Building Trade, Applicants chiefly belonged to the, 2082.—Depression in, less in London than in other parts, 1601, 1602.—Decrease of work in the, 1585 *et seq.*—Effects of severe winter on, 2045.—Evidence as to the, 1581.—Exceptional want of employment in the, 1608.—High wages ensure better work, 1607.—Higher wages in London than the country, 1594 *et seq.*—Generally bad except in Colonies and America, 2117.—Increase of wages, *see* Wages.—Inferior, more depressed, 1666.—Work in, 1668 *et seq.*—Majority of applicants were employés in the, 1094.—Many applicants belonged to the, 1297.—Mode of procedure as to employment of hands, 1594, *et seq.*—Not greatly affected by machinery, 1625, 1673.—Wages in the 320, 321, 522, 1603 *et seq.*, 1607.—Wages lower in the country, 1606

Cadgers (*see* Ragamuffins, Loafers, &c.), Decrease of number of, 738.—Not relieved, 627
Cabinet-makers (*see also* Furniture Trade), Distress chronic among, 2471.—Employed in cheaper work, 2381.—Large firms of, have abandoned the trade, 2464
Cabinet-making, Cape and Australia markets for, 2468.—Depression in, general all over London, 2464.—Evidence as to the, 2381 *et seq.*—Good field in Australia for, 2452
Camberwell, Evidence as to, 393
Cape, The, market for cabinet-making, 2468
Carpenters do not suffer much from foreign material, 2062 *et seq.*—Emigration of, 2094 *et seq.*—Foreign, 2060.—Large number applied, 2244.—Large number out of work, 248.—Rate of wages and hours of labour, 2059.—Some were out of work who never were before, 2256.—Slack trade among, 2037.—Trade, Improvement of, 2069.—Wages were not lowered, 2038 *et seq.*
Cases (*see also* Applicants and Applications), Great number of, 195.—More or less chronic, 61, 62 *et seq.*—Not appreciably different from those ordinarily applying for relief, 69.—Percentage of improper, 95.—Assisted, Returns of, 83 *et seq.*—Relieved would have been relieved under ordinary circumstances by ordinary relief agencies, 132
Character of Applicants, No instructions in the Rules of the Fund as to the, 208.—Inquiry into, 1470, 1510
Charities, Combination advocated of, 2206.—Want of co-operation between local, *see* letter from Mr. Valpy, 15

Charity Organisation Society, Applicants have strong feeling against, 1631.—Applications to the, 31.—Co-operation between Poor Law and, 683, 749, 793.—Co-operation with the, 82, 1461, 1462, 1615.—Could have met distress with larger funds, 1391, 1392.—Fund distributed at the office of the, 32.—Fund not distributed according to principles of, 65.—Machinery sufficient for purposes of investigation, 237.—Not too rigorous in their inquiry, 793.—People will not apply to the, 633.—Question as to distribution relieving the funds of the, 59.—Reason why applicants in Soho objected to apply to, 664.—Special meeting to consider steps to be taken, 283.—Strong feeling of workmen against, 2277
Charity Relief Works, *see* Metropolitan Public Gardens Association, also Labour Test, &c.
Charity was undertaking Poor Law work, 2259
Cheap Work, *see* Work
Chronic, Bulk of distress was, 2134
Chronic Cases, Application of labour test to, 972.—Applications mostly from, 992, 995, 2337.—Clergy inclined to assist, 270.—Could not be met by the Poor Law, 2426, 2432.—Difficulty of dealing with, 1694.—District Visitors relieve, 1681.—Jewish Board of Guardians would not send to the Poor Law, 2151, 2152.—Not assisted, 231, 939, 1231.—Out-of-work poor detest, 1363.—Relief of, 821, 2152, 2178, 2219.—Rules did not sanction relief of, 62.—Should be sent to the Poor Law, 2540.—Tendency of Fund to relieve, 1610
Chronic Distress, 1477.—Among Cabinet Makers, 2471.—Can only be met by Thrift, 1145
Church and Chapel Attendants, Fund relieved, 1610
City Missionary, Recommendation of case by, not sufficient, 210
Clapham, Evidence as to, 1286
Clare Market, Evidence as to, 200
Classes, Direct statement wanted as to which should be relieved, 1285.—Should be brought into contact with the masses, 2112
Cleanliness, Increased, 1486
Cleansing Streets, 722, 763 *et seq.*, 851; *see also* Roads
Clement Danes, Evidence as to St., 200.—Rector of, distributed doles, and would not co-operate, 231, 232
Clergy, in St. Marylebone, Action of, 35.—Anxious to relieve their own cases, 2361.—Chief Almoners, 41.—Co-operation of, 163.—Forms sent in large bundles to the, 298.—Gave doles, *see* letter from Mr. R. A. Valpy, p. 15.—Gave useful information, 304, 344, 346—Great number of applicants were those who are continually relieved by, 1639.—Have small knowledge of great majority of applicants, *see* letter from Mr. Valpy, p. 16.—Issue of forms to, *see* letter from Mr. Bramly, p. 22.—Objection to applying to the, 1629, 1630.—Recommendation of case by, not sufficient, 210.—Refused to be Almoners, 284.—Should be on the Committees of the Fund, 2304 *et seq.*—Some undeserving cases recommended by, 344
Clerks, Applications from, 114.—Great number of applied, 403
Club Arrears, amount spent to pay, 877.—Arrears paid, 1242, 1267, 1531, 1969, 2359
Clubs (*see* Friendly and Benefit Societies, also Thrift) for dock labourers, No solvent, 813.—Large amounts should be given to members of, than to non-members, 884.—Majority of applicants did not belong to, 877.—Membership of, 354, 377, 378, 1488.—

Clubs—*continued.*
Relief given to enable applicants to join, 879.—
Very few applicants belonged to good, 211
Coal Trade, Evidence as to the 2309 *et seq.*—
Fund not required for the, 2323.—No out-of-work in the, 2319.—Scarcity of hands in the, 2354.—Severe winter increased employment in the, 2315 *et seq.*—Wages in the, 2319.
Coffee Tavern Company, Relief given through, 268
Collie, Evidence of Mr. G., 1756
Colonies, Building Trade generally bad except in, 2117
Combination of Charities advocated, 2206
Committee composed of persons unaccustomed to dealing with distress, 868
Committees of the Fund, Clergy should be on the, 2304.—Composition of, 561, 846, 1184, 1190, 1236, 1237, 1447, 1448, 1459, 1461, 1610, 1612, 2429; *see also* letter from Mr. Bramly, p. 22.—Head of Family required to attend before, 827, 869.—Procedure of, 858 *et seq.*—Small and irregular attendance of members of the, 892.—Working men not welcomed upon, 2289, 2290
Common Lodging Houses full, 740, 741.—Residents, in not assisted, 208, 830
Competition, Chief cause of slackness, 1682.—Slackness in Building Trade caused by, 1589, 1591.—The cause of distress, 1689.—Would be increased by lowering of wages, 1602.
Country, People prefer the, if they can get work, 1499.—Wages lower in the, *see* Building Trade.
Covent Garden, Cases of labourers, &c., from, 216

Daily News Enquiry, Alleged harm at Camberwell by, 433
Davies, Action of Rev. Llewellyn, 36, 152
Depression of Trade (*see also* Trade) causes ow prices, 2397.—Demand for cheap work causes, 2463.—Evidence of, 115 *et seq.*—Not exceptional, 198.—Not sufficient to justify establishment of Fund, 198 (*see also* Fund not required)
Deptford, Evidence as to, 1224, 1380.
Desert of cases not so much considered if really unemployed, 262
Dew, Evidence of Mr. G., 2034
Dinner Tickets, relief by, 268; *see* Tickets, also Kind
Distress (*see also* Depression of Trade), Among artisans not discovered, 2083.—Among Jews caused by lack of work, 2135.—Amount given by the Fund sufficient to meet, 1260.—Exceptional among the Jews, 2133.—Cause of, should be removed rather than distress itself relieved, 798.—Caused by competition, 1689.—Caused by general depression, 1901.—Caused by slack work, 1436 *et seq.*—Caused more work than usual for the Metropolitan Public Gardens Association, 1699.—Causes of, 1559, 1560.—Character of, 2399.—Charity Organisation Society could have met, with larger funds, 1391, 1392.—Chiefly caused by arrears of rent, 1174.—Chronic, 1477.—Cold weather greatest cause of, 1258.—Confined to artisan class, 1102.—Could be met by existing organisations, 954, 1391; *see also* Organisations.—Discovered by inquiry, 1366.—Evidence of great, 1392.—Evidence of Pawnbrokers as to, 575.—In Camberwell, 443.—Fund did not touch some of the, 1890.—Gradual approach of, 1443, 1554 *et seq.*—Great, but not so exceptional as reported, 287, 323, 325, 371, 372.—Great in North London, 1628.—Is Chronic, 2471.—Likely to recur, 1463.—Local agencies could have met exist-

Distress—*continued.*
ing, 291.—Mostly chronic, 1131 *et seq.*—None in Coal Trade, 2315 *et seq.*—Not exceptional, 245, 291, 325, 670, 679, 760, 780, 987, 1133, 2332, 2473.—Not exceptional until commencement of Fund, 397, 398, 453 *et seq.*—Occurred before establishment of Fund, 510.—Parish authorities said was not exceptional, 589.—Pawnbrokers did not think exceptional, 1191.—Period of, 1419.—Prolonged, 1421.—Poor Law should in the main relieve, 842.—Recurrence of, feared, 514, 1917, 1865.—Recurrence of, not apprehended, 2070.—Should be met locally, 1109 *et seq.*—Subsided with the winter, 540.—Thought exceptional, 1400 *et seq.*—Was caused by bad trade, 1096.—Was exceptional, 502, 522, 527, 630, 1055, 1240, 1241, 1909 *et seq.*, 2251.—Well-directed charitable effort required to meet, 922.—Work created in consequence of, 1718.—Work given to relieve, 1804.—Would not have been met by local effort, 1565, 1566.—Would not have caused great hardship if Fund had not existed, 988.
Distribution, Mode of (*see* Procedure), Unsatisfactory nature of the, 189.
District Boards of Works and Guardians, Co-operation of, 799, 1119.
District Visitors, Application Forms issued by the Clergy through, 294.—Applications through 1262. Distributed application forms, 432.—Recommendation of case by, not sufficient, 210.—Relieve church-goers and the permanent poor, 1681.
Dock Labour decreased, 734, 735.—More regular than formerly, 774.—Status of men employed in, 770.—Temporary work, 769.
Dock Labourers (*see also* Labourers), 1180.—Cannot be thrifty, 2342.—Distress not exceptional among, 758.—Large number of, 1956.—Medical Clubs for, 814.—Mode of life, 1192.—No small solvent clubs for, 813.—Not worse off than usual, 1273.—Should be sent to the Guardians, 2355
Docks, Increase of warehouses round the, 776.—Rate of wages at the, 1220.
Doles given, 858.—Given by Clergy in St. Giles's, *see* letter from Mr. Valpy, p. 15.
Doubtful Cases relieved in kind, 1284.
Dove, Evidence of Mr. F. J., 1581.
Drink, Relief given sometimes spent in, 1222., 1187.—Relief when given in money spent in, 1947.— Sale of tickets for, 1966.
Drinking people should be relieved only in kind, 2067.
Drunkards begged as unemployed with boxes at Lewisham, 387.—Families of, relieved, 858, 861.—Only excluded from relief, 375.—Nothing in the Rules of the Fund to exclude from relief a, 108.—Should be sent to the Workhouse, 2068
Drunkenness of those who refused to accept offer of work, 1035.—Small amount of, among men employed, 1819.

East London (*see also* Whitechapel), Not many persons able to help the poor in, 712
Education, Increase of, 1652.—Technical, will do good, 2458
Emigrants, Maintenance of intending, *see* letter from Mr. Bramly, p. 23
Emigrate, Best men would, 2255.—Difficulty of getting men to, 1029.—Few applications to, 1356.—Many good workmen, 2451.—People not willing to, 1463, 1558.—Some shipwrights would, 1940 *et seq.*, 1986, 2006

Emigrated, Care required as to cases, 2162 *et seq.*
—Many applicants had, 1742
Emigration, 1006 *et seq.* - Applicants not suitable for, 2377.—A remedy for want of work, 2270.—By Jewish Board of Guardians, 2162, 2163, 2186 *et seq.*—Of carpenters, 2094 *et seq.*—Should be State-directed, 2270.—Suggested, 1424
Employed, Applicants mostly irregularly, 1180.—Cases were relieved whilst still, 1513
Employers complain that men refused to work in order to pose as unemployed, *see* letter from Mr. Valpy, p. 15.—Do not interest themselves in the poor, 922 *et seq.*—Enquiry of, 247, 405, 406, 966, 905, 907, 1254, 2214, *et seq.*, 2371.—Enquiry could not be made of, 1297—Enquiry made of, 529, 569, 607, 835.—Enquiry not made of, 1512—Had difficulty in getting workmen because of the Fund, 266.—Large, few resident, 922.—Not on Committee, 2362.—Served on Committee, 1190
Employment (*see* also Labour Test, Work), Alternative, 1642; *see* also Trades.—As plentiful as usual, 689.—Advocated in time of distress, 2066.—Better to find, than to relieve distress, 1634.—Difficulty of relieving by way of, 1377.—Men left, to obtain relief, *see* letter from Mr. Valpy, p. 15.—Men should be taught supplemental, 1149 *et seq.*, 1166; *see* also Trades.—Mode of, unsatisfactory, 1724.—Provided by District Board of Works, 1119.—Provision of, 1634 *et seq.*—Provision of, strongly advocated, 1647 *et seq.*—Should be by piecework, 1695.—Should be given in times of distress, 1654, 1656, 1724.—Should be provided for better-class artisans out of work, 1688.—Suggestion as to providing, 2070.—Want of, caused distress, 530
Energy, Lack of, among people, 1560
Enquiry (*see* also Investigation), A farce, 1186.—Amount of, 375, 376.—Charity Organisation Society not too rigorous in their, 793.—Difficulty of sufficient, 1354, 1414 *et seq.* — Discovered distress, 1366.— Imperfect, 1948.—Into cases, Extent of, 72.—Into character, 1470, 1510.—Into distress, skilled work, 2418.—Lessens need for relief in kind, 2220.—Metropolitan Public Gardens Association do not ordinarily employ men without, 1856.—Money not given without, 57.—Objection of applicants to, 637, 639.—Officers, No paid, employed, 2415.—Officers should be paid, 2406. —Of trade societies, 2087 *et seq.*—Organisation wanting, 483.—Plan of, 72, 163, 122, 160, 399, 457 *et seq.*, 831 *et seq.*, 963 *et seq.*, 1095, 1232 *et seq.*, 1265, 1294 *et seq.*, 1388, 1458, 1511 *et seq.*, 1568, 1572 *et seq.*, 1620, 1628, 1720, 1725, 1773, 1839, 1889, 1952, 2209, 2212 *et seq.*, 2366 *et seq.*, 2402 *et seq.* — As to men at work, 1857 *et seq.*—Jewish Board of Guardians, 2123 *et seq.* — Relief not given without, 57. — Staff necessary for, 659. — Strict, necessary, 1027, 1889 *et seq.*, 1952 *et seq.*, 1959.—Suggestions as to, 1194, 1367, 1369, 2086 *et seq.*—Was sufficient, 626 2209
Exceptional Distress, *see* Distress; also Pressure

Family, Head of, required to attend before Committee, 827, 869
Fletcher, Evidence of Mr. A. P., 1
Food cheaper, 695
Foreign Jews, Fund did not attract poor, 2192
Foreign Material, Carpenters do not suffer much from, 2062 *et seq.*—Not employed by speculative builders, 2065.—Speculative builders use, *see* Builders

Foreign Work, Bad quality of, 1676 *et seq.*—Influence upon trade of the importation of, 1679—Workmen in fancy trades, 2060
Foreigners affected by distress, 506.—Employment as servants of, 168.—Many, 505
Forms (*see* Application Forms).
Fraud, Great amount of, *see* letter from Mr. Valpy, p. 15
Friendly Societies (*see* Clubs, Benefit Societies, Thrift), Enquiry of, 913. — Not increasing, 790
Fund (*see* also Mansion House), Administration of, too much for individual effort, 2405.—Administrators should be local, 1694.—Advertisement of, necessary, 1611.—Advocated, if distributed by the Charity Organisation Society, and other existing organisations, 1405, 1406. — A mistake, 1634.—Amount given by, was sufficient, 1260.—Amount sent to Jewish Board of Guardians from the, 2142.—Appeal for, not justified, 2898.—Applicants increased after establishment of, 591.—Applicants preferred applying to the, than to the Poor Law, 418.—Applications not increased by the, 784.—Assisted cases not touched by ordinary relief agencies, 241.—Bad effect of the, 1634.—Badly distributed at first, 941.—Benefited artisans, 2247.—Benefited shopkeepers, 2473.—Better administration of, wanted, 1319, 1320.—Better organisation of, would prevent rush of applicants, 2439.—Caused applications which would not otherwise have been made, 326, 373, 374.—Caused many new applications, 2145.—Caused people to migrate to London, 671 *et seq.*—Caused people to remain idle, *see* letter from Mr. Valpy, p. 15.—Clergy should be on the Committees of the, 2304 *et seq.*—Composition of Committees of, 561, 1184, 1190, 1236, 1237, 1447, 1448, 1459, 1161, 1610, 1612; *see* also letter from Mr. Bramly, p. 22.—Co-operation of, with District Board of Works, 1119.—Co-operation of, with Relieving and Sanitary Officers, 1186.—Co-operation of, with the Poor Law, 1105.—Creation of, should be prevented, 841.—Deserving cases not brought out by publicity given to, 1571.—Did good, 413, 1435, 1546, 1960, 2143, 2435, 2473.—Did harm, 1412, 1413, 1545, 2259.—Did not attract poor foreign Jews, 2192.—Did not reach better-class workmen, 912, 986.—Did not touch some distress, 1390.—Difficulties of administering, 188 *et seq.*, 1335 *et seq*, 1570.—Distributions other than the, 1562 *et seq.*—Effect of the, 2052, 2058.—Expectation created by the, 1012.—Expected by ragamuffins, 332.—Forced upon locality, 823. —Full amount granted from, not distributed, 618.—General scramble to participate in the, 969.—Induced large number of people to remain out of work, 263.—Large number of worst class applied to, 1617.—Large, undesirable, 902.—Lowering tendency of, 1962.—May cause migration to London, 2055.—May prevent advisable migration, 1502, 1503, 1918, *et seq.*—May lessen a man's energy, 1557.—Mode of distributing, *see* Procedure.—Much more subscribed to, than was necessary, 2364.—Not advocated, 155, 197, 226, 356, 385, 545, 612, 1108, 2164.—Not necessary, 137, 198, 818, 982, 989, 1106, 2323, 2332 *et seq.*—Not satisfactory, 1195.—Of great service, 1969.—Only dealt with an imaginary crisis, 1423.—People soon knew of existence of, 555.—Policy of, should have been more clearly stated, 169.—Prevented applications to labour-yard increasing, 1118.—

v

Fund—*continued.*
Prevented people becoming paupers, 1104.—
Proposals for working a future, 899 *et seq.*—
Publicity given to, did harm, 1407.—Publicity necessary as to, 1301, 1331, 1332.—Quick spread of news as to the, 296.—Mr. Acworth's Opinion as to Recurrence of, 433.—Reached the right people, 2082.—Recurrence of, advocated, 1320, 1467.— Relieved church and chapel goers, 1610.— Rules issued by the, *see* p. 7.—Rules of the, not adhered to, 1628.—Rules of the, not much considered, 1680.—Should be collected privately, not by advertisement, 898, 1245.—Should be subscribed locally, 360, 2365.—Should not be advertised, 1209.—Should not be an institution, 2109.—Should not be raised periodically, 2258—Should not relieve distress, but remove the cause, 2109.—Simply decreased number of applications to other charitable agencies, 134, 137,—Sources of relief other than the, 1495, 1547, 1562, *et seq.* 1579.—Success of, depends upon time taken in preparation for it, 1692.—Suggested mode of working a future, 2290 *et seq.*—Suggestion as to composition of Committees to administer a, 2429.—System of, as good as was possible, 2067.—Tendency of, to bring about feelings of dependence and expectation of relief, 794.—Tendency of, to relieve permanent poor, 1610.—Too much money was not sent by, 1522.—Unsatisfactory nature of the distribution of the, 189.—Warning should be issued that people were not to expect recurrence of, 2110. Was beneficial, but many undeserving cases were relieved, 953.—Was of great benefit, and did good, 2143.—Was useful, 1435.—Was wisely administered, 1106.—Whole of the grant from the, spent on unremunerative work, 1129.—Would not help in removing real distress, 387. —Work provided would not have been offered but for the, 1719.—Working men not welcomed on Committees of the, 2280, 2290.—Working men should serve on Committees of, 2084
Furniture, Description of wood most used for, 2478, 2479 *et seq.*—Large importation of foreign wood for, 2477.—Large increase in value of walnut wood for, 2479—Not exported to America, 2469
Furniture Trade (*see also* Cabinet-makers), Amount of work not much less than ordinary, 2441.—Evidence as to the, 2378.—Lower class of work in the, 2381 *et seq.*—Mahogany not much used in the, 2478.—Slackness in, 2381.—Winter does not stop work in the, 2379.—Work different in kind rather than amount, 2442.—Workman must keep to his particular department in the, 2453

Gardeners, Want of employment among, 1866 *et seq.*
Gardens Association, *see* Metropolitan
Gardiner, Evidence of Mr. T. Gage, 815
Gee, Evidence of Miss, 1380
George-in-the-East, Evidence as to, St., 1170
Giles's, Evidence as to, St., 200
Guardians (*see also* Relieving Officers, Poor Law, &c.) and District Board of Works, Co-operation of, 799.—Co-operation between Charity Organisation Society and, 683.—Co-operation with the, 80, 839.—Functions of the, 1514 *et seq.*—Not consulted, 177.—Suggestion as to setting on foot of relief works by, 490

Hayward, Evidence of Rev. W. Curtis, 502
Heale, Evidence of Mr. W., 1286
Hop-picking, People go, 1552, 1553

Houses for Poor, Improved, 692 ; *see also* Dwellings

Idle, Fund caused people to remain, *see* letter from Mr. R. A. Valpy, p. 15
Imposture, Evidence of great, 1892 ; *see also* letter from Mr. Valpy, p. 15
Improper Cases, Proportion of, 95
Individual Judgment as to cases best, 622
Individuals did not assist cases, 341
Investigation, *see* Enquiry
Irregular Work, *see* Labourers, Casual
Islington, Evidence as to, 581
Isolated Action of the Almoners, 42, 50, 56, 139, 175

Jack, Evidence of Mr., 935
James's St., Evidence as to the parish of, 502 ; *see also* Soho
Jewish Board of Guardians, Amount expended annually in relief by, 2171.—Amount received from the Fund by, 2142.—Composition of Relief Committee of, 2130.—Emigration by, 2162, 2163, 2186 *et seq.*—Evidence of Secretary of, 2118.—Mode adopted of raising funds by, 2148 *et seq.*—Mode of procedure of, 2156 *et seq.* —Organisation of, quite complete, 2161.—Would not have sent cases to the Poor Law, 2151, 2152
Jewish Population, Evidence as to, 2121 *et seq.*—Relief Societies, Co-operation amongst, 2180
Jews, Exceptional distress among, 2133.—Trades followed by, 2137

Kenny, Mr., distributes broadcast forms for applying for relief, 156
Kind, Doubtful cases relieved in, 2219.—Enquiry lessens need of relief in, 2220.—Relief not generally in, 1282.—Relief in, 215, 268, 2473, 2475 ; *see also* Tickets.—Relief Chiefly in, 186.—Relief in, mischievous, 1656.—Relief of chronic cases in, 2219.—Relief in, seldom resorted to, 786.—Small advantage of relief in, 861.

Labour (*see also* Work), Badly paid, 1204.—Relief provided by, 1122, 1126.—Supplemental, 1424 ; *see also* Trades.—Whole grant from the Fund spent on unremunerative, 1129
Labour Market, Complete information as to state of, desirable, 1363.—Influence of the Fund upon the, 263
Labour Test, 309 *et seq*, 473, 474, 808, 809, 811, 821, 822, 850, 893 *et seq.*, 970 *et seq.*, 993 *et seq.*, 1177, 1196 *et seq.*, 1217, 1226, 1249 *et seq.*, 1303 *et seq.*, 1318, 1347, 1372 *et seq.*, 1640, 2078, 2079, 2408 ; *see also* letter from Mr. Bramly, p. 23.—Amount of relief wage necessary, 978 *et seq.*—Advisable, 1248.—Approved, 944.—Classes to which not applicable, 2294.—Difficulty of Applying, 1219.—Good class of workmen would not accept a, 2267.—For women, 1177, 1217.—Hard, 1374.—Men skulked and got drunk while at the, 984.—Not adopted, but advisable for some cases, 2197 *et seq.*, 2200.—Rate of payment and hours, 2296.—Should not be at lower wages, 1643
Labour-yard, 366, 753, 840, 854, 855, 1658, 1660 —Advocated, 1832 *et seq.*, 1852 *et seq.*—For some cases, 2009, 2032.—Cases in the, helped, 411. —Dissatisfaction with the, 1515 *et seq.*—Dock labourers would shirk, 2031.—For dock labourers and the unthrifty, 2557.—Loafers should go to the, 1688.—Many employed by Metropolitan Public Gardens Association might have been at the, 1738.—Men object to go to,

Labour Yard—*continued*.
1853, 1929 *et seq.*, 1999.—No, 603, 1177.—Not required, 752.—The only out-relief to able-bodied, 1089, 1167.—Too demoralising for a respectable man, 994.—Would have been no hardship to some of the applicants, 993
Labourers (*see also* Dock), Applicants mostly, 942, 1028.—Casual, were relieved, 1955.—Fund did not reach better class of, 986 (*see also* Artisans, Workmen)
Landlords, Pressure put upon tenants for back rent by, *see* letter from Mr. Walpy, p. 15
Laymen in St. Marylebone, Appointment as Almeners of, 40
Legge, Evidence of Hon. and Rev. Canon, 1036
Letter, Applications received by, 467
Lewisham, Evidence as to, 273, 935, 1036
Limehouse, Evidence as to, 1878
Loafers, Decrease in number of, 738.—Should be given piece-work, 1734 (*see also* Cadgers, Ragamuffins)
Loan, Suggestion as to raising, to relieve distress, 1651
Local Administrators required to distribute Fund, 1694.—Charities, communication with, 258.—Effort would not have met distress, 1565, 1566.—Fund should be, 477, 478, 2365.—Magnates did not fulfil their responsibilities, 2363
Locally, Distress could have been met, 1160
Lodging-houses, *see* Common
London Docks, *see* Docks
London, Fund caused a migration to, 671 *et seq.* Fund may cause migration to, 2055.—Great migration to, 2053.—Wages in the Building Trade higher, *see* Building

Machinery and the Building Trade, *see* Building
Machinery, Special, not wanted for the distribution of a special fund, 174; *see also* Organisation
Mackay, Evidence of Mr. T., 1170
Mahogany not now much used for furniture, 2478
Mansion House Fund, *see* Fund
Marchant, Evidence of Mr. T. W., 1224
Mary, St., Newington, Evidence as to, 815
Marylebone, Evidence as to St., 1
Masses should be brought into contact with the classes, 2112
Mechanics, deserving applicants generally, 1896; *see also* Artisans, Workmen
Medical Clubs for Dock Labourers, 814.—Relief, Statement as to, 788, 790, 791
Menservants, Lack of employment for, 142
Metropolitan Public Gardens Association, Amount received by the, 1722.—Evidence as to, 187, 1697 *et seq.*, 1756.—Plan of procedure, 1697, *et seq.*, 1805 *et seq.*—Rate of wages paid by the, 1706, 1799, 1805 *et seq.*—Work provided by, 998 *et seq.*
Metropolitan Visiting and Relief Association, Circular issued by, 22.—Fund and the, 9
Migration advisable, 1484, 1485.—Fund may prevent advisable, 1502, 1503, 1918 *et seq.*—Not noticed, 1256.—Of better class 1429.—Of workmen from London, 1658.—Relief given for, 881.—To London, Fund caused, 671 *et seq.*—Fund may cause, 2055.—Great, 2053
Money, Best to pay for work done in, 1024.—Objections to relief in, 1468 *et seq.*, 1504.—People had less to spend, 1554 *et seq.*—Relief advocated in, 186, 1656, 2067.—Relief given in, 409, 1282.—Relief not advocated in, 1905, 1047, 2475, 2476
Moss, Evidence of Mr. Nathan, 2378

Newington, Evidence as to, 815, 1426.

North and North-West of London, Sub-Committee for, 25
North London, Distress great in, 1628
Notice-board set up, 827
Notices of places of distribution, Wide issue of, 18
Nugee, Distribution by Father, 1562

Occupation, Changes of, in bad times, 2456
Olney, Distribution by Mr., 1563
Organisation, Better, would prevent rush of applicants, 2439.—Of Jewish Board of Guardians quite complete, 2161
Organisations, Combination advocated of, 2206.—Distress could be met by existing, 214, 613, 636, 680, 761, 804, 867, 954, 1324, 1391.—Existing, should administer the Fund if it recurred, 1400.—Should be strengthened to meet exceptional distress, 842, 1109
Outdoor Pauperism, Increase of, 1057, 1069
Outdoor Relief, 748, 750, 1908; *see also* Parish, Poor Law, &c.—Benefit of, 2030, 2033.—Confined chiefly to the aged, 1255.—Evil effects of lavish, 703.—Free, to widows, would reduce women's wages, 747.—Given freely, 1657.—Not given, 1188
Out of Work, A great deal of, not being helped, 1425.—Applicants for employment were *bonâ fide*, 1825.—Bad effect on a man of being, 1634.—Cases and the Poor Law, 2279 *et seq.*—Cases, Mode in Whitechapel of dealing with, 683.—Cases must apply to the parish, 1130.—Cases, Recurrence of, 2222 *et seq.*—Cause of waterside labourers being, 1842.—Difficult to find out whether applicants are, 1184.—Some were, who never were before, 2256
Overlapping, Question of, 178 *et seq.*

Painters, Distress among, 1628, 1641
Parish Authorities said distress was not exceptional, 589; *see also* Poor Law, &c.—Relief supplemented, 821
Pauperism decreased, 676, 906.—Returns, a good indication whether distress exists, 906, 912.—Statement as to, 702, 704 *et seq.*
Paupers, Fund prevented people becoming, 1104
Pawn, Redemption of tools from, 2262, 2359, 2431.—Redemption from, 1267, 1968.—Relief not given to redeem things in, 2228, 2229
Pawnbrokers did not think distress exceptional, 1191.—Said distress was great, 575
Pawning and Pawnbrokers, 220 *et seq.*—Great deal of, 1899.—Statements of applicants as to, 1192
Pawntickets, 890, 921.—Large amount of, *see* Letter from Mr. Bramly, p. 23.—Not verified, 223
People, Improved condition of, 1427 *et seq.*, 1486, 1532.—Lack of energy among, 1560
Periodic Cases, *see* Chronic
Permanent Poor, *see* Chronic
Personal Service to the Poor, Value of, 714, 270
Pledge, *see* Pawn
Police required to keep order among applicants, 1181
Political Motives displayed by persons offering help in the distribution, 254
Poor (*see also* Working Classes), Condition of, not different from previous year, 70.—Districts Pauperism, less in, than in rich, 695.—Improved condition of, 690.—Sanitary Condition of, 693, 780.—Increased care for the, 783, 801.—Less sickness among the, 694.—The, help the poor; 715
Poor Law (*see also* Guardians, Parish, Relieving

vii

Poor Law—*continued.*
Officers, Out-door Relief, Pauperism, Workhouse), Administration, Improved, 782.—Applicants did not care to apply to, 415, 416, 417, 418.—Cases assisted by, not helped by the Fund, 260.—Cases at first mostly those for the, 825.—Cases for the, did not apply, 573.—Cases sent by but not to, 1621, 1622.—Cases were relieved, 822, 825, 889.—Chronic cases referred to the, 939.—Chronic cases should be sent to the, 2340.—Co-operation between Charity Organisation Society and the, 683, 749, 793 ; of the Fund with the, 1105.—Dock labourers should be sent to the, 2355.—Functions of the, 798, 1343, 1696.—Inadequacy of relief given by the, 2433.—Lower class should be left to the, 2106, 2107.—Many cases not suitable for the, 361.—Not sufficient to deal with exceptional distress. 339.—Officers, *see* Relieving Officers.—People will not apply to, 633, 1370, 1504.—Unthrifty applicants should be sent to the, 2258.—Would not meet chronic cases, 2426. 2432.—Work, Charity was undertaking, 2358.—Working men know little about, 1696
Population Question deserves attention, 919, 920
Post Office Savings Bank, Few deposit in, 1490
Powell, Evidence of Mr. J. D., 2230
Praed, Relief given by Mr., 1443, 1523, 1526, 1547, 1575, 1579
Press, Advertisements in the, 19
Pressure (*see also* Distress), Ordinary relief agencies not sufficient for, 241
Procedure, Plan of, 92 *et seq.*, 358, 408, 420 *et seq.*, 457 *et seq.*, 960, 1079, 1184, 1231 *et seq.*, 1324, 1411
Providence, *see* Thrift
Provident Societies, Increased membership of, 330
Public Gardens Association, *see* Metropolitan
Public-house Trade, Decrease of, 726, 727, 742.—Did not suffer, 392, 577, 2392
Public-houses, Tickets of the Fund sold in, 268, 269
Public Works, *see* Employment, Labour Test, and Relief Works

Ragamuffins expect recurrence of Fund, 332
Relations should help, It should not be a cardinal point that, 641
Relief, Advertisement that it was to be given, 468.—Agency, Fund was merely an additional, 133.—Amount annually expended by Jewish Board of Guardians in, 2171.—Amount of, 1216, 1222, 1223, 1228, 1290, 1520, 1530.—By tickets, 1450, 1504, 1506 *et seq.*, 1949 ; *see also* Tickets, Kind.—Committee, suggestion as to a permanent, 227.—Direct statement as to classes to whom it should be given, 1285.—Enquiry lessens need for, 2220.—Extent of, 441, 442.—Given by weekly allowances, 368.—Given to many who ought not to have had it, 1187.—In kind, 2473, 2475, *see also* Kind.—In money, 409.—In money advocated, 1656, 2067.—In money inadvisable to give, 2476.—In money, objections to, 1468 *et seq.*, 1504, 1947.—Manner of, 862, 863, 1079 *et seq.*, 1230, 1267, 1450, 1468 *et seq.*, 2135 *et seq.*—Mischievous, 1656.—Mode and Scale of, 2178 *et seq.*—Necessary because people have no energy as to emigration, &c., 1559, 1560.—Not generally in kind, 1282.—Number of cases, and amount given in, 1452 *et seq.*—Of the ablebodied, 1505, 2204.—Rules as to, 1294, 1338, 1339.—Sources of, other than the Fund, 1495, 1547, 1562 *et seq.*, 1579.—To artisans, temporary, 2141.—Withheld because it would be spent in drink, 1548

Relief Works, *see* Labour Test, also Works, 1634, 2374.—Endeavour to establish, 434 *et seq.*
Relieved, Percentage, 1202
Relieving Officers (*see also* Guardians, Poor Law &c.), Additional, appointed, 1076
Relieving Officers, Co-operation with, 72 *et seq.*, 225, 461, 822, 840, 929, 930, 940, 1186, 1188, 1361 *et seq.*, 1572 *et seq.*, 1957, 2373.—Enquiry not made of, 572, 610.—Have small knowledge of majority of applicants, *see* letter from Mr Valpy, *p.* 15.—Not always to be relied upon for evidence as to distress, 1311, 1313.—Sent cases to the Fund which they had refused to relieve, 1612.—State nothing indicating exceptional distress, 330.—Working men will not apply to the, 1312, 1313, *see also* Poor Law.
Rent, Application for payment of back, 100, 156—Arrears of, greater than usual, 1397.—Back, paid, 621, 874, 1174, 1215 ; not paid, 1278 *et seq.*, 1531, 2105, 2218.—Too high, 585.—Evidence as to payment of back, 654, *et seq.*—Increase of, 691.—Much arrears of, 456.—Pressure put by landlords upon tenants for back, *see* letter from Mr. Valpy, p. 15
Residence of Applicants, Length of, 475.—Rule as to length of, 207, 1294
Resident Cases only relieved, 1256
Respectable Poor did not care to personally apply, 1270.—Would not come forward on account of crowd of ragamuffins, 212
Returns of Cases assisted, 83 *et seq.*
Rich districts, Pauperism larger in, than in poor, 719
Riverside Work, Slackness of, 1864
Roads, Making and cleansing of, Relief by, 945 *et seq.*, *see also* Streets and Cleansing
Roberts, Evidence of Mr. R., 1581
Roman Catholic Clergy, Cases sent by, mostly ineligible, *see* letter from Mr. Valpy, p. 15
Rules, Delay in issuing, 239, 1173
Rules of the Fund, 61 ; *see also* p. 7.—Do not exclude drunkards from relief, 108.—Not adhered to, 62, 1628.—Not much considered, 1680

Sailors pretty well employed, 2349
Sanitary Condition of poor, Improved, 693, 789.—Officers, Co-operation with, 1186
Savings (*see also* Thrift, Banks, Post Office, Increased membership, 330.—Of the people, exhausted, 1903
School Board Visitors distributed application forms, 432
Schoolmasters and Visitors, Valuable information received from, *see* letter from Mr. Valpy, p. 15.
Servants, *see also* Men.—Employment of foreigners as, 168.—Great number of, 101.—Out of place, Applications from, 101, 141
Sewing-class Test, 1177, 1217
Shipbuilders, Want of work among, 1210 ; *see also* Shipwrights
Shipbuilding Trade, generally bad, 1913 *et seq.*, 1972 *et seq.*—Gone, 1989
Shipping Trade, Bad state of, 2344.—Depression of, 759.—Not exceptionally depressed, 1193
Shipwrights (*see also* Shipbuilders). Bad state of trade of, 1917 *et seq.*—How is supply of, kept up, 2020.—Number of, 1972 *et seq.*—Only employed three days a week, 1983.—Some would emigrate, 1940 *et seq.*, 1986, 2006.—Trade gone from London, 1912.—Very few apply for charity in the winter, 2000.—Wages and number of, 1925, 1926, 2003 *et seq.*—Wages not lower, 1926, 1981

Shopkeepers (*see also* Tradesmen), Distress amongst, 587, 591.—Great depression among small, 2473.—Suffered, 742, 7=3.—The principal sufferers, 684.—Tickets given to applicants should be apportioned generally among, 2474
Shoreditch, Evidence as to, 2401
Sickness among the poor, Less. 394
Slackness the cause of want of employment, 128
Society for the Relief of Distress almoners first had money from the Fund, 546.—Mansion House Fund and the, 9.—No almoners, 337.—No co-operation with, 1614
Society men, in Building Trade, Easier to get employment for, 2049
Soho, Evidence as to, 502
Speculative Builders, *see* Builders
Staff not sufficient at first, 820
Starvation Cases, 463.—Did not exist, 1211.—No bad cases of, 1565
Stephany, Evidence of Mr. M., 2118
Stoke-on-Trent, Experiment at, 1203, 1372
Stoneyard, *see* Labour-yard
Streets, Cleansing of, 722 *et seq.*, 763 *et seq.*, 851 (*see* also Roads)
Summer, Trade bad in the, 1099
Superior class would not come forward on account of crowd of ragamuffins, 212
Supervising men at work, Mode of, 1844

Temperance, Considerable progress of, 1536.—Movement, Good done by, 1=34
Thrift (*see also* Benefit and Friendly Societies, Clubs, Savings), Applicants should show, 2238, 2257, 2284, 2341.—Amongst applicants, Want of evidence of, 211.—Attempt to promote, 1275.—Dock labourers cannot show, 2342.—Evidence of, 352.—Increase of, 726, 1142.—Inducements to, 1488 *et seq.*—More, desirable, 2472.—Necessity of, 2266.—Test, 500, 501, 652, 663, 805, 883 *et seq.*—The only remedy for chronic distress, 1145
Tickets do not carry same value as money, 1988.—For relief were sold, 864.—Issued by the Fund sold in public-houses, 268, 269.—Of the Fund publicly exposed for sale, 268.—Relief by, 186, 268, 269, 1222, 1223, 1450, 1504, 1506 *et seq.*, 1907, 1949, 1965.—Sale of, 1966.—Tradesmen did not always give value for, 1506 *et seq.*
Tools, Purchase of, 2226.—Redeemed from pawn, 2262, 2359, 2431.—Were pawned in many cases, 2388
Trade, Bad state of, 1353, 1432, 2252 *et seq.*—Depressed, 908 *et seq.*—Depression of, General, 2254.—Depression of, might not affect artisans, 917.—Distress caused by bad, 1096.—Evidence of depression of, 115 *et seq.*—Exceptionally depressed state of, 2077, 2345.—Gradual decline of, 2253.—Improvement of, 2067, 2147, 2350, 2427.—Leaving St. George's-in-the-East, 1193.—No signs of revival, 1164.—Not improved. 2400
Trade Societies, Advisability of cases being sent by, 2015.—Do not care to have to do with charity matters, 2086.—Enquiry of, 2087 *et seq.*—Evidence as to help given by, 1664.—Relief given to members by, 2248, 2273.—Would not officially co-operate with charities, 2260, 2261
Trades followed by Jews, 2187.—Nature of, 1481.—Supplemental, 1149 *et seq.*, 1166, 1424, 1690, 1691, 2007 *et seq.*, 2091 *et seq.*, 2297 *et seq.*, 2453 *et seq.*
Tradesmen (*see also* Tickets), Did not always give value for tickets, 1506 *et seq.*—Give

Tradesmen—*continued.*
money for tickets instead of food for which issued, 268

Undeserving cases recommended as deserving, 344, 347

Vallance, Evidence of Mr. W., 665
Valpy, Evidence of Mr. R. A., 200
Vestries, Men employed by the Metropolitan Public Gardens Association were sent by the, 1768
Visitation (*see also* Enquiry) of cases, 497 *et seq.*
Visitors of cases not sufficiently numerous, 484

Wages (*see also* Work), Amount of, 1551.—At relief works should be adequate, 2296.—Decrease of, 918.—Evidence as to, 119.—High, ensure better work, *see* Building Trade.—Higher in the Building Trade in London than in the country, 1594 *et seq.*—In the Building Trade, *see also* Building.—In Building Trade, Increase of, 1671.—In Building Trade, Mode of fixing, 2046 *et seq.*—In Building Trade, Rate of, 1596.—Labour test should not lower rate of, 1643.—Lowering of, would increase competition, 1602.—More work in proportion done for high, 1710 *et seq.*—Necessary Rate of, 1846, 1850 *et seq.*—Not reduced, 696.—In the Coal Trade, 2319.—Of Carpenters, not lowered, 2038, 2041.—Of Shipwrights, not lower, 1926, 1981.—Of Shipwrights, Rate of, 2003 *et seq.*—Of Women, reduced, 696.—Questions as to past, 643 *et seq.*—Rate, &c., of, 1727 *et seq.*—Rate of Carpenters, and hours of their work, 2059.—Rate of, in Building Trade, 1667.—Rate of, paid by Metropolitan Public Gardens Association, 1706, 1799, 1805 *et seq.*—Reduction of, 569.—Standard of, 2040.—Work would not be increased by reduction of, 2042
Walnut Wood, Increase of value of, 2479
Walworth, Evidence as to, 815, 1426
Wandsworth, Evidence as to, 2286
Waterside Labourers, Cause of want of work among, 1842
Weekly Allowances given, 368
Well-to-do, Migration of, 1429
Westbrook, Evidence of Mr. G. T., 1878
West Ham, Committee of the Fund at, 2275
Westminster, *see* James's, St., also Soho
Whitechapel (*see also* East London), Evidence as to, 665
Widows, Free outdoor relief to, would lower women's wages, 747
Wife and Children of Drunkard, Mode of dealing with, 2079
Wilkinson, Evidence of Miss, 1697
Women, Labour test for, 1177, 1217
Women's Wages reduced, 696.—Would be lowered by free outdoor relief to widows, 747
Wood, Large importation of foreign, 2477.—Used for furniture, Description of, 2478, 2479
Work (*see also* Employed, Employment, Labour, Wages, &c.), Apprehended recurrence of slackness of, 1640.—Change of, in bad times, 2456.—Character of men engaged to do the, 1776.—Competition the chief cause of slack, 1682.—Decrease of, 729.—Demand for, 2400.—Demand of cheap, causes depression in trade, 2463.—Demand for cheap, lowers character of, 2462.—Description of men employed at the, 1776 *et seq.*—Difficulty of getting men to do the, 1712.—Distress caused by want of, 599, 2135.—Emigration a remedy for want of, 2270.—Exceptionally slack, 1441.—Extra, made

Work—*continued.*
1718.—Given to relieve distress, 1804.—Great deal of out of, not being helped, 1425.—Greater demand for cheaper, 2445 *et seq.*—Greater number of men than necessary employed to do, 1764.—Hours of, 1706, 1707, 1727, 1752, 1805, 1814, 1818, 1861, 1862.—Irregular, *see* Dock, also Labourers, Casual.—Men given, mostly of the class always out of work in winter, 1830 *et seq.*—Men left their, to obtain relief, *see* letter from Mr. Valpy, p. 15.—Men refused to, in order to pose as unemployed, *see* letter from Mr. Valpy, p. 15.—Mode of procedure of Metropolitan Public Gardens Association in providing, 1805 *et seq.*—Mode of supervising men at, 1703, 1844.—More men than necessary employed to do the, 1764, 1779, 1781, 1861.—Neglected in order to participate in fund, 1545.—No reason given for slackness of, 1537.—Of fund too great for individual effort, 2405.—Plan of Inquiry as to men at, 1857 *et seq.*—Plan of Metropolitan Public Gardens Association in providing, 1697 *et seq.*—Provided by the Metropolitan Public Gardens Association, Description of, 1783 *et seq.*—Provided was greatly overpaid, 1708, 1738.—Provided would not have been offered, but for the Fund, 1719.—Refused by unemployed, 1939.—Scarce in summer, 516.—Scarcity of, 871, 918.—Should be given, rather than money, 438.—Slack, but people morally improved, *see* People.—Slack in the Building Trade, 1585 *et seq.*—Slackness of Riverside, 1864.—

Work—*continued.*
Small number accepted offer of, 970, 1032.—Some who refused the offer of, got drunk, 1035.—Want of, *see* also Out of Work
Workhouse full, 1069 *et seq.*—Relief given sufficient to keep applicants from the, 363.—Test, 1063, 2279, 2282, 2357; *see* also Labour Test.—Test, Difficulty of applying, 1212.—Test not applied, 1176
Working Classes (*see* also Artisans, Poor, and Working Men), Improvement of the condition of, 726.—Increase of thrift among, 726.—Morally rather than materially improved, 732
Working Men as members of the Committees of the Fund, 234—Committee, *see* letter from Mr. Bramly, p. 22.—Know little about the Poor Law, 1696.— Labour-yard degrading to, 1659 *et seq.*—Members of Committee did not introduce cases, 1360.—Not welcomed in Committees of the Fund, 2289, 2290.—Population composed of, 1316.—Served on Committee, 1237, 1359, 1447.—Should serve on Committee of the Fund, 2084.—Will not apply to the Relieving Officer. 1312, 1313
Workmen, Good, applied, 2431.—Description of, employed, 1709.—Good, had to do inferior work, 2395, 2397, 2443 *et seq.*—Many good, out of work, 2421 *et seq.*
Works, Question as to future establishment of Relief, 486, 487.—Suggestions as to the Guardians setting on foot Relief, 490 *et seq.*
Written Applications, *see* Letter

[APPLICATION FORM A.*

_____Committee.   No._____

Date_____

Name in full_____

Address_____Time in district_____

Previous Address_____

Age_____ Married_____ Single_____ Widowed_____ Occupation_____

Ages of Children at home_____

Earnings: Man_____ Wife_____ Children_____

Present Means of living_____

Name and Address of last Employer or Foreman_____

_____ Time there_____

How long out of work during last twelve months_____

Reference: Name and Address_____

Club or Trade Society_____ Arrears_____

Relief from Club_____ Parish_____ Other Source_____

Weekly Rent_____ Let off_____ Rent due_____

Debts_____ Pawn Tickets_____

Remarks_____

Visited by_____ Date_____

Report_____

N.B.—Visitors will, so far as possible, verify the above statements, and report especially on the state of the home and any signs of thrift.

Decision_____

* NOTE.—At the back of this form, when printed for use, is a form of receipt, with spaces for 'Date,' 'Relief Granted,' and 'Signature of Applicant.'

[FORM B.

INQUIRY OF EMPLOYERS.

Confidential.

OFFICE:

_____ 18

Si ,

of

who has applied to this Committee for assistance, states that up to _____ ,
18_____, he was in your employ as _____ and that h weekly wages
were _____, that h left you on _____ ,
and that the cause of h leaving was _____

Will you therefore kindly inform the Committee whether these statements are correct?
and whether h was steady, regular, and did h work efficiently?

Your obedient servant,

REPLY OF EMPLOYER OR FOREMAN,

Date _____

_____
_____
_____
_____

Signature _____

[FORM C.

_____ DISTRICT. No. _____
_____ RELIEF FUND.

VALUE **ONE SHILLING.**

FOR FOOD AND FUEL ONLY.

STAMP.

Any _____ tradesman presenting this Ticke
at _____ any _____ between _____ an
_____ o'clock will receive cash.

PRINTED BY
SPOTTISWOODE AND CO., NEW-STREET SQUARE
LONDON

www.ingramcontent.com/pod-product-compliance
Lightning Source LLC
Chambersburg PA
CBHW020259170426
43202CB00008B/437